G000094781

Re-Imagine

India-UK Cultural Relations in the 21st Century

Re-Imagine

India-UK Cultural Relations in the 21st Century

Editor

Shrabani Basu

BLOOMSBURY

LONDON • NEW DELHI • NEW YORK • SYDNEY

© British Council, New Delhi, 2014

First Published, 2014

All rights reserved. No part of this publication may be reproduced or transmitted in any form or by any means, electronic or mechanical, including photocopying, recording, or any information storage or retrieval system, without prior permission in writing from the publishers.

No responsibility for loss caused to any individual or organization acting on or refraining from action as a result of the material in this publication can be accepted by Bloomsbury India or the author/editor.

BLOOMSBURY PUBLISHING INDIA PVT. LTD.
London   New Delhi   New York   Sydney

ISBN: 978-93-82951-34-6

10 9 8 7 6 5 4 3 2 1

Published by Bloomsbury Publishing India Pvt. Ltd.
Vishrut Building, DDA Complex, Building No. 3
Pocket C-6 & 7, Vasant Kunj
New Delhi 110 070

Laser Typeset by FORTUNE GRAPHICS
WZ-911/2, Shankarlal Street, Ring Road, Naraina, New Delhi

Printed at REPLIKA PRESS PVT LTD

The views and opinions expressed in this book are those of the editor and authors and do not necessarily reflect the position of the British Council.

The publisher believes that the contents of this book do not violate any existing copyright/intellectual property of others in any manner whatsoever. However, in case any source has not been duly attributed, the publisher may be notified in writing for necessary action.

Contents

Preface

This book emerged out of a project of the same name and attempts to understand what the relationship between India and the UK will perhaps look like in the future. Trend forecasting of a relationship is not an easy task, some would say it should not even be attempted, since it grows organically and the troughs and peaks can have no indicators based on hard facts. We therefore took recourse to opinions and perceptions to feel the pulse.

As part of the project we held a series of debates and dialogues in Delhi, Mumbai, Chennai, Hyderabad, Kolkata, London and Edinburgh, listening to a wide range of stakeholders in the relationship, including business leaders, civil servants, development workers, academics, cultural entrepreneurs and artists both from India and the UK over a span of 14 months. We also listened to a wider group of audiences through an online survey. Feedback was received from over 350 individuals. Facebook, Twitter, Picasa, YouTube, blogs, podcasts and films were an essential part of the process involving young people. We engaged with 7,000 people through our website, our online videos attracted over 3,000 views, about 100 blogs were written around the project, and over 28,000 accounts were reached through Twitter. In this initiative, our partners were Counterpoint, UK; King's India Institute, London; and the Indian Council for Cultural Relations (ICCR). The findings are available at our website: *http://www.britishcouncil.in/programmes/re-imagine*

We found that the relationship would score 6 out 10 on a scale of 1-10. Two hundred years of shared history had a period of recess, neither country investing actively in building a contemporary relationship. The result: India does not know contemporary Britain and Britain has little idea of how the new India is emerging. The past offers a strong platform for rebuilding a new relationship, but it has to be based on an equal footing, recognising the cultural nuances and current ambitions of both nations.

The book re-affirms this but does so by delving deeper. The essays here draw on historical anecdotes, personal history, current policies, and impending behavioural shifts to reflect the change. Shrabani Basu, who as editor provides the overview that strings together all the essays, is also on the committee of Project 400 that commemorates the arrival of the first Indian in England and the departure from India in 1614 of the first ambassador to the Mughal Court, Sir Thomas Roe. She traces the people to people links over four hundred years that create the overlapping history of the two nations and raises the question how a relationship forged on a common love for cricket, curry, parliamentary democracy and the English language can be taken forward gainfully in the twenty-first century, at a time when both countries face uncomfortable problems as they look into the future.

Mike King, one among many descendants of people who made India their home, sea captains, merchants, missionaries, educators, writers, engineers, civil servants and soldiers, is still unravelling family history to discover new links. Phillip Knightley writing about the media's attitude and influence in India and the UK, maintains that Britain's love affair with India and all things Indian never abates, whilst today's Indians aspire towards a cobbled image of Britain's sometime greatness, a mutual affection underpinning the relationship that will long endure after the reveries are over. Indrajit Hazra, playing on the title of a popular Bollywood film, *English Vinglish*, where the actress Sridevi plays the role of a housewife constantly teased by her children and husband for her poor English, argues that the growing acceptance of Hindi as the link language of India, irrespective of region, has led to a less complex-ridden approach to the way Indians speak, understand, read and write in English these days: 'Hindi no longer embarrasses young India: English no longer daunts them.'

Tom Bird, producer of the Globe to Globe festival as part of the Cultural Olympiad, went in search of Shakespeare in India and found that in India Shakespeare has transcended Englishness and become a writer like Ibsen or Tagore or Borges, who people read as writers of the world, as great singers of the human condition and that Indian theatre-makers offer a new insight into the works of Britain's national playwright. Sanjoy Roy's essay is a reminder that intervention through the Arts creates wealth in a sustained manner, allowing people and their communities to find new ways of overcoming odds and finding unique solutions. Nasreen Munni Kabir, who produced and directed the first television series on Indian cinema on British TV, records the emotional response of the diaspora to their country of origin. Sita Brahmachari explores the complex identity of the young readership for whom she writes and how they connect to a wider world.

Pradeep Kar provides a view of Geek India largely concealed to outsiders, a quiet but busy nation, focussing on innovation, connecting the dots to draw new and exciting futures that has special relevance to the UK. Indian science can have a positive influence globally with regard to the intrinsic value of science in society, writes K. Vijay Raghavan, and this provides great avenues for collaboration between India and the UK, which continues to be a world leader in science and innovation. Nirmalya Kumar of the London Business School and currently on lien with the Tata's, recounts the extraordinary experience of collecting Jamini Roy in London and through it discovering his own identity after having visited sixty countries, holding three nationalities and calling four countries home. Jack Spence's article is about stretching the mind of both the teacher and the student and acknowledging the moral and political complexities of international relations.

Mihir Sharma in attempting an analysis of the young in India says that the basic divisions in India's young population are three: the interlocutors for cultural exchanges with the rest of the world; the real middle class many of whom have grown rich in the past two decades; and the solid core who hover around the official poverty lines. It's the third category that the country needs to address urgently if the demographic dividend is to be prevented from becoming a demographic curse. So is young Britannia living on the edge, argues Kapil Komireddi, without the defining stabilities of adult life – job security, economic independence, family, parenthood and property ownership.

William Crawley and David Page while recounting the heydays of BBC in India tend to conclude that with the growing dominance of local TV channels in India, the BBC does not have the impact it once had, which in the context of BBC-India relations is to be welcomed as a sign of new equality. Jo Johnson's paper focuses on the trade and investment relationship with India, in the context of the UK's need for export and business investment-led growth and the on-going negotiations for an EU-India Free Trade Agreement. He concludes by offering suggestions in which the UK can strengthen an already strong relationship by focussing on a few core areas where it needs revitalising.

The book makes fascinating reading and is recommended for all who are interested in the special relationship between India and the UK. I would like to thank the editor and all the contributors for their generosity with time and thought. My colleagues Stephan Roman, Sujata Sen, Shonali Ganguli and Aatreyee GuhaThakurta worked on it behind the scenes. Sunil Khilnani and Kriti Kapila of King's India Institute and Catherine Fieschi of Counterpoint believed with us that it should be written. Anuj Bahri of Red Ink, and Suresh Gopal and Jyoti Mehrotra of Bloomsbury India made it happen. My thanks to all of them individually and to many others who have contributed in their special way.

Rob Lynes
Director India, British Council

Acknowledgments

I am grateful to Sujata Sen of the British Council for asking me to edit this book on a subject that is close to my heart. Thanks to Rob Lynes, Director of the British Council for his support. My grateful thanks to Shonali Ganguli of the British Council for her help with the publishing process and for skilfully coordinating with fifteen authors.

I would like to thank all my contributors who gave their time and energy for this book despite their busy schedules. Thank you for putting up with my relentless demands and deadlines.

My thanks to the British Library Board, The Royal Pavilion and Museums, Brighton and Hove, the Imperial War Museum, Hidayat Inayat Khan and the Museum of the International Sufi Movement, Shakespeare's Globe Theatre, Teamworks, Hyphen Films, English Heritage, Dartington Hall Trust and the BBC for use of the images from their archives.

It was a wonderful experience to work with writers and thinkers from both India and Britain and I would like to thank the British Council Re-Imagine project for providing me the opportunity to do so.

Shrabani Basu

Introduction

Shrabani Basu

*I*n the summer of 1614, Patrick Copland, a chaplain in the East India Company, returned to England after spending two years in India. On the ship with Copland was a young Bengali boy who would create history. Copland had spent a year teaching him chiefly by signs 'to speake, to read and write the English tongue and hand'. The nameless Bengali would be the first Indian to arrive on English soil, four hundred years ago.

Educated at the Aberdeen Grammar School and Marischal College, Copland believed in the power of education as a process of civilisation. When the East India Company established a trading post in Surat, in Gujarat, in 1612, Copland immediately joined the Company as a chaplain and left for India. Part of his mission would be to educate a native. To him, educating the young Bengali boy in both the English language and Christianity, was an evangelical duty; the boy, he thought, would help him to convert his own people; the British, he believed, were 'civilising the natives'.

The arrival of the first Indian in 1614 caused a stir in London. As the young Bengali walked down the streets, he would be followed by children staring at him open-jawed; women would watch through tiny cracks in their doors. Even Shakespeare is believed to have alluded to this disposition of Englishmen to stare at an Indian. In his play *The Tempest*, the ship-wrecked Trinculo says on first seeing the dark-skinned native Caliban:

Journal of Sir Thomas Roe 1614

Courtesy: British Library Board

'What have we here? A man or a fish? Dead or alive? A fish! ... Were I in England now, as once I was, and had but this fish painted, not a holiday fool there but would give a piece of silver. There would this monster make a man. Any strange beast there makes a man. When they will not give a doit to relieve a lame beggar, they will lay out ten to see a dead Indian.'

Copland's student proved remarkably clever at picking up both the English language and the Christian faith. After two years in England, Copland wrote to the Company that his pupil had increased his knowledge of Christianity, and suggested that he be publicly baptised 'as the first-fruits of India'. The Company consulted the Archbishop of Canterbury, George Abbot, who agreed to the proposal.

On Sunday 22 December 1616, a boisterous crowd surged towards the Church of St. Denis on Fenchurch Street. The week before Christmas was usually a busy one in this area, with people passing through doing their shopping, but the crowds that day were particularly excited. They had come following the announcement that a native lad of Bengal was to be initiated into the Church of Christ. The members of the Privy Council, the Lord Mayor and Aldermen, the shareholders of the East India Company and its sister company in Virginia, all waded through the 'sea of upturned faces' to reach the densely packed congregation. The rite was administered by Dr John Wood and the boy from Bengal was christened Petrus Papa or Peter Pope, a name chosen for his baptism by King James I himself.

Peter Pope remained a diligent pupil and was soon translating from Latin to English. He successfully translated from Latin the sermon delivered by his teacher in a church in Cheapside to the Honourable Virginia Company in 1622. The English translation was printed and sold at a shop in Cornhill near the Royal Exchange and duly credited: 'Peter Pope, an Indian youth, borne in the Bay of Bengala, who was first taught and converted by the said P.C. And after baptised by Master John Wood, Dr in Divinitie in a famous Assembly, before the Right Worshipfull, the East India Company at St. Denis in Fan-Church Streete in London, 22 December 1616'. The sermon was called 'Virginia's God be Thanked' and dealt with the success of the affairs in Virginia over the last year. It could be classified as the earliest work by an Indian to be published in England.

Copland had successfully imported and recognised the 'first-fruits of India'. Over the next four hundred years, many more would come, and the two nations would be tied together by history. This book attempts to look at how the relationship will go forward in the twenty-first century as the balance of power shifts in the world and India and Britain find their space in a rapidly-changing global village.

But first, the beginnings. It was as early as the sixteenth century during the reign of Queen Elizabeth I that the merchants of London had listened to the tales of the wealth 'of Ormus and Ind' and dreamt of travelling to and trading with the Orient. Flush with victory after the defeat of the Spanish Armada in 1588, the English began to see themselves as a naval power. The dreams of sailing to far-away lands was becoming a reality and a group of London merchants sent a petition to Queen Elizabeth I for permission to sail to the Indian Ocean. On 31 December 1600, the Queen gave them her blessings and granted the Royal Charter. It was one of the last acts of her reign. The group of merchants gathered at the Royal Exchange in London and proudly announced the setting up of the East India Company. It was to be a joint-stock company, with shares owned by the wealthy merchants and aristocrats; 1,218 subscribers raised a total of £68,373, no small sum in those days. The Company was to trade in spices, indigo, salt, cotton, silk, tea and opium. Little did the merchants know then, that the company would change the course of history and lay the foundations of an Empire.

In 1608 the first East India Company ship landed in Surat, a port in Gujarat in western India. On board was a minor officer of the Company, Captain William Hawkins, who was seeking permission to set up a trading base in the port city. But the Portuguese had already established themselves and Hawkins failed to get permission. He returned to England with a message for the King: send better gifts for the Emperor and a powerful fleet to defeat the Portuguese. The second fleet was despatched in 1612. It easily defeated the Portuguese fleet off Surat and the East India Company made its first inroad in India. On board that fleet was Patrick Copland, the chaplain, who was seeking to 'civilise' the natives.

Two years later, as Copland was escorting the young Bengali boy on to a ship bound for England, Sir Thomas Roe, Member of Parliament for Tamworth, was preparing to sail in the opposite direction: from England to India. He was to be the envoy of King James I to the court of the Mughal Emperor, Nur-ud-din Salim Jahangir. On 2 February 1615, Roe stepped on board the *Lion* at Tilbury docks with fifteen attendants. The voyage took six months, the *Lion* navigating round the Cape of Good Hope. On 14 September, the ship dropped anchor off the port of Surat and an emissary was sent to prepare for the arrival of the new ambassador. Roe's brief was simple. He had to win over the Mughal Emperor and secure the trading post of Surat. He would be the first Englishman to be stationed in the Mughal court of Agra. On 25 September, the preparations were over. The *Lion* was decked with colourful streamers and flags and a 48 gun-salute heralded the arrival of the ambassador. He was received in a splendid tent by the chief of Surat. The port city at that time was ruled nominally by Prince Khurram, son of Jahangir, who had given the powers to the local chief Zulfikar Khan and Mukarab Khan. They preferred the Portuguese to the English, so Roe would have to cut his diplomatic teeth in some tricky waters.

Wasting no time, Roe journeyed north bearing the gifts for the Mughal Emperor that had been sent by King James I. He finally had the audience with Jahangir in Ajmer on 10 January 1616 and requested a treaty that would give the East India Company the rights to reside and build factories in Surat and other areas. In return, the Company would provide the Emperor with goods and rarities from the European market. Jahangir, impressed with the British fleet's defeat of the Portuguese, immediately granted permission. Roe looked like the sort of person Jahangir could do business with. Besides, the Emperor calculated that it would be useful to have the British play off the Portuguese who had been fanatic in their religious outlook. Roe remained as envoy from 1615–1619 and greatly enjoyed his time at the Mughal court, frequently dining and drinking with the Emperor who he described in his journals as 'very merrie and

Mural in the Houses of Parliament showing Sir Thomas Roe at the court of Mughal Emperor Jahangir in 1615

Courtesy: explore-parliament.net

joyfull'. In 1618, the first British factory was started in Surat. Many more would follow over the next three centuries.

In 2010, when the newly elected Conservative government under David Cameron came to power and he chose to visit India with a high-power trade and industry delegation, there were many in the Indian media who compared that mission with that of Sir Thomas Roe to the court of Jahangir in 1615. Had history come full circle? Did Britain once again need India, and had India in Britain left its mark? In Britain, the Tata Group – with their takeover of Corus, followed by their acquisition of iconic British brands like Jaguar, Land Rover and Tetley tea – has become the largest single employer in the manufacturing sector; the richest man in Britain is an Indian named Lakshmi Mittal and curry is the national dish of Britain. Bollywood dancing is a staple at gyms across the country. The 2011 census has established that Indians are the highest ethnic minority in Britain (the total ethnic minority population, comprising of Indians, Pakistanis, Bangladeshis, Afro-Caribbean and other ethnic minority groups is 4.6 million). Has the post-Empire curtain-call brought the Indian summer permanently to Britain?

The engagement with Britain, pre-Independence, may have been one of master and colonised, yet the dialogue between the people of the two countries had always been a reason for optimism. It was, famously the link between Rabindranath Tagore and the artist William Rothenstein which eventually led to the publication of the *Gitanjali* in an English translation by Tagore in 1912 in London. The Nobel Prize swiftly followed in 1913, making Tagore the first person outside the West to win the prize. The *Gitanjali* had been published in Bengali in India in 1910 and it was during a journey to London that Tagore began translating some of the verses into English. He did these in a notebook which he carried around with him. The manuscript was once left behind by his son in a briefcase on the London Underground. Had it not been for the honesty of a fellow passenger and the remarkable efficiency of the Lost Property Office at Baker Street Station, the manuscript would have been lost to the world.

Tagore's friend and host, Rothenstein, requested to read it. Amazed by the spiritual richness of the verses, Rothenstein sent it to the Irish poet William Butler Yeats. Yeats came to London soon after receiving the verses and was so moved by it he wrote: 'I have carried the manuscript of these translations about with me for days, reading it in railway trains, or on the top of omnibuses and in restaurants, and I have often had to close it lest some stranger see how much it moved me.' He wrote the foreword to the edition that was published by the India Society, in London in 1912, in a limited edition of 750 copies of which only 250 were for sale. Tagore dedicated the English *Gitanjali* (translated as Song Offerings) to William Rothenstein.

The Hampstead circle around Tagore may have been famous, but the poet also left his mark on a young Englishman, Leonard Elmhirst, who he had met in the US. Tagore – by then a Nobel laureate – had so impressed Elmhirst that he visited Shantiniketan to see Tagore's work with rural reconstruction and education. He became Tagore's private secretary and travelled with him around the world and created a department for rural reconstruction in Sriniketan near Shantiniketan. In 1922, after marrying

American heiress, Dorothy Whitney, Elmhirst bought Dartington Hall and the surrounding estates near Totnes in Devon, to try out his innovative ideas in education, social reform and rural regeneration on

Leonard Elmhirst and Rabindranath Tagore in the grounds of Dartington Hall
Courtesy: Dartington Hall Trust

the lines of Tagore's Shantiniketan. Thus, a corner of Devon became forever Bengal. Since the celebrations of Tagore's 150th anniversary in 2011 in Dartington, the Tagore festival has now become an annual event.

In the field of science, this interaction between India and England was carried on by pioneers like Jagadish Chandra Bose who went to Christ's College Cambridge to study natural sciences and worked closely with Lord Rayleigh to make deductions about microwaves in plant tissues. Bose is considered the father of radio waves and microwave technology and is widely seen as the fore-runner to Marconi. Bose returned to India in 1884 after obtaining his Tripos from Cambridge and a year later conducted his ground-breaking experiment in Calcutta Town Hall, lighting some gunpowder in the hall and transmitting signals that made a bell ring some distance away. Two years later, Marconi conducted his experiment with radio waves in the Salisbury Plains. Today there is a bust of Bose in Christ's College outside the Yusuf Hamied Centre (a gift of a gallery and auditorium to Cambridge by another Indian alumni of Cambridge, the scientist Dr Yusuf Hamied, chairman of the socially-conscious generic drug company Cipla, which has provided life-giving drugs for cancer, AIDS and diabetes to the third world at affordable prices). In December 2009, the first academic session at the Yusuf Hamied Centre, fittingly, was a symposium on the life and work of J.C. Bose.

The genius of Srinivasa Ramanujan and his work with Prof G.H. Hardy is also legendary. The shy mathematician from Erode in Tamil Nadu, famously dropped out of formal education and while working as a clerk in the Madras Port Trust, sent nine pages of his theorems to Prof G.H. Hardy in Cambridge. Hardy was amazed, consulted his colleague J.E. Littlewood, who confirmed Ramanujan's genius, and immediately invited the young mathematician to work with him in Cambridge. Ramanujan stayed for five years in Cambridge, became a fellow of Trinity College and a Fellow of the Royal Society, only the second Indian to do so at the time. Ramanujan's formulas excite mathematicians even today and one of his last problems was solved at the end of 2012, ninety-two years after his death at the age of 33. While on his death bed in 1920, Ramanujan had sent a letter to Hardy outlining several new mathematical problems never heard before, along with a hunch of solutions as to how they may work. Mathematicians from the Emory University in Atlanta, Georgia, solved the formula and have claimed that it can explain the movement of black holes. The discovery is another first for Ramanujan, since no one in the 1920s was talking about black holes.

Women, too, were part of the quest for education and scientific research. Kadambini Ganguly (nee Basu) and Chandramukhi Basu became the first women in India to graduate from Bethune College in Calcutta, making them also the first women graduates in the entire British Empire. Ganguly would go on to study medicine, getting another feather in her cap as India's first woman doctor. In 1886, she received a degree in medicine from the Bengal Medical College. But faced with opposition from the teaching staff and orthodox sections of society, she went to Edinburgh to obtain her LRCP degree. It was a prolonged campaign by women, leading to a virtual riot outside Surgeon's Hall in Edinburgh in 1870 – that finally led to the Scottish Universities opening their gates to women in 1892. Dr. Ganguly returned to India with degrees from Edinburgh, Glasgow and Dublin and went on to set up her own private practise in Calcutta.

Gaining a degree in medicine at the same time was Anandi Gopal Joshi, who went to the US with the help of a Christian missionary and got a medical degree from the Medical College at Philadelphia in 1886. Addressing a gathering in Serampore College near Calcutta, before her departure, Joshi told the orthodox Hindus and the sceptics, that she wanted to study medicine as there was a great need for Hindu women doctors in India. She told the gathering that she wanted to start a medical college for women in India on her return. Her speech moved many and contributions flowed in (including Rs. 200 from the Viceroy). She was just 17 at the time. On her graduation, Queen Victoria sent her a congratulatory message. Joshi returned to India due to ill-health and tragically died in 1887 at the age of 21. She never practised as a doctor.

Another young woman, Rukhmabai, married in 1876 at the age of eleven to Dadaji Bhikaiji, made history when she challenged her husband's plea for 'restitution of conjugal rights' in the Bombay High Court when he asked her to come and live with him when she had come of age. Rukhmabai refused to join him, saying that she wanted to study medicine instead. The case caught the attention of the British media as it raised the issue of child marriage and the rights of women. Rukhmabai won the case, though her husband won the appeal. By then, moved by her determination, people contributed for her to travel to England, which she did in 1889, enrolling in the London School of Medicine, and qualifying as a doctor in 1894 (having also studied at the Royal Free Hospital in Hampstead). Returning to India, Rukhmabai became a medical officer for women in Surat and worked there for twenty-two years and in Rajkot for fifteen years. In the fifties and sixties, several Indian doctors would join Britain's National Health Service, becoming the backbone of the service. Indian GPs worked and served the local community in areas that no one wanted to go to: in deepest Wales, the Midlands and Northern Ireland.

It was her English friends who persuaded Cornelia Sorabji, the first female graduate from Bombay University, to get special permission by Congregational Decree to allow her to take admission in Somerville College, Oxford, to study law. In 1892, Sorabji became the first woman to graduate in law in Oxford. She was not allowed to practise for another 32 years simply because she was a woman. She became the second woman in Britain to be called to the Bar in 1924. A bust of hers was unveiled at Lincoln's Inn in 2012 by Lady Hale, the first woman judge in the Supreme Court of England.

Of the women who travelled to England from India in the nineteenth century, few were as remarkable as Toru Dutt, whose family in India had converted to Christianity and in 1869 left for Europe. The Dutt family (father Govind Chunder Dutt, mother and sister Aru) lived in France and Britain, and Toru – a natural linguist – became proficient in both English and French, as well as Bengali and Sanskrit. The Dutts lived in Cambridge between 1871–1873, where Toru attended Higher Lectures for Women at the University. She died young (at the age of 21 in 1877), leaving behind the manuscript for two unpublished novels *Bianca* or *The Young Spanish Maiden* (thought to be the first novel in English by an Indian woman) and *Le Journal de Mademoiselle d'Arvers* written in French (also possibly a first by an Indian writer). Her volume of poetry, *A Sheaf*

Gleaned in French Fields (translations of French poetry into English), had been published in India in 1876 and in London in 1880 (after her death). She also left behind a volume of poetry *Ancient Ballads and Legends of Hindustan*, translations and adaptations from Sanskrit literature.

Cornelia Sorabji
© British Library Board

Another woman who travelled to England with her husband in 1882, was Krishnabhabini Das. While her husband, Debendranath, taught Indian history, culture and religion to those Indians who wanted to take the Indian Civil Service exams, Krishnabhabini spent her time in the British Library reading and researching. In 1885, she published her travelogue *Englande Bangamahila* (A Bengali Lady in England), the first Bengali travel document authored by a woman. Her name was kept anonymous by the publisher. She gave a fair and objective account of British life, customs, institutions for young Bengali women confined to their homes and those wanting to venture abroad. In 2012, her name was included in the Oxford Dictionary of National Biography as an 'author and social activist'.

The nineteenth century saw Indian involvement in Britain on many levels. In 1887, Queen Victoria received a special gift for her Golden Jubilee from

Queen Victoria and Abdul Karim
Courtesy: Royal Collection
© HM Queen Elizabeth II

the superintendent of the jail in Agra: it was a gift of two Indian servants who would stand behind her at table, looking grand in their Indian clothes and turbans, their purpose purely decorative. Abdul Karim and Mohammed Buksh were the first Indians to work in the Royal Palaces. The younger Abdul Karim was rapidly promoted, quickly becoming the Queen's closest confidante and Munshi (Indian secretary) and causing a storm in court because of his closeness to the Queen.

Karim cooked Queen Victoria her first authentic curry and taught her to read and write in Urdu. The Queen continued her lessons right till her death in 1901, completing thirteen Hindustani Journals. Her last entry – a half page entry in Urdu – was written at the age of 81, only two months before her death. His lasting influence on the Queen can be seen in Osborne House on the Isle of Wight, the Queen's holiday home (now an English Heritage property), where she built an Indian-style Durbar Hall to use as her banqueting room. Here she would serve the curries prepared in the Royal kitchens by her coterie of Indian servants

The Durbar Hall in Osborne House on the Isle of Wight
Courtesy: English Heritage

and speak in Hindustani to visiting Indian royalty, living out her role as Empress of India. It was in her beloved Osborne House that she died, ending an era that had transformed Britain. Her favourite Karim became the last person to see her before her coffin was closed, a moment of history frozen in time.

In 1810, a flamboyant Indian called Sake Deen Mohammed, started the first Indian restaurant in Britain. Called the Hindostanee Coffee House, it

Sake Deen Mohammed
© British Library Board

was situated in George Street in Portman Square in London and advertised itself as a place 'for the entertainment of Indian gentlemen, where they may enjoy the Hoakha, with real Chilm tobacco, and Indian dishes, in the highest perfection...' The Hindostanee Coffee House catered to those returning nabobs of the East India Company who missed their Indian food and ambience. Mohammed decorated the restaurant with cane chairs and the walls with paintings of Indian scenes. A room inside had hookahs or water-pipes for customers. Unfortunately, the restaurant was unsustainable and he had to close it down in 1812.

The enterprising Deen Mohammed moved to Brighton where he set up a bath house and offered Indian style shampoo, aromatherapy and head massage. Mahomet's Bath House, set against the Brighton seafront and close to the Pavilion, became the place for the rich and famous to be seen, and he included amongst his clients, the Prince of Wales.

In cricket, a young Indian prince, Ranjitsinhji, became the first Indian to play for England. So popular was he that songs were written and music composed in his praise. Ranji joined Trinity College, Cambridge at the age of 17 in 1889, and won his first cricket blue in 1893. He soon became the champion batsman for the All England team, earning the newspaper headline 'Ranji saves England' during a match against Australia in 1899 when the rest of the team had collapsed early. Ranji was second only to W.G. Grace in popularity as a cricketer in late nineteenth century Britain.

In politics too, Indians were making slow but steady inroads. It was the Indian reformer, Raja Ram Mohan Roy, who made the first political petition in Britain, when he submitted a memorandum to the Parliamentary Committee of Indian Affairs in 1831 about the renewal of the East India Company's charter. He also appealed to the Privy Council against the re-introduction of sati. Roy became immensely popular in Britain and was even asked to stand for parliamentary elections, but he declined. He died in Bristol in 1833 after a short illness. In 1839, The British India Society was formed by a group of sympathetic Englishmen who sought to improve the conditions of the Indians and sought to bring pressure on the East India Company. It was followed by the London Indian Society in 1865. The first attempt to stand for elections in England would be made by a Bengali, Lalmohun Ghose, who stood from Deptford as a Liberal candidate in 1883, but lost. In 1892, it was Dadabhai Naoroji who became the first Indian MP to be elected to the House of Commons when he won the seat of Finsbury Central as a Liberal candidate by a hairline majority of five votes over his Tory opponent.

Naoroji had shown the way. In 1895, Mancherjee M. Bhownaggree became the second Indian to win a seat. Bhownaggree won Bethnal Green Northeast for the Conservatives. The following century would see Shapurji Saklatvala, one of the founders of the Workers League of India, winning the seat of Battersea for Labour in 1922. In 1924, Saklatvala contested the same seat for the Communist Party of Great Britain and won again, becoming the only Indian MP to sit as a Communist in the House of Commons. Decades later, Keith Vaz would become the first Asian MP in the House of Commons after India's Independence, winning the seat of Leicester East in 1987 for Labour. He retains the seat with a large majority.

While Indian women like Princess Sophia Duleep Singh (daughter of Duleep Singh, the last Maharajah of Punjab), were active in the Suffragette movement, marching at the head of the Black Friday deputation to Parliament in 1910 alongside Emmeline Pankhurst, it would be another century before women of South Asian origin would win a seat in the House of Commons. In 2010, five Asian women MPs were elected to Parliament: Valerie Vaz, Priti Patel, Rushanara Ali, Shabana Mahmood and Yasmin Qureshi.

With the twentieth century came the two World Wars and the call on Indian soldiers to play their role for King and country. One and half million soldiers were sent to the frontline, fighting in battles in far flung places, for a war that had little to do with them. By 1918, Indian troops had been in action in France, Belgium, Gallipoli, Mesopotamia, Palestine, Egypt, Sudan, East Africa, Persia and Kurdistan. Twelve soldiers were awarded the Victoria Cross for their bravery. Twelve thousand wounded Indian soldiers were brought to Brighton during the war and many were housed in the Brighton Pavilion which was set up as a hospital for them.

Indian soldiers outside the Royal Pavilion, Brighton, 1915
Courtesy: The Royal Pavilion and Museums, Brighton & Hove
Credit: A.H. Fry

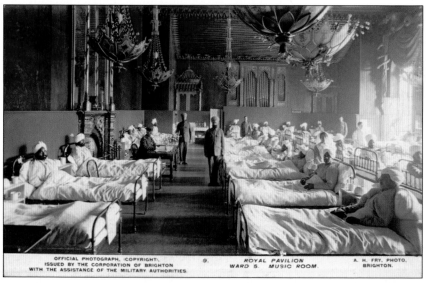

Injured Indian soldiers lying in the Music Room of the Royal Pavilion, Brighton, 1915
Courtesy: The Royal Pavilion and Museums, Brighton & Hove
Credit: A.H. Fry

Highly-publicised visits to see the Indian soldiers by King George V and Queen Mary were aimed at raising their morale. Efforts were made to ensure that the Hindus, Muslims and Sikh soldiers could have their dietary requirements and wrote cheery letters home. Fifty-three Hindu and Sikh soldiers who died there were cremated on the Sussex Downs in Patcham near Brighton and nineteen Muslim soldiers were taken for burial to the Shah Jehan Mosque in Woking, the only purpose-built mosque in Britain those days. In 1921, a Memorial was built in Patcham, on the site where the soldiers were cremated, in the style of an Indian Chhatri. A service is held there to honour the dead Indian soldiers every June.

World War II saw two-and-half million Indian soldiers volunteer for the Imperial forces, the largest volunteer army in recorded history. They suffered the highest casualties. Once again, they served in far-away places like Italy, North Africa and the Far East and twenty-eight Victoria Crosses were awarded to them during the course of the war. Nine were awarded

the George Cross, including the most famous recipient, Noor Inayat Khan, who was infiltrated into occupied France as an undercover radio operator for the Special Operations Executive, and who was eventually betrayed, captured, tortured and executed in Dachau Concentration Camp. Following a three-year campaign to have a personal memorial for her in London, the bust of Noor Inayat Khan was finally unveiled by Princess Anne in November 2012 at Gordon Square Gardens in a moving ceremony. It is the first statue of an Asian woman in Britain.

Noor Inayat Khan in her WAAF uniform
Courtesy: Imperial War Museum

Sixty-five years after Independence, Britain and India remain bound together as a result of their shared history. Indians are the single largest ethnic group in Britain, contributing to British society through business, services, art and culture. British politicians whenever addressing gatherings of British Indians (a crucial vote-bank), inevitably go through

Noor Inayat Khan playing the veena
Courtesy: Museum of the International Sufi Movement

the jokes on the British love for cricket and curry as a standard. Prime Minister David Cameron once told a gathering of the Conservative Friends of India that his most precious possession was a cricket bat signed by Sachin Tendulkar and that he would not even let his wife touch it. Conservative cabinet minister, Eric Pickles, repeats his curry joke at every Indian function. The former Labour foreign secretary, the late Robin Cook, became famous for what was his 'chicken tikka masala' speech when he described Britain's favourite dish as being representative of multi-cultural Britain.

But beneath the surface optimism, Britain and India face some uncomfortable problems as they look into the future. Britain faced a summer of riots in 2011, exposing the seething underbelly of social and economic tension that could flare up within hours and leave a trail of wanton destruction. The phone-hacking scandal put the media in the spotlight, and revelations of serial abuse by the late BBC presenter, Jimmy Savile, collectively horrified the nation. While the Royal wedding, the Queen's Diamond Jubilee celebrations and the Olympics provided some sweeteners, the economic forecasts have provided no relief from the doom and gloom. The rise in university fees means that even less people have applied for university admissions in 2013 than they did the year before, when the fees first went up. The consequences of this could be far-reaching. Meanwhile, unemployment and benefit cuts are hurting the youth and the vulnerable.

India, too, has been tainted. It may be aspiring for a permanent seat in the United Nations and celebrating its growth rate, but unrest is spilling over into the streets as the youth express their anger first against corruption, as they did in 2011, and then recently, in the wake of the tragic rape and death of a 23 year-old physiotherapy student in a bus in Delhi, at the unsafe environment in which women have to live and work in India. The image of 'Incredible India' has taken a battering, as it is outed as a country which has little or no respect for women. As Britain and India move forward in the second decade of the twenty-first century, they will have to look for ways to motivate and inspire the youth, or face more summers of riots and discontent. Both countries also face the constant threat of terrorism. Working together might just help. The following chapters try to provide some insights into how a relationship forged on a common love for cricket, curry, parliamentary democracy and the English language can be taken forward gainfully into the twenty-first century.

Select Bibliography

Basu, Shrabani. *Victoria & Abdul, The True Story of the Queen's Closest Confidant* (The History Press, Gloucester, 2010)

_____ *Spy Princess, The Life of Noor Inayat Khan* (Sutton Publishing, Gloucester, 2006)

_____ *Curry, The Story of the Nation's Favourite Dish* (Sutton Publishing, Gloucester, 2003)

Elmhirst, Leonard K. *Poet and Plowman* (Visva-Bharati, Calcutta, 1975)

Fisher, Michael H. *The Inordinately Strange Life of Dyce Sombre*(Columbia University Press, New York, 2010)

Neill, Edward D. *Memoir of Rev Patrick Copland* (Charles Scribner & Co, New York, 1871)

Vadgama, Kusoom. *India in Britain* (Robert Royce, London, 1984)

Visram, Rozina. *Ayahs, Lascars and Princes, Indians in Britain 1700-1947* (Pluto Press, London, 1986)

Oxford Dictionary of National Biography

www.cwgc.org

1|

My Family and India

Mike King

I was standing outside Rawalpindi Railway Station on a beautiful Saturday afternoon in February 2009, admiring the architecture and feel of a place many members of my family had passed through in their time. A smiling Corporal in the Pakistan Army stepped forward, shook my hand and welcomed me to the area where my uncle was born more than 80 years ago. Later, when visiting the immaculately maintained Commonwealth War Graves cemetery to pay my respects to the war dead of undivided India, I was met by the cemetery keeper who offered to make me some chai. Had I not been on such a tight schedule that afternoon, I would have gladly stayed on to talk to this gentleman and learn more about that special place which was the final resting place of so many brave people.

Years before this, when I lived in Canada, a distinguished gentleman who had been a Regimental Sergeant Major in World War II, met a friend of mine from the Indian Army and said admiringly, 'I was in Italy with the Indian Army. They were fine men.' And so they were. Ancestors of mine served alongside their Indian brethren in two world wars where people of all races and religions united to serve the King Emperor in a great common cause which ensured the defeat of tyranny on two occasions, at great cost to the people concerned.

My grandfather's loyal Punjabi sappers followed him all the way to German East Africa for the duration of World War I and then on to the North West Frontier for the Third Afghan War of 1919 without a complaint. In World War II, when Britain was in deadly peril, two and a half million men (and a good number of women) enlisted in the Indian Forces and did their part for world freedom. As my father once said to me, 'With loyal people like this behind us, how could we go wrong?' It

WH King after the award of his MBE by King George V at Buckingham Palace
Courtesy: Mike King

was a pity that Prime Minister Winston Churchill, great man that he was, failed to see this quality in the King's Indian subjects who rendered so much by way of valuable service to Britain and the Empire.

As the descendant of people who made their home in the Madras (now Chennai) region over two hundred years ago with the East India Company, I am fortunate to count as ancestors, men who were sea captains, merchants, church missionaries, educators, writers, engineers, police officers and soldiers, all of whom contributed something of worth to India in their time. While I have conducted extensive research on my family's historic links to India, I have been unable to determine how my great great great grandfather died on East India Company service in Nagpur in 1835. Similarly, I can find no record in the India Office files held by the British Library in London of my great grandmother's death in Coonoor. Locating her grave is a task I have set myself for full retirement when I shall have time to travel across India and investigate this particular family mystery.

This vast and exotic land was at the height of its imperial splendour when my father was born in the Punjab in 1910. His own parents had been born in St. Thomas' Mount in Chennai, and both were fluent Tamil speakers. By the time my grandfather had been posted to the North West Frontier, he had mastered four more Indian languages including Pashtun which he could read, write and speak fluently. This ability to pick up languages served him in good stead when he worked his way across India on government service, dealing with all manner of people, many of whom knew nothing of the English language. He would clearly have marvelled at the proficiency of modern day India and its people's mastery of English in all forms, whether written or spoken.

In 1922, my grandfather organised and led the laying of the telegraph line from Gyantse to Lhasa in what was then Free Tibet. The whole project was a great success and Tibet was now linked to the outside world by a telegraph line that led from Lhasa to Delhi via Gyantse. Historically, some form of contact had always existed between India and Tibet but now they were linked by technology, something the Tibetan government welcomed. The 13th Dalai Lama received my grandfather in the Potala

Palace and presented him with a gold and silver prayer wheel which is still in the family's possession to this day. The first telegram from Delhi to Lhasa was actually sent by the grandmother of actress Joanna Lumley who knew my grandparents well in those days. In recent years, both my cousin and I have had the pleasure of meeting Ms Lumley and talking about our respective families' historic links to Imperial India and the events they witnessed in those special times. The first telegram from Lhasa to Delhi and thence to England was sent by the Dalai Lama to King George V in London.

While all these engineering and other advances were taking place in British ruled India, cracks had begun to appear in a once comfortable imperial setting. The shooting of unarmed men and women in Jallianwala Bagh in Amritsar by Gurkha riflemen, on the orders of Brigadier General Reginald Dyer in 1919, changed everything. My father, who was then happily ensconced at Bishop Cotton School in Simla, the Raj's summer capital, realised that this unfortunate action was the beginning of the end and that things could not go on as they were. Indian independence was inevitable. British administrators seemed unable to understand the aspirations of educated Indians such as Nehru and Gandhi and treated them with what amounted to derision, little realising that they would one day be the leaders of an independent India. By the time my father entered Cambridge University in 1928, India's Independence movement was well under way.

When World War II started, India, in common with other members of the Empire family, threw its weight behind Britain and saw the whole process through until the very end. In 1944, a force of British and Indian troops successfully took on the Japanese army at Kohima and Imphal, and repulsed the invaders after much bitter fighting. Once again, Indian forces had proved their worth in battle just as they had in the Middle East and Italy two years previously. They fought their way through Burma and were present at the Japanese surrender in Rangoon in 1945, a ceremony witnessed by my uncle who was then a young officer in the Indian Airborne Forces.

As a man born and brought up in India, my father understood the desire of his fellow Indian citizens to be free of colonial rule. Nevertheless, he always hoped India would remain part of the family and not sever its links with Britain. He rejoiced in the achievements of individual Indians of whatsoever group, and loyally supported the land of his birth until his untimely death in 1972. His great and abiding wish was for India to modernise and shake off the worst aspects of casteism that he believed, held the country back. He openly regretted the fact that the Imperial government of British times had failed to break the power of the money lenders and not instituted peoples' banks to serve the needs of the poorer members of Indian society.

The Partition of India in 1947 was, in my father's view, a disaster that pitted one group of Indians against another. It resulted in a terrible loss of life for a questionable result. While India has forged ahead economically and built up its democracy since those dark days, Pakistan has lagged behind and has had to endure years of unpopular and unrepresentative army rule along the way.

For India to become a democratic bulwark in the world and a buffer to the power of China, some things will have to change. Serious attention must be paid to the issues of public health, transportation and employment. Large scale illiteracy will have to be tackled and education made available to all. Wealthy people will need to engage in philanthropy and satisfy the need for basic fairness in Indian society so that families can be decently housed and receive quality medical care that we in Britain take so much for granted.

India has everything it needs within its own borders to be a great force in the world, but until all these basic issues are addressed, it will not be regarded as a fully developed nation. Space rockets are a visible manifestation of a modern India in the making but until progress in real terms comes down to poor farmers and labourers in the remotest parts of the country, it will be difficult for India to advance in the way that it should. Forty years after my father's death, I know he would be pleased to see his beloved India rising, but he would be disappointed at the on-going daily struggles of the poor, something he always deplored and longed to see changed. India has already done so much for world freedom. Let it now move on to the next plane and be the nation it deserves to be.

2

Reporting India

Phillip Knightley

*B*ritain's love affair with India and all things Indian never abates. India remains the Jewel in the Crown of the Empire, still a source of fascination for historians, novelists, playwrights and film-makers, a well of inspiration and controversy tinged with fear that promises never to run dry. Its influence has penetrated deep into British society. If you doubt this, next time you are with a group of British people, casually ask who among them has any connection, however remote, with India? You will be amazed at what comes tumbling out: from grandfathers who served there in the Second World War, to uncles who worked in Indian branches of British banks in the 1950s, to cousins who were with the British Council, or who served with Kodak, or the British India Steamship Company, or had a spell teaching at one of the major Indian schools. I also cite as evidence of this fascination Khushwant Singh's book published in 2009, *Sahibs Who Loved India*, a collection of pieces he commissioned in the 1970s as editor of *The Illustrated Weekly*, a popular Bombay-based magazine. Week after week, British writers, politicians, socialites, members, actors and members of the Royal family were given space to pour out their affection for India.

They wrote more lyrically about this relationship than the Indians themselves. Who would have imagined a hard-headed journalist like Ian Jack describing in *The Guardian* recently, his memories of an Indian market place:

'Certain habits in Indian life once gave an illusion of permanence. On hot afternoons thirty years ago, for example, you could lie on your bed under a slow-turning fan and hear noises from the street that had been the same for at least a century. The lonely wife in Satyajit Ray's film *Charulata* heard them as she flitted about her Victorian mansion in 1870s Calcutta like a trapped butterfly and in 1982 you could hear them still: some rhythmic chanting, the hollow patter of a little drum. And if, like Charulata, you went to the window, there in the dusty lane you would see a gang of coolies shouting something like a work song as they pushed a wooden-wheeled cart with a heavy load, or a street entertainer drumming up business with his tabla. The most common sounds, however, were the singsong calls of peddlers selling fish or vegetables, or milky sweets and ancient biscuits. These were scenes that looked as if they had existed for centuries and would never be expunged by modernity.'

It is probably bad taste to claim that Britain regarded India more highly than any other nation of the Commonwealth. But despite the hidden racism at that time of organisations such as the English Speaking Union, whose original aim was to draw Britain and the English-speaking part of the Commonwealth closer, I believe that Britain paid more attention to India than it ever did to Australia, New Zealand, Canada, or South Africa. True, in the First and Second World Wars it had little choice. But it was not entirely because of political and military pressure. The two nations were bound together for all sorts of reasons. The lives of so many British at the height of the Empire depended on India. Generations found careers there in the Indian Civil Service (ICS), the army, and as tea planters and businessmen. And their lives and careers were recorded by generations of British and Indian journalists, from Rudyard Kipling to Mark Tully, from Sunder Kabadi to Saeed Naqvi.

The book *Fifty Years of Reporting South Asia*, 2009, produced by the Foreign Correspondents Club in New Delhi makes a stab at assessing with hindsight how accurately the British end of this effort succeeded in catching historical and political events, in describing what it was like living in India, and in understanding that elusive quality, the Indian character. You have to remember that being despatched to report on India was not always considered the plum posting it has been in recent years. When Robert Stimson, later the BBC's first correspondent in India, decided after the Second World War to go to Bombay to take a job on *The Times of India*, his British friends thought he was mad. They told him that it would be a different matter if he were going into the Indian Civil Service or even the Indian Army. 'Then at least you'd have some kind of status in a country where the right labels are important. But as a newspaperman, no. You'll be an object of suspicion to the Indian. The pukka sahib will look down his nose at you. You'll certainly take to drink.' They were wrong, of course, and Stimson found the story a full one with 'on the whole a happy ending'.

But you never knew in advance. Take as an example events that were to lead up to the liberation of Goa, the last of the European colonies on Indian soil. After Indian Independence, the Portuguese made it clear to the Indian government that they had no intention of leaving quietly. Fearful of the example that a bloodless departure would set for its African colonies, Lisbon announced that it planned to remain in Goa indefinitely, calculating that Nehru would value his international reputation far above the political gains to be had from the liberation by force of a small enclave on the western coast of the country. Instead, Nehru devised a plan to persuade the Portuguese to go peacefully: three thousand Gandhian 'satyagrahis' (non-violent protesters) were to cross the border into Goa, confront the Portuguese troops and appeal to their conscience. This could have been a story of international importance; so accompanying them in the dust and heat was the bulk of the New Delhi foreign press corps, led by Gerald Priestland of the BBC, which according to Krishna Menon, was run by 'a bunch of bloody pukka sahibs'. The reporters made it to no-man's land, half a mile of sandy scrub marking the border. But there they were marooned because their Indian taxis refused to cross it.

As Priestland recalled, 'So we heaved our suitcases and typewriters and staggered off down the track, the Indian army outposts rattling their rifles at us as we passed. Round a bend in the road, we saw the border chain and, just beyond it, a Portuguese wagon laden with chilled beer. At the sight of this, the foreign press corps broke into a shambling trot, pursued by Indian jeers.'

In this little anecdote, Priestland captures the essence of trying to report India for a Western audience: the complicated politics, the uncertain scale of events, the distances, the confusion, the mutual incomprehension, the frustration and the capacity for violence lurking behind the mundane. In fact, that was probably why foreign press clubs have always thrived in India; they provided a place for the foreigner to have a few beers, let off steam about the locals and thus remain sane. James Cameron was infuriated by the senseless war between India and China over a disputed border. 'It is heart-breaking that in the twilight of his great authority, Jawaharlal Nehru should be saddled with this intolerable dilemma. . . the last time I saw Chou En-Lai was in Delhi with his arm around Nehru. The cry then all over India was "Hindi Chini bhai bhai" – India and China are brothers, they shouted, and how splendid it sounded and how far away today.'

Despite the difficulties, the impossibility of containing one's temper and occasional disillusionment, correspondents in India felt they led a privileged life. If the correspondent was married, then his wife and family usually accompanied him on his assignment. They could look forward to superior living accommodation, servants and home leave in Britain. They could boast of a wide following both in India and Britain, 'hundreds of thousands, if not millions, of readers who depend on us for news and views'.

Not any more. Alas, foreign correspondents stationed abroad are a dying breed. News organisations claim that they can no longer afford the cost of posting a correspondent to a foreign capital and instead engage a freelance to cover for them or despatch a 'fireman' when a big story breaks. Some British newspapers these days manage to cover India without a single full-time correspondent. Others expect one correspondent to cover several nations in the sub-continent and be an expert on all of them. The Australian journalist Tony Clifton returned to Australia after forty years of international reporting, thirty of them for *Newsweek*. When he left his final posting in Delhi, the once globe-girdling network of *Newsweek* correspondents had shrunk to one.

The Indian media sets a better example in its reporting of Britain and traditionally, always has. I remember when I first arrived in Britain in 1954 being amazed at the number of Indian correspondents working in London. They all belonged to the Commonwealth Correspondents' Association and were active in arranging lunches and dinners and in persuading leading British figures to give talks and interviews. Its doyen was Sunder Kabadi who had come to Britain for the first Round Table Conference in 1931 and had stayed on. During his long career, he was correspondent for the *Indian Express*, the *Navhind Times* and *Amrita Bazaar Patrika*. It was Kabadi who made the Association such a force in Indian journalism, succeeding, for example in persuading Lord Mountbatten and Douglas Fairbanks Jr. to address a luncheon, a remarkable double bill. I felt, however, that he was pushing his luck when I found him in his office in one of the Inns of Court, busy addressing an invitation to Harold Wilson to attend a lunch on the eve of that year's Labour Party conference. I suggested the Prime Minister would be too busy with conference affairs to find the time. 'Yes, yes. I know', Sunder said dismissively. 'But I have to ask him anyway. Otherwise he'll go around saying those bloody Indian correspondents have given me the snub.'

Kabadi may have been exaggerating the care he took to keep politicians on side. But in recent years Britain has shown the same effort to cultivate Indian goodwill. I gave a talk to a group of leading Indian journalists who were on a visit to Lincoln University as part of a study programme on Britain. They were in the care of a Foreign Office official who was frank about the main aim of the programme. 'It's to show them how Britain functions in the hope that they will report on British affairs a little more sympathetically than would otherwise be the case.'

India has no such programme for British journalists and leaves them pretty much to themselves except during politically sensitive times like the Emergency that Indira Gandhi declared in 1975 following civil disorder over election malpractices. In fact, the bane of the press in both countries appears to be more the antagonism between editor and proprietor than government interference with editorial freedom.

In his revealing memoir, *Lucknow Boy*, noted Indian editor Vinod Mehta tells of his many years of falling out with proprietor after proprietor when he refused to bow to their ideas of what should be in the paper. Sometimes the proprietor's interference came early on in the relationship and sometimes only after Mehta had mistakenly come to believe he had at last found a boss who genuinely believed in editorial freedom. Not that British proprietors were much better, as evidence presented to the Leveson inquiry demonstrated.

At least Indian journalists were untainted by the 'hacking scandal' that so engrossed the British press as celebrities and politicians complained to Lord Leveson that newspapers had eavesdropped on their telephone conversations in search of scandalous stories. This may have been because Indian journalists lacked the technical know-how to follow suit rather than any ethical objections. Instead they became involved in a different sort of scandal, so typically Indian that it left their British colleagues amazed.

In 2001 a new website called Tehelka.com created a sensation when it exposed match-fixing in Indian professional cricket. It followed this up the same year with a 'sting operation' that exposed bribery and corruption in Indian defence procurement. The story attracted international attention and led to the resignation of the Indian defence minister. Re-launched in 2003 as a weekly newspaper funded by well-wishers and using its well-rehearsed 'sting tactics', it captured on hidden cameras several people who had taken part in the 2002 Gujarat riots admitting that the riots were part of a well-planned political conspiracy. Of almost as much interest as the stories themselves, was the reaction of the Indian authorities to them. Executives of *Tehelka* were suddenly subjected to income tax investigations and their tax returns for several years were audited. Rumours circulated that *Tehelka* was staffed by agents of Pakistan and it was accused of extortion by offering to kill stories in return for cash payments.

Tehelka was a sign of a new attitude by newspapers to those in power. Gone was the traditional subservience expected from journalists who benefited from government-subsidised housing (the so-called 'journalists' colonies') and other favours. From now on the Indian government would have to face the fact that at least some of the media would do its best to hold it to account.

Nothing illustrates this change as much as the difference in attitudes expressed by the arrival on the media scene of the editor, activist, publisher and journalist, Julian Assange. The 41 year old Australian, shot to international prominence in 2010, when in partnership with leading newspapers in Britain, the United States and Europe, his organisation, Wikileaks, began to publish secret United States military and diplomatic documents.

The military documents revealed that a US helicopter in Iraq had wantonly opened fire on a group of unarmed Iraqi civilians. The details of the attack, including video shots from the helicopter had been revealed by Bradley Manning, the US Army private, since then accused of leaking state secrets. At first Assange was viewed as something of a hero by the British media. He received the Amnesty International Media Award, *Time* Magazine's 2010 Person of the Year Award, the Sydney Peace Foundation gold medal and the 2011 Martha Gellhorn Prize for Journalism. But some sections of the media in Britain turned against him, largely over his demands that he have total control over the way in which his material was released and handled.

Then damaging accusations about his sexual behaviour on a lecture trip to Sweden surfaced when two Swedish women made complaints to the police about him. The Swedish authorities issued a European arrest warrant seeking his extradition to Sweden so that he could be questioned about the complaints. Assange challenged the extradition procedure and took his case to the highest court in the United Kingdom but lost.

All this cost him and Wikileaks public support, as the media conflated the man and the sex allegations, with the campaigner and his work. Newspapers were full of articles taking one side or the other on the question of whether Assange was guilty of rape or only poor sexual etiquette, the difference between sexual attitudes in Sweden and those in Britain. The wider issues raised by Wikileaks were overlooked and disappeared from the news. The Indian media, on the other hand, was non-judgemental of Assange the man, and stuck to the issues raised by the documents. Under editor Narasimhan Ram, *The Hindu* published the India-related US diplomatic cables released by Wikileaks, triggering corruption inquiries which continue to this day. And the Indian media was in general supportive of accounts that suggested there were 'dark forces' at work which had made it their business to cause Assange as much trouble as possible, so as to discourage others from following the example of Wikileaks. When Assange sought political asylum in the Ecuadorian embassy, the British press found it strange and wondered what his supporters thought of the move. The Indian press highlighted the threat by the British government to forcibly enter the embassy to arrest Assange and ran criticism of British 'neo-colonial' attitudes.

This goes against the trend in the Indian media which does not have a reputation for standing up for Freedom of Speech (for example, their attitude to controversy over Salman Rushdie and his book, *The Satanic Verses*, 1998). I think this dates back to the 1950s when India was an interface between the West and the Soviet bloc at the height of the Cold War. India tried to maintain good relations with both sides, leaning a little in favour of Moscow. This made her a prime target for the Central Intelligence Agency because it was one of the few countries where American intelligence officers could find ways of examining Soviet weapons (for instance, the Larkin brothers spy trial). Both sides ran sophisticated 'cultural' programmes to try to influence Indian public opinion. These programmes also provided cover for espionage activity so that the more sophisticated Indians tended to avoid them from worry that they might be compromised.

Sovexportfilm spent its time arranging film festivals in India and promoting the best Soviet films. It also ran a minor intelligence operation hoping to recruit Indian agents. *Imprint* was a small American-run publishing company which put out a monthly magazine offering 'the best of books each month' to its Indian subscribers and publishing books for children about American folk heroes. It was a CIA-run propaganda operation. As far as intelligence operations go, both were fairly benign affairs. Indian film-goers got to see some Russian masterpieces. And

30,000 subscribers to *Imprint* got to read some good books that they would not have otherwise been able to afford.

If one had to weigh the Indian media's influence today against that of the British media, I think the scales would favour India, not least because there is so much more of it. In Britain, newspapers struggle to survive, as readers switch to other sources for their news. Most are losing money and quality journalism is slowly dying. Whereas in India, new newspapers open almost every month and the circulation of established newspapers is still rising (the only other large countries where this is so are China and Brazil). A new generation of Indian journalists and intellectuals of global stature, such as Pankaj Mishra, are starting to influence our world-view.

And as broad as modern India's vision is, it still has a point of special focus. The burgeoning middle classes are visiting Britain in unprecedented numbers, with Heathrow Airport's Terminal 4 looking like a futuristic version of the bustling Victoria Terminus of old Bombay. These are not just tourists souvenir-shopping in Selfridges and Harrods; Indian entrepreneurs and industrialists are buying up classic marques from Tetley Tea to Blackburn Rovers Football Club. Bollywood has followed, casting London's landmarks and Victorian terraces as backdrops for its musical blockbusters.

Look down the credits of any BBC TV show from *Eastenders* to *Panorama* and you will see that second and third generation Indian immigrants are colonising the corporation venerated by their grandparents for its World Service broadcasts. India has seized the other most sacred of British institutions, the game of cricket, and has turned it from a sedate pastime to perhaps the most exciting team sport in the world.

So whilst Brits of my generation bask in nostalgia for the India of the Raj, an attitude that invites the accusation of archaic elitism, today's Indians energetically aspire towards a cobbled image of Britain's sometime greatness, which in our post-Empire climate of jaded self-doubt seems naive. But underlying the wish-fulfilment is a mutual affection that will endure long after the reveries have faded.

3 |

English Vinglish:
A Far Cry from Mimicry

Indrajit Hazra

यह पंक्तियाँ कम लोग समझ पायेंगे। এই পংক্তিটা এথানে আরও কম লোক বুঝবে।[1] And yet, it is *this* line that you're reading now that will be understood by everyone interested in this essay, even if (especially if) you are an Indian sitting in India and will never confuse 'Eve-teasing' for anything remotely Biblical or will know immediately when someone's 'acting pricey'.

This observation underlines the fact that as users of the English language in India, we are members of a rather sprawling internationalist but exclusive club. A club that provides various levels of membership, some barely recognizable as member groups except to themselves. But the operative words 'by most people interested in this essay' in the first paragraph highlights much of how English works in India: as a blind assumption that *only* a certain level of English users are interested in this kind of (hopefully) intellectually stimulating discussion. In other words, if I had written this in Gujarati – which I can neither speak, understand, read nor write – no one would have bothered to read it. This, as I have learnt from various British sit-coms, is bollocks.

More Indians use Hindi – by which I mean speak, understand, read and write – than they understand, never mind speak, English (English users of various proficiencies are far less in number.) My mother tongue and first language, Bengali (in which the second line of this essay has been written), is a regional language used by Bengalis living in the eastern region of the country (and in the neighbouring country of Bangladesh) and at least partially used (spoken and understood) by non-Bengalis in that region, as well as by Bengalis scattered across the world. Unlike Bengali or Hindi or, for that matter any other language used in India, English comes from another part of the world. Technically, it should have been like Klingon. But thankfully, it isn't. Far from it, actually.

Much has been made of English as a 'link language' in this Babel of 1.3 billion people. In a country of 23 official languages and 1,576 mother tongues that fall under 114 languages, it would seem practical to have one language that is communicable by all. One would have assumed that this honour would have gone to a home-grown language, especially to one spoken in its variously related forms by 422 million-odd Indians: Hindi. After all, most Indians will know a smattering of Hindi as compared to a smattering of English. But even in the majority-celebrating democracy of India, such thinking hits a wall thanks to two features: representation and aspiration. As the Tamil leader C.N. Annadurai stated during the anti-Hindi agitations in the 1960s in response to the fact that more Indians spoke Hindi than any other language in India, 'If we had to accept the principle of numerical superiority while selecting our national bird, the choice would have fallen not on the peacock but on the common crow.'² And to understand how English was anointed the 'peacock' in the fluttering aviary of languages in India and remains so, one has to first go back in time to investigate its roots in language politics and powerplay.

The issue of which language independent India's Constitution was to be written in, which language was to be spoken in Parliament, and which language would be designated as 'national', was debated furiously in 1946. English had, since the primacy of the East India Company and subsequently under direct British rule, been the language of elite Indians. As historian Michael H Fisher writes pithily in *Counterflows to Colonialism*: 'The ability of British ideology to convince Indians that associating with them, especially in Britain, would bring improvement and justice, often in the face of much evidence to the contrary, suggests one power of colonialism.'[3] But many Indian traders, primarily the Parsis in Bombay and Bengalis in Calcutta, initially learned English to take advantage of commercial and administrative opportunities created by British rule, even as they retained sartorial and dietary habits, speaking Gujarati and Bengali at home as their first language, a trend that would resurface without all the post-colonial heart-burn in the late twentieth century and that continues to this day.

But English was a loaded language in the years leading up to Indian Independence in 1947. Historian Ramachandra Guha, in *India After Gandhi, 2007,* writes of how R.V. Dhulekar, member of the Constituent Assembly from the United Provinces, started to speak in Hindustani (an admixture of Urdu, itself an offspring of Persian and Arabic, and Hindi, which has its source in Sanskrit) before being reminded by the chairman, that many in the audience did not know the language he was speaking.

Dhulekar's riposte set the tone for the 'language war' that would follow: 'People who do not know Hindustani have no right to stay in India. People who are present in this House to fashion a Constitution for India and do not know Hindustani are not worthy to be members of this Assembly. They had better leave.'[4] In today's contemporary terms, that would be like an American music programming director declaring that anyone who is not a Justin Bieber aficionado should get out of music programming. So English was the elephant in the room, in which propagators of Hindi as a national language, and its detractors, were lugging it out.

As Guha points out, despite Jawaharlal Nehru's comfort level with the English language – the Harrow and Cambridge University graduate was far more comfortable in English than he was in Hindi, unlike his political mentor Mohandas Karamchand Gandhi – he had believed that there should be an all-India language of communication without 'infringing in the least' on the domain of the many provincial languages. English was not the language understood by an overwhelming number of Indians. So, as far back as 1937, the man who would become India's first prime minister had envisaged Hindustani as a 'golden mean'.

But he hadn't reckoned for the opposition to the perception of the 'hegemonic north Indian' language being imposed on the country as a whole. In the face of loud protests against 'Hindi imperialism' from various parts of the country, it was decided that the 'official language' of the Union would be Hindi, but for 'fifteen years from the commencement of the Constitution, the English language shall continue to be used for all the official purposes of the Union for which it was being used immediately before such commencement'. Procrastination as politics had begun.

Growing up in the non-Hindi-speaking Bengali middle-class milieu of Calcutta in the 1970s and 1980s, I was well aware of a palpable anti-Hindi sentiment. I was a willing, enthusiastic participant.

Even as a large proportion of Calcutta's population comprised non-Bengali speakers – whether it was the rich Marwaris who had migrated from Rajasthan generations before, or the day wage-earning migrants from adjoining Bihar who formed much of the city's floating labour force – Hindi was considered the language of 'north India', not of Bengal. When I flunked my Hindi third language exam in middle school, the disappointment of my parents was so minimal that it bordered on a secret, perverted pride.

The decision of my entering an English-medium, Jesuit-run school itself had been a matter of some deliberation for my parents. My father harboured the notion of admitting me in a Bengali-medium school. After all, he himself had gone to one without having problems later in engaging with the world at large when he went to study, and then work, abroad. My mother, a post-graduate in Bengali literature and not as proficient in speaking English as my father, was hesitant about this. She completed the pair of a fully Bengali-using household (along with my Bengali-only using grandmother) in which I would speak only in Bengali at home. Eventually both my parents decided on an English-medium school believing that it would impart a *better* education than its Bengali counterpart. The idea of English as a key language to explore opportunities later – that would exist outside my immediate home milieu – must have played a large part in that decision.

In such a scheme of things, English was the medium of teaching in school, Bengali being the second language and Hindi the third (to be studied only for two years out of the ten), while Bengali ruled effortlessly at home and outside the artificially Anglicised realms of school.

Hindi in 1970s and 1980s Calcutta – and I would presume in non-Hindi cities such as Madras, Hyderabad and Guwahati as well – was the language that 'other' Indians spoke. This had a not-so-invisible veneer of cultural superiority attached to it. One spoke to rickshaw-pullers and restaurant waiters in (mangled) Hindi, but never to one's peers even when the latter happened to be natural Hindi-speakers. But to speak to non-Bengalis of one's own social milieu – or those above – one needed a 'third' language. And that superior, class-cum-communicative function was provided by the English language which we had been making our own in school.

My maternal grandfather owned a cinema that ran the latest Hindi movies. Through the late 1970s and 1980s, I would watch pretty much every film, acting out and singing all the Amitabh Bachchan roles and songs during the regular power outages that were part of 1980s Calcutta life. I would pick up most of my (dodgy) 'Bombayaa' Hindi not from 'ridiculous' textbooks but from these films which I, along with my aunts, loved to watch in those pre-VCR days. These movies not only provided a gateway to understanding a language that we secretly wanted to spew and which we publicly disdained, but they also became our window to 'India'. But out in the open, we depended on Bengali. And increasingly, as a mark of our rising street cred, on English.

On the artificially maintained 'political' front, the newly elected communist government of West Bengal, had decided in 1977 to wage a war against the English language. One can somewhat understand even by looking at the elite in today's Calcutta, in their colonial-style clubs and almost anal worship of everything 'English' (as opposed to American or Indian), where this was coming from. By attacking English, the preferred language of the gentrified classes – the bhadraloks (literally, gentlemen) and executives in Anglophilic companies and their gin-sipping, English-speaking wives – the communist government was seeking a legitimacy from the non-English speaking masses.

The first communist government that came to power in 1977 (and was re-elected right until 2011) decided it wasn't a good idea to teach a foreign language to children in primary schools. The government operationalised a directive in 1981 to abolish English language teaching in primary schools – from Class 1 to Class 6 – the very years I was being taught how to pronounce English words properly, and sing songs such as the British 1953 chart-topper by Patti Page, *(How Much Is) That Doggie In The Window?*

The government had essentially used the same principle that South Indian politicians had in 1965, fifteen years after Nehru's 'Let's take a look at English as an official Indian language 15 years later' policy had resulted in full-blown, anti-Hindi agitations including self-immolations in the southern state of Tamil Nadu. Looking back, it is both amusing and shocking that not too many people made much of the well-known fact that Jyoti Basu, the chief minister of the elected communist government, sent his own children and grandchildren to English-medium convent schools and, later, abroad for higher studies.

It was only in 1998, after coming under much pressure for enhancing an English-Bengali 'class divide' among students by the time they entered college, that the government appointed a committee headed by Professor Pabitra Sarkar that decided that English language learning would be formally reintroduced into primary schools from Class 3 onwards from 1999. The reasons cited for this incremental turnaround included 'the opening up of the country's economy to foreign multi-national and transnational corporations as a precondition for economic liberalization... [having] contributed to the high profile of English which it enjoys'.[5] By 2004, the reversal was complete after another committee headed by Professor Ranjugopal Mukhopdhyay recommended the reintroduction of English as a 'compulsory, second language' to be taught from Class 1.

There are some educationists today – and I tend to agree with them – who believe that the 'negative effects' of English language education being denied to government school-going children in the 1980s and 1990s are exaggerated. Not learning a language in one's formative years does not necessarily close the doors on learning the language in middle school. My parents, uncles and aunts, all went to schools where the medium of teaching was in Bengali, and where they were taught English the same way I was taught Bengali in my school: as a second language with separate classes rather than the medium of learning of all subjects. That had been enough for a higher education for them in English and for the workplace later in life. My father would go to Britain in the mid-1970s and became a practising psychiatrist there, and then to English-speaking New Zealand, before returning to India, and he did fine. In any case, one still doesn't expect German or Chinese kids to learn English, the global language, until later.

But what did happen as a result of the 'no-English in government-run primary schools' policy was the accentuation of the division between English-medium and Bengali-medium school education. The issue wasn't just a matter of kids turning out more prepared to face the world armed with a universal language. It was that the quality of government school education (conducted in Bengali), in general, had collapsed, and would, except in certain individual schools, lag behind to this day.

Things like the quality of science textbooks and of teachers in Bengali-medium schools would dip drastically. So even beyond the ability of an English-medium school student being able to conduct a conversation or a debate perfectly with his counterpart in Edinburgh or Philadelphia, the matter of *what* was being imparted as education, regardless of the language it was being imparted in, started to matter more than ever before. A boy in Calcutta being able to speak fluently in English and know lines from Shakespeare's *The Merchant of Venice* and Matthew Arnold's *Dover Beach* clearly became a byword for being better equipped than his non-English language medium school counterpart.

I first realised the power of English in India as a social status indicator at the age of twelve. Our class teacher had asked me a question – in English, of course – and instead of responding with a 'Beg your pardon?' or 'Sorry?', I had grunted out a 'Huh?', or more precisely, the Bengali response, 'Aanh?' That response, in a society that still held on to the idea of English and English values in its largely Victorian England avatar, was that of the unreconstructed Indian-English user.

The story of English as a status-enhancing tool for Indians, beyond its primary purpose as a common currency of communication, has its origins – predictably, if under-rated – in British imperialism and expansionism.

In 1800, Governor-General Richard Wellesley established the Fort William College in Calcutta. Here, recently arrived East India Company employees and British civil servants, would be taught Persian, Hindustani, and Bengali. Like any multi-national corporation opening a major branch in a new country, the East India Company also expected its employees to have a working knowledge of the language(s) of the places where they worked. It is only natural for an American oil company executive posted in Russia to pick up basic Russian.

Soon after Fort William College in Calcutta, the East India Company decided to open two colleges in Britain itself for young newly appointed officials and officers to learn introductory Persian, Hindustani, Arabic, Bengali and/or Sanskrit before they set sail for India. The first one was for civil servants in 1806 at Haileybury and the other one for military cadets in 1809 at Addiscombe in south London. The faculty was overwhelmingly made of British 'Orientalists', with a handful of Indians joining.

But the direction of 'Indian education' changed with a new focus on an English-based administration. 'The total ignorance of the English language on the part of the Native Indian and Persian teachers... deprives them of the power of being useful to beginners (which all the Students necessarily are) in the study of Persian and Hindostanee', stated the Addiscombe College Committee Reports of 1826.[6] This was like the students in the 1980s British sit-com *Mind Your Language* complaining that their teacher was teaching them a foreign language – English – by only speaking in English in the class without explaining matters in their mother tongues.

In 1830, Fort William College, which had already been reduced in size and budget after Haileybury and Addiscombe had opened its doors, was shut down. Fort St. George College in Madras, however, opened by the East India Company in 1812, continued to teach British officials and officers South Indian languages.

Thomas Macaulay's 1835 'Minute on Indian Education' turned the tide completely. The reliance on Persian as the official-administrative language was replaced by English for both Britons and Indians. In 1837, the official language of the East India Company, which had been Persian, became English. One can mark this date as when the English language officially became the aspirational language for Indians hoping to move up the socio-economic ladder.

Out of this powerplay came the curious case of English-using Indians who looked down on fellow Indians who were ignorant of or apathetic towards the English language and what was perceived to be its accompanying set of accessories. Thus was born the notorious 'brown saheb', a simulacrum of the Englishman (or, to a lesser extent, the Englishwoman) moulded out of Indian ingredients.

Perhaps the first proper 'brown saheb' was a Kashmiri gentleman in Delhi by the name of Mohan Lal who worked as a munshi (Urdu for a writer or secretary, although he preferred the English term 'Persian Secretary') for British officers, after his family lost their hereditary land grant from the Mughals. In 1828, the East India Company reorganised the existing Delhi College and opened the Anglo-Arabic College with a new English language course added to its existing Persian course. Mir Shahamat Ali, a contemporary and fellow student of the first batch of the English course at Delhi College with Lal, wrote in 1847, 'Molvies [maulvis or Islamic scholars] objected either from jealousy or from the excess of prejudice, [and] declared that, by beginning to receive an English education, we had lost our creed....'[7] And yet, as historian Michael Fisher observes, 'the attractions of this new Anglicised education, and the employment prospects it brought, convinced some three hundred young men to join Delhi English College over the next five years'.[8]

Mohan Lal, who would travel in the 1830s with Scottish explorer and British political agent, Alexander Burnes, and with other British officials in secret missions in north-west India and Afghanistan, and would later visit England in 1844, can be described as the first Indian who made his way up the social status ladder because of his knowledge of English. His British patron, Charles Edward Trevelyan, would write rather pointedly, 'What has given Mohan Lal so decided an advantage over the generality of his countrymen? What is it that had gained for him a willing acknowledgement of his personal superiority by the princes of Central Asia, and enables him to enjoy, on terms of equality, the society of European gentlemen? It is simply his knowledge of the English language. Not a critical knowledge...but such knowledge as enables him to read and understand English books, and to converse intelligently with English gentlemen on ordinary subjects.'[9]

Echoing his brother-in-law Thomas Babington Macaulay's 1835 'Minute on Indian Education' – in which Macaulay had infamously written that 'all the historical information which has been collected from all the books written in Sanskrit language is less valuable than what may be found in the most paltry abridgments used at preparatory schools in England' – Trevelyan added, '...and can it be doubted that, under the Divine blessing, the same means which have produced such a decided effect in raising an individual in the scale of civilization and honour, will, if properly applied, lead to the same result in regard to the entire population of this great country?'[10]

Mohan Lal, a product of this 'Divine blessing', would go on to write about how he found 'partly Anglicised Hindus' embarrassing. This self-deracinated Indian would describe people who 'continued to rub mustard oil over their bodies, which makes them disagreeable to those whom they approach to converse with'. Lal also ridiculed 'fellow' Hindus: '[They] worship the pictures of their deities, which were painted on walls, some of them being represented with four heads, and others with monkeys' heads, which they presented with offerings of flowers and fruits.... Here is a display of utter ignorance and prostitution of all sense – rational creatures turned fools, and deceived into a belief in stones, water, and fire, all of which I am sure can do them no good.'[11]

Mohan Lal wrote two books, both in English, *Travel in the Punjab, Afghanistan and Turkistan to Balk, Bokhara and Herat and a Visit to*

Great Britain and Germany (1834) and the two-volume, *Life of Amir Dost Mohammed Khan of Kabul* (1846). Both were generally admired in Britain, although some reviewers, such as that writing in *Quarterly Review*, paradoxically criticised him for his 'absurd...mimicry of John Bull phraseology' as well as for 'the thoroughly Asiatic modes of thinking and feeling which have survived all his Feringhee training'.[12]

But it was Mohan Lal, a proto-V.S. Naipaul and Nirad C. Chaudhuri rolled in one, who believed that 'Anglicization' was the need for India. 'India will never regain the zenith of its former glory, nor even prosper, until the whole population becomes acquainted with the language of the government, and then, entertaining the pacific sentiments of loyalty and homage to her present honourable masters, claim and enjoy her rights like the other subjects of Britain.'

He would discover, however, that knowing the English language – and picking up many aspects of British culture – was not enough to get the status he wanted in imperial Britain.

Thankfully, India has moved on from the halcyon days of the 'brown sahib' and the faithful mimicry where elocution and Wren & Martin-regulated English grammar were the elite Indian's essential handrails to professional and social progress.

English in India today is no longer as tightly held in the hands of the English-language-walas as it was, say twenty years ago. Much of the country's English-users now come from not the English-medium educated upper class or upper middle class milieu but from new layers of a multi-level aspiring India. Ironically, the post-colonial angst of many fluent English-users, products of Oxbridge or St Stephen's College, Delhi – who felt it necessary to indicate their 'authenticity' by quoting in Sanskrit or Urdu or looking down upon 'Indian writing in English' as a kind of mongrelised entity that they themselves needed to create a distance from[13] – have segued into an English-using population that uses the language less for status-enhancing purposes and more for opportunities and being comfortable with the world, including an expanded India, at large.

Also, in the higher spectrum of contemporary literature, a Booker-winning, best-selling writer of the calibre of Salman Rushdie, constantly using hybrid words that mine both Eastern and Western cultural reference points, has made it easier for Indian writers writing in English to push aside an earlier generation whose role models were of the E.M. Forster and Somerset Maugham vintage and aesthetics. Amitav Ghosh's novels are praised for being 'Bengali novels in English', which a generation ago would have been a harsh criticism. And Jeet Thayil's 2012 Booker shortlisted novel, *Narcopolis*, is riddled with the Hindi cuss word 'chyut' that is as tripping off the pages as 'fuck' is in James Kelman's books.

The ready usage of English mixed with Hindi or Bengali or other Indian languages is no longer seen as a bastard child to be scoffed at. Accent and pronunciation of English may still be a dead giveaway as to one's proficiency with India's primary link language which itself is a handle to where one is socio-economically coming from. But once again, with an increasing number of Indians speaking English the way they see it fit, and in a manner that *does* open up doors to them in areas otherwise difficult to get a toe-hold into, English in India is less an annual ticker on the Oxford English Dictionary's latest entry of an 'Indian word' into the language and more a calling card.

The sniggers can still be heard though. More than anyone else, it is the English-medium educated Indians who still find 'Indian-English' signs and utterances – 'Chilled Bear', 'Lock Before You Sleep', 'Enter Through the Back Side' – more than just funny. They see these as mutant sub-English-users trying to break into their club and failing miserably. But as these folks still groan at the general use of 'prepone', 'revert back' and 'half pant', even they realize that it is a nervous laughter of those still worshipping at an altar that has turned into a raucous bazaar, as English itself is always malleable and hungry to ingest words and usages from other languages. *How* you speak English in India still matters almost as much as *what* English you speak.

And the politics of not speaking English fluently enough is occasionally still the matter of concern for some who conflate, rather than correlate, prowess in English with success. Not too long ago, before the Gujarat state elections, a commentator in an English business daily,[14] quoting a report by the consultancy firm KPMG, bemoaned the fact that there was a 'lack of proficiency in English' in the state. 'When I go home to Surat', he wrote, 'I can speak with friends only in Gujarati and even those educated in English speak a pidgin in an accent that other Indians will be familiar with ("snakes in the hole/snacks in the hall" as the old joke goes)'. He goes on to point out that as a mercantile culture, Gujarat has not needed English because its elite did business and that the lack of English means 'Gujarat still doesn't have a proper middle class as Mumbai, Delhi and Bangalore do'. Then he comes to the nub of what he sees as the problem: 'No white-collar, Anglicised, urban Indians.... It is why there is little social mobility for the lower middle class.'

Really? Calcutta with its long history of Anglicised English language-usage among the middle-class and elite still has remnants of an English-speaking, Anglo-Indian, lower middle class, not to mention ossified social status despite the knowledge of Tennyson's poetry. And would the author – like so many other Indians who don't speak English only as a 'link language' but also as a comfort language – have frowned so deeply about Gujarati-speaking Gujaratis, if the context was Swedes speaking in Swedish, or Japanese speaking in Japanese?

The case that the writer ultimately tries to make is that the economic growth of a state like Gujarat is held back because of a lack of Information Technology (IT) and IT enabled Services (ITeS). In the context of Indian IT service industries – that boom box of the Indian economy story – it boils down to call centres, which is really more about accents and learning catchphrases (essentially mimicry) than about innate English language skills. Which, in any case, Gujarat with its manufacturing and industry-based economy, like say, the state of Rio de Janeiro in Brazil, may be fine without mastering.

The media in India holds up a mirror to the disproportionate importance given to English language in India. I work for the English language daily, *The Hindustan Times* (Its rival, *The Times of India*, is the world's largest selling English language daily). *Hindustan*, its sister publication in Hindi, has a higher circulation than *Hindustan Times* and is growing. And yet, it is *The Hindustan Times* which gets more play because of its wider English bandwidth. But on television it is the Hindi news channels – not to mention the entertainment channels – that are the biggest and most far-reaching in India.

Which takes us back to the matter of English as an aspirational device. The quality of English being used increasingly across the length and breadth of India may vary from the split infinitive-catching, William Wordsworth-spouting, English-walas to the 'Hello, how do you do? You wish to see Taj Mahal?' English communicators. But going by the mushrooming of 'Spoken English' schools (taught by teachers with a barely passable knowledge of standard English, let alone standard spoken English) in every city and small town, more and more Indians are taking to English, the way youngsters took to typewriting and shorthand lessons when I was young.

There is a great apocryphal story about Kapil Dev, the Indian cricket captain, who won India their first Cricket World Cup in 1983. The same year, after leading his side to a Test match victory against the visiting West Indies side in Ahmedabad and notching up career-best figures of nine wickets for 83 runs, the young man from Haryana who could barely string two sentences together in English, was intensely nervous as he faced the media in the after-match press conference. When a foreign journalist enquired about whether India had other pace bowlers like him and asked: 'When will there be another Kapil Dev?' India's greatest all-rounder answered, 'Father dead. Mother aged 62. There cannot be another Kapil Dev.'

The same Kapil Dev would go on to be the biggest endorser and beneficiary of the English guide series, Rapidex English Speaking Course, that was published from the late 1970s and whose success, according to its publisher, Ram Avtar Gupta, still rests on 'the craze of learning English that has been prevalent in India for many decades'. Kapil Dev now speaks cracking English without having to take recourse to friendly interpreters (which was strangely absent during his time). But more importantly, he has gained in the strange confidence that many Indians lack when they are unsure of speaking English 'correctly'.

Paradoxically, the growing acceptance of Hindi as the de facto 'link language' of India's people, irrespective of region and, more importantly, class, has led to a less complex-ridden approach to the way we speak, understand, read and write in English these days. The demarcation between Hindi as a growing link language (even in the Hindi-phobic South and East) and English as an aspirational language coupled with the mother-tongue in non-Hindi-speaking regions, has ushered a golden age of communication and discourse in India that can be seen in platforms as diverse as television shows, Facebook posts and English newspaper headlines (which once had a ban on any Hindi-isation in its content). Hindi no longer embarrasses young India; English no longer daunts them.

In Gauri Shinde's moving film *English Vinglish*[15] – the title playing on the Indian habit of adding a rhyming nonsense word after a word, to suggest the meaning of 'somesuch' eg. '*phool-tool*' (in Bengali denoting a flower), or '*bhoot-shoot*' (in Hindi denoting a ghost), or 'barking-sharking' (in English to denote barking) – the housewife played by Sridevi is constantly teased and riled by her two school-going children and executive husband, all three of whom are proficient English-users.

She is especially hurt when her children at the breakfast table start rolling with laughter and make fun of her pronunciation of 'jazz', which she pronounces as 'jaaj'. The conflation of proficiency in English with social standing is brilliantly displayed in a scene where the Hindi-speaking wife is approached by the mother of another girl in her daughter's English medium convent school who keeps talking to her in English which she simply cannot follow. Her daughter, in sheer embarrassment, saves her by 'reminding' her that she had wanted to go to the bathroom.

The shortcomings of not being able to follow or speak English in modern urban India are not romanticised or patronised in the film. At no point is there a message – as may have been the case in earlier Hindi movies of the 1970s and 1980s – that speaking English is a synonym for being 'un-Indian' or 'Westernised'. The housewife ultimately goes to an English language class when she's visiting her sister in New York and stumps everyone in a climactic scene when she is able to make a wedding speech in English.

It says something about how things have changed when it comes not only to the way Indians view English, but also to the way they view Hindi, considering the family depicted in the film is Marathi (the grandmother breaking into Marathi from time to time) and we hardly register the internalised translation job we are made witness to in a film about arming oneself with English, as if it was a credit card or a statement-making accessory, in twenty-first century India.

Notes

1. The first sentence is in Hindi and says 'This line will be understood by few people here'. The second sentence is in Bengali and says, 'Even fewer people will understand this line here.

2. Annadurai's quote from Ramachandra Guha's *India After Gandhi: The History of the World's Largest Democracy* (Picador India, 2007).

3. Michael H. Fisher, *Counterflows to Colonialism: Indian Travellers and Settlers in Britain, 1600–1857* (Permanent Black, 2004).

4. Dhulekar's quote from Guha's *India After Gandhi*.

5. Pabitra Sarkar Report on English in Primary Education in West Bengal (Government of West Bengal, 1998).

6. Addiscombe College Committee Reports, from Fisher's *Counterflows to Colonialism*.

7. Mir Shahmat Alis' quote, ibid.

8. Ibid.

9. Charles Edward Trevelyan's quote, ibid.

10. Ibid.

11. Mohan Lal's quote, ibid.

12. Ibid.

13. Most notably, this desire to stamp one's 'authenticity' as an Indian was displayed recently by Kannada playwright, actor and Rhodes scholar graduate from Oxford, Girish Karnad, who accused Trinidadian-British

Nobel Prize – winning writer of Indo-Trinidadian heritage, V.S. Naipaul, of being 'tone deaf – which in turn makes him insensitive to the intricate interweaving of Hindu and Muslim creativities [in India]...'.

14. Aakar Patel, 'How Modi is hampering Gujarat's growth' (Mint Lounge, December 15, 2012) www.livemint.com/Leisure/XIDIWhMGYHB804qvr BVRlK/How-Modi-is-hampering-Gujarats-growth.html

15. *English Vinglish*, DVD, Eros International.

4 |

Looking for Shakespeare in Mumbai and Delhi

Tom Bird

*I*n the spring of 2012, I was invited to appear on the BBC's *Breakfast* programme in order to talk about the forthcoming *Globe to Globe* festival, in which we would invite theatre companies from all over the world to the Globe, to perform a Shakespeare play in their own language. Whilst waxing on the extraordinary popularity these sixteenth and seventeenth century English dramas still enjoy all around the world, the presenter, Charlie Stayt, threw me a curveball 'Is there anywhere that Shakespeare *isn't* popular?'

The best answer, in that situation, would have been just to say, 'no, not really, Charlie'. Instead, however, I looked flummoxed and sank sweatily into the sofa, mumbling that the plays really were popular everywhere, but that if there were places where his work is less popular, those were probably the places that had ancient, distinct and still-existent theatre traditions of their own-places, I said, 'like India'.

It's rather fortunate that there weren't any other Shakespeareans on the sofa with me that morning, because that was one of the most inaccurate statements that has ever been made to BBC *Breakfast*'s millions of cornflake-munching viewers. Why it popped into my head as an answer to that particular question, I will never know. I was tired. Hurriedly, I backtracked, in order to avoid justified complaints from the many people who would be watching *Breakfast,* aware that Shakespeare has been played in India for nearly two hundred years, and that Indian adaptations of his work have never been stronger, or more plentiful.

I had been on the *Breakfast* sofa because of *Globe to Globe,* the festival I was directing at Shakespeare's Globe Theatre in London for the 2012 Cultural Olympiad. We were planning to host 38 international companies on the Globe stage, each to do one of Shakespeare's plays in their own language, and thus end up with the complete works being performed over a madcap six weeks. We were always aware of the prevalence of Indian languages in London, and therefore were set on having at least two productions from India taking part in the festival, in addition to a production each from Pakistan and Bangladesh. The catch, however, was that we had ten months to programme the whole thing.

Particularly in the past year, many commentators–infinitely more qualified than me–have written or broadcast on India's spectacular relationship with Shakespeare. They have examined the history of Shakespearean performance in the subcontinent, and have looked at how his work is taught and performed in India today – from Bollywood adaptations to *King Lear* in Kannada in a Mysore jail.[1] Instead, what I aim to do here is to describe the real process of bringing Indian adaptations of Shakespeare to the Festival in London: how does a previously uninformed theatre producer go about finding the Shakespearean performers in India? What are your options when you have to choose only two productions? What does it *mean* to produce a Shakespeare in India in the twenty-first century? Furthermore, I would like to write in a bit of detail about the two productions from India that formed part of the festival, and their impact on audiences, critics and the wider London Cultural Olympiad.

For people of my age, who have grown up watching theatre in the UK, 'Indian Shakespeare' doesn't mean the Kendals and Kapoors and *Shakespeare Wallah*. The first time I heard of that film was when I began talking to people about the festival. Rather, a single production I saw in 2007 seems to have defined this sub-genre in more recent times:

Tim Supple's *A Midsummer Night's Dream*, produced by the Royal Shakespeare Company and the British Council. Tim's multilingual production involved lots of research in India, many Indian actors, and the help of many theatre-makers who I subsequently met–most of whom seemed to have been thoroughly energised by their involvement with that project. What we wanted to do with the Indian work in *Globe to Globe*, however, was not to produce 'Indian' work ourselves, as it were, but to bring the work as a whole from active Indian theatre companies, work that might have existed anyway, whether or not the festival existed; to find companies keen to work with Shakespeare off their own backs (or those already doing it), and to invite them to bring their own take to the Globe, with no creative input from us, and little production support from us besides the fee we paid them.

My search for an Indian Shakespeare production began thousands of miles from India, on my doorstep in east London in early 2011. The Hackney Empire, a gorgeous late Victorian theatre, at that time almost going out of business, nevertheless had the gumption and risk-taking prowess to stage a radical re-working of *Hamlet* by the Company Theatre of Mumbai, entitled *The Clown Prince*. Atul Kumar, the Company's artistic director and one of the finest comic actors I have ever seen, played his absurd role with aplomb in this heartfelt, clowning take on the tragedy, performed in English and gibberish. It was Kumar's relationship with the audience that immediately made me certain of his company's suitability for the Globe: he spoke to us about the Hackney traffic, and moaned about the sirens, bugbears of his audience. Most importantly, when the lights first came up, he just waited a beat, and then smiled as though we were all sitting opposite him at a chai stand in Delhi. To see this in a proscenium arch theatre with the house lights down is thrilling enough; but this kind of honest, open, conversational playing soars when transferred to an Elizabethan-style playhouse where 1500 audience members and a company of actors share a common light.

When the curtain came down at Hackney, the small but enthusiastic audience leapt into raptures. On a side note, it's interesting that curtain calls in London always seem to be louder and more enthusiastic when a work has come from abroad. I think this is a combination of: (1) bravo for getting all the way here; (2) we're from India/Poland/Kenya too, so let's support our actors here; and (3) gosh, that was fantastic. I've never seen anything like that before. Whatever it is, it's surely evidence that this city, for all its theatrical richness, still remains something of a theatre bubble, honourable exceptions like the Barbican aside. Legacy was the most overused word in London in 2012, but if there is a theatrical legacy to be had, I hope it is that producers open our theatres up to the world more and more.

It seemed like the whole audience of *The Clown Prince* were being squeezed into the Empire's Harold Pinter Room for the post-show drinks. The conversation was very much centred on 'how do we save Hackney Empire?', but, without wishing to be rude, I needed to get to Atul, the star of the show, to pique his interest in playing some Shakespeare– not *Hamlet*, for we already had one – at the Globe. It is unfettered and inexcusable arrogance, but when you work for a famous theatre and you ask what you perceive as a small company to produce for your stage, you cannot help expecting an overenthusiastic 'yes!' in return. Certainly, this is what had happened in many of my other conversations with theatre- makers around the world. I was almost sick of hearing what an honour it would be, how their destiny would be fulfilled, etc. But Atul was different, in that he seemed totally *in*different, at first, to the idea of the Company coming to Bankside. 'That would be nice', he said, moving his head tiredly, 'we should talk'. A conversation the following day in the bar of the Arcola Theatre failed too, as far as I could see, to raise much enthusiasm in him for the project. He didn't reject my overtures, not at all; he just mildly acquiesced, and evaded the subject when I tried to talk specifics: plays, money, details. I needed to change my tack. I needed to get on a plane.

Mumbai is one big theatre, with twenty million overexcited actors. The first time I had visited, in 2008, this wild city was in the aftermath of the attacks on the Taj Hotel and other sites in Colaba. Huge boulevards and tiny alleys were closed off, policemen chewed *paan* and held machine guns threateningly in front of the barriers. Through the streets there marched hundreds of people denouncing the Pakistani government and people, who they said were behind the attacks. India was urged to retaliate. In 2011, I returned to something closer to the real Mumbai, grinning, rushing and no longer looking over its shoulder. Intense cricket matches took place on the Oval Maidan and in the Wankhede Stadium behind Marine Drive, where the local team were playing. The 2008 attacks had so shocked Mumbai that even the cricket had stopped, for a while at least. Last time I had come here to get my head in order following an emotional wurlitzer back home; this time I was here to work, and for a blessed time between January and September of 2011, work meant travelling around the world finding theatre companies to play Shakespeare at the Globe.

With the help of the British Council in Mumbai, I had arranged meetings independently with a number of theatre-makers from the city, and from further afield in Pune and Gujarat. I was curious to discover early on that everyone seemed to want to meet at exactly the same location, as though it was a formality: the Prithvi Cafe at Juhu Beach. This is a shady oasis amidst the hustle of Mumbai, shaded by big-leaved trees, crucial for my survival in the blasted heatwave of late May. It surrounds the Prithvi Theatre, a hub for India's theatre scene, run at the time by Sanjna Kapoor, a visionary who seemed to want to give the chance to as many artists as possible to perform on the professional stage in this madly competitive city. That said, I was told by many of the directors I met, that getting a show on in the Prithvi is not exactly straightforward: it was booked up for the foreseeable future, they lamented. Even if they can't get a show booked in, Mumbai's theatre wallahs hang here, in the café; it is their sometime address. They drink Pepsi and tea, eat *biryani*, and talk stage stage stage all day and long into the night. There is no equivalent in London – *everyone* seems to call in there at some point during their day, if they're in town. And so I set up camp for days on end, a sweating red-faced Shakespeare nut in the corner of the garden. I needed to come away from India with at least two prospective – most probably new–productions of Shakespeare plays. I had, at least, come to the right place.

Like a good James Bond film, things really started when I began to talk to Q. Thin and tall with piercing eyes and a cheeky smile, Q is Quasar

Padamsee: Manchester United supporter, cricket obsessive, theatre man. He had assisted Tim Supple on the *Dream*, and was the boy who knew everybody who was anybody making theatre, not just in Mumbai or the cities, but throughout India. And best of all, every time he mentioned someone, he took a swig of Pepsi, reached for his mobile, and gave me their number. Though an exciting young director, he didn't seem interested in pitching for the gig himself, or in needlessly discrediting his colleagues and competitors. By the end of our conversation, I had a kind of scribbled road map through Indian contemporary theatre, the kind of thing it could have taken months to research.

And so began a giddy, memorable, hilarious and moving series of conversations in the Prithvi Cafe between myself, melting under a sweaty sunhat, and a series of directors, actors, producers, almost all of whose work would have thrived back at the Globe. I met Mohit Takalkar, whose work in Marathi with Aasakta is hugely respected; Arun Kakde who directed a legendary production of *A Midsummer Night's Dream*; Akarsh Khurana, whose group Akvarious work in English and Hindi but whose links with Punjabi actors opened up the possibility of a Shakespeare production in that great language; Yogesh Sanghvi, a commercial producer from the Gujarati theatre; Sunil Shanbag, one of the luminaries of Indian theatre, someone who you can just sit and listen to for hours; and Atul, who brought his whole family with him to the Prithvi, to eat biryani with me. He seemed a lot happier with the idea of *Globe to Globe* this time round, and we began to talk through various Shakespeare plays to see which might work for him, and his clowning, passionate group, the Company Theatre. Mumbai, for all the sardine train journeys from Churchgate to Santa Cruz, for all the nights crouched alone and exhausted in the corner of Colaba bars writing up notes, had been spectacularly good to me: I had a plethora of options to take back to London, an excitement about these companies' seeming fondness for the silliness and sincerity of Shakespeare, which mirrored the silliness, sincerity, sin and soul of the city in which they worked.

Rural Gujarat buckled past me through the blue-barred windows of the *August Kranti Rajdhani*, the express train taking me to Delhi for the next leg of my Indian search. I drank a thousand cups of spiced tea while we spun through Surat and Baroda. When the train terminated at Hazrat Nizamuddin station, I realised that Delhi in summer is an altogether different proposition from Mumbai. The heat was outrageous, 45 degrees, like permanently standing under a ginormous hairdryer. No more outdoor interviews.

Roysten Abel met me in the cafe of a bookshop in Khan Market. Famed for various productions, one of which was an irreverent take on *Othello*, I had been desperate to talk to him for some time. I had seen videos of his work, which showed off the man's extraordinary stagecraft. We ate cake, and talked of London, of his background in the *kathakali* form of dance and his new work, which included a musical performance about the Manganiyar community in Rajasthan. Roysten, like Q, seemed uninterested in doing the work himself, and advised me to 'be careful' when looking for shows in India, as, unlike Q, he was critical of the work of theatre-makers in the country in general. In contrast to the carefree attitude I had encountered in Mumbai, he was cautious and seemed almost suspicious of much of the work he saw. But he did have one recommendation: when we had finished our cake, Roysten sent me to the National School of Drama, which everyone calls the NSD, to talk instead to Abhilash Pillai, a Royal Academy of Dramatic Art (RADA) graduate who directed Shakespeare both professionally and with students in Delhi. We walked around the shady courtyards of the NSD, chatting about the work in Delhi generally, about the graduates of the NSD and what kind of future they could expect. Like so much in India, he is full of optimism for the future, and that positivity recharged my batteries for the rest of my time in the hairdryer city. It seemed fitting that my last port of call was this drama factory, where India's theatrical future – a future that is spectacularly promising – was being moulded.

There are three general observations I had made in course of talking to colleagues in India about the real business of putting on a Shakespeare play. The first has to do with a slightly debilitating divide between 'commercial theatre' and 'experimental theatre'. Personally, I like to think the two aren't necessarily mutually exclusive, but in India it seemed to me that they are regarded as different art forms, different industries, different worlds. A recent review in *The Hindu* for a production of *As You Like It* began: '...[t]here are two views on theatre: one that it is meant for a niche audience, the other that it is meant to entertain.'[2] Such a dichotomy strikes me as both odd and damaging, but it is certainly very present in the discourse of Indian theatre today. One is either a commercial producer or an experimental one, and the crafting of the artwork is totally at the mercy of this. During the conversations I had, almost everyone explicitly defined themselves as one or the other. The *problem* is: where does this leave Shakespeare, who is both the finest experimenter in the history of drama and the playwright who has sold the most tickets in the history of drama? The man who brought us *Hamlet* – solipsistic meditative masterpiece – also brought us *The Merry Wives of Windsor*, a sexually tense sitcom with cheap jokes. Indeed, even Hamlet has its fair share of cheap jokes, crowd-pleasers, ticket-sellers. I think it's fair to say that Shakespeare as a producer would have been flabbergasted by the idea that one set of theatre-makers forge new paths, and another set aim to line their pockets. From the little we know of his life, it seems that he did both, and I think Indian theatre might be in a healthier position going forward if it abandoned this great divide.

The second observation has to do with English language. A large part of the intention behind *Globe to Globe* was always to show how energising and enthralling it can be to watch a Shakespeare play in a foreign language, and therefore one of the festival 'rules' we made very early was: absolutely no English. No one at the festival (save an American hip-hop show) broke this rule more than Atul Kumar's company, who brought the Hindi-language production. Atul wrote to me long before the festival, and asked that the actors be allowed to 'slip into' the odd bit of English now and again. At first, we rejected this for the sake of fairness, but the actors did it anyway, and it was remarkably successful. At the end of the famous '[i]f music be the food of love' speech, translated into Hindi, the actor playing Orsino winked at the audience, adjusted his rakish hat and said, in the unmistakable Mumbai English: 'my name is Orsino, by the way'. The reason this works for Indian Shakespeare, of course, is that this is the real language of many people in India today: their own mother tongue is so often peppered with English words and phrases, and in the end it was a credit to Atul's show that he broke the rules and recognised that language in India (indeed, language anywhere) is never pure and always a tapestry.

Finally, there was history. I wondered, on my way to India, about the postcolonial politics of performing Shakespeare, whose work (alas) was used for empire-building. I knew that there was lots of his work performed, but I didn't know whether there was also an anti-lobby, rejecting one of the accidental heroes of British colonialism. It was a relief, then, to find that in India, as elsewhere, Shakespeare has transcended Englishness and become a writer like Ibsen or Tagore or Borges, who people read most often as writers of the world, great singers of the human condition, rather than Norwegians or Bengalis or Argentines. Indeed, many people I met on my travels in 2011 insisted that Shakespeare was much better in Hindi/Lithuanian/Maori.

The Company Theatre from Mumbai perform *Twelfth Night* in Hindi at the Globe to Globe Festival in 2012

Courtesy: Shakespeare's Globe
Credit: Simon Annand

In the end, we invited Atul Kumar's Company Theatre, who performed *Piya Behrupiya* or *Twelfth Night* in Hindi; and the Arpana theatre,

The Company Theatre's *Twelfth Night* at the Globe Theatre
Courtesy: Shakespeare's Globe
Credit: Simon Annand

directed by Sunil Shanbag, with *Maro Piyu Gayo Rangoon*, their take on *All's Well That Ends Well* in Gujarati. We were overjoyed with both. Atul's production took sex and silliness as it's starting-off points, a very wise angle from which to approach *Twelfth Night*. Mansi Multani's middle-class Mumbai Olivia sang *'Cesario!'* into the pouring London rain, shielding her head when she came downstage. Geetanjali Kulkarni, a slapstick presence throughout as Viola, engendered one of the festival's most touching moments when, during a quiet moment while nothing but the harmonium played in the background, she loosened her hair from its knots and shook it out, pining for her true identity in this madcap world of cross-dressing and lust.

The Arpana production also featured musicians sitting on stage, and rich golden costumes as the action moved between rural India and Burma. Mihir Bhupta's adaptation retained the play's soul while transporting the setting to locations more relevant to the cast and audience (on both nights, the theatre was full of Hindi and Gujarati speakers). Whenever the plot moves on, an actor reflects on it with a song, whether they are old or young. It is a staggeringly thoughtful, elegant reading of the play that remembers that, in theory, all *is* well that ends well.

I found the critical reaction to both productions particularly fascinating. To *The Guardian*'s credit, they reviewed every single *Globe to Globe* performance – no mean feat. However, Lyn Gardner and Andrew Dickson, the reviewers of *Twelfth Night* and *All's Well* respectively, both came to a similar conclusion. Gardner missed 'the beguiling, melancholy heart of the play' which she wrote was replaced by 'non-stop jokes',[3] while Dickson (albeit at the end of a glowing and intelligent review) felt that 'Shakespeare's suggestion that fairytale endings are more complicated than they seem passes by without qualm. In this most problematic of comedies, you're left wondering: what's the problem?'[4] I fear these reactions say more about what Shakespeare has become in Britain than how the work is being produced in India. One has to search long and hard to conclude that the heart of *Twelfth Night* is 'beguiling and melancholy' rather than sexy and silly, and too often the dark heart of Shakespearean comedy in this country is nothing more than a director's projection of his or her own melancholy onto a comedy full of cheap gags. What I find undeniable is that all the pathos generated by these great comedies is

Arpana Theatre from Mumbai perform *All's Well That Ends Well* in Gujarati at the Globe to Globe Festival

Courtesy: Shakespeare's Globe
Credit: Ellie Kurtz

brought into *sharper* focus when the comedy is played true and daft, as in both these cases.

India's gift to *Globe to Globe* was the two productions' insistence that, to bring delight to an audience via a Shakespeare comedy, you start with the comedy to establish a shared humanity, and I reject the notion that this method steamrollered the sadness present in both dramas. Writing this, I cannot help concluding that Indian theatre-makers have rather more to teach us about our national playwright than we have to teach them.

Notes

1. http://www.bbc.co.uk/news/world-asia-india-18036002
2. http://www.thehindu.com/arts/theatre/a-georgian-magic/article4077442.ece
3. http://www.guardian.co.uk/stage/2012/apr/30/twelfth-night-shakespeares-globe-review
4. http://www.guardian.co.uk/stage/2012/jun/01/alls-well-that-ends-well-review

5 |

May a Million Fireflies Rise

Sanjoy Roy

Our weekly Saturday afternoon meetings were routine affairs. Our producer and director colleagues used to collect at the office to discuss the past week's problems and plot for the week ahead. Over samosas and chai, crucial decisions were made: which character should be killed off, who were the most annoying, what celebrity shoot or food choice needed lining up for next week, etc. Back then, we were primarily a television production company, churning out weekly soaps, satirical news, food and talk shows, enjoying the first spring of Indian television. Policies had changed, new channels were starting up almost on a daily basis and the entertainment industry was abuzz with possibilities and awash with fresh capital. Those of us who had climbed aboard the roller coaster, sped into the future with virtually no brakes on.

Six years on, we were a factory, churning out formats, inventing soaps, re-imagining game shows which were a precursor to today's reality programmes. The weekly meetings were an opportunity to catch your breath, let your hair down and assess (and occasionally scream and shout). Our colleagues, Sharupa Dutta and Manika Berry Asgaonkar, who were leading a handful of projects, looked tired and stressed; sixteen-hour days that included an arduous journey to Noida's film city was taking its toll; television itself tended to make you brain dead, or kept you lonely and single. They wanted a break, and in unison, suggested we stop!

STOP? How did that work? My partner, Mohit Satyanand, mulled over the thought, and having done some number crunching, announced that in his opinion, the only people making money from the shows were the channels, who used to pay us in 90–120 day cycles. In essence we could, if we wished to, take a break. A flurry of letters, followed by threats and heated arguments with a slew of channels, brought this chapter to a close.

Hara-kiri has many forms: this was its finest! The channels, unhappy about our decision, delayed payments even further. As we began winding down our programmes, the overheated TV scene collapsed with channels sputtering out, sacking people and financially ruining the producer fraternity. We were lucky to have got out when we did (or so we consoled ourselves). We were cash strapped, overstaffed and having to paddle hard to stay afloat.

It was 1995. Mohit had calculated that given our outstanding payments across channels and money owed for an ongoing Television Awards project sponsored by Onida, we would have enough to keep us afloat for a while, till we reinvented ourselves. Founded on a principle of peers voting for each other, with a jury to celebrate excellence, these awards would have been the best of its kind. Unfortunately, Onida ran into serious financial problems and decided to wind down the awards.

Stung by non-payments, many of our trusted colleagues left in search of fresh pastures. Sharupa went on to work with Pan Nalin in his various film projects and set up a new channel in Bangladesh: Manika began writing scripts; Charu Sharma Singh crossed over and joined the television channels: Tarun Laroia worked with Miditech.

In 1995 Mohit, his sister Kanika and Val Shipley had begun a bi-monthly get together at Mala and Amit Sharma's home, where friends and family would gather to listen and make music. Not Bollywood, nor hard rock, it quickly became a space for Indi and alternative music. The Friends of Music (FOM) group was born. A slew of today's stars, Susmit Sen and Indian Ocean, Mohit Chauhan, Bobby Cash strummed and sang their way to stardom from those early concerts. We took heart and expanded our work to include dance and theatre. We commissioned Astad Deboo,

India's celebrated contemporary dancer, to work with traditional Thangta martial arts performers and commissioned new writing in theatre, some of which won awards, and others found audiences. By 1999, we had created content but there didn't seem to be adequate platforms to showcase these acts.

In the eighties and nineties, the British Council in India was a hub of activity. Sushma Bahl, British Council's Director of Arts, had boundless energy, a rare vision, and the experience to work across international borders. Having seen me perform in Primetime Theatre's *Me and My Girl*, she invited me to visit the Edinburgh Festival Fringe as part of the British Council showcase programme in 1999. This set the agenda for our first cross-festival presentation in 2001.

Working closely with the Festival Fringe, the International Film Festival, the Edinburgh Tattoo and the Edinburgh International Festival, we created an annual platform of work from across India, enlarging our presence from six productions to sixteen. Many thought we were mad, but our long-term objectives paid off in more ways than one. We presented an array of artists: Aditi Mangaldas who returned year on year to great acclaim, Mrigaya, the world music group which went on to win the Herald Angel award at Edinburgh in 2002 and a five star review from *The Scotsman* newspaper, Indian Ocean, Lillette Dubey and her Primetime Theatre group, Adi Shakti, Lushin Dubey, Dadi Pudumjee and the Ishara Theatre Company, to name a few. Even Shah Rukh Khan, made his way to Edinburgh, in a celebration of the best of Indian arts.

It took some convincing to get the Edinburgh International Film Festival to agree to move Shah Rukh's 'In Conversation' to a larger venue. They cited examples of having presented the biggest stars including Sean Connery, in a 300-seat venue. Tickets went on sale and sold out minutes after the box office opened, only to be resold at £100 a ticket! The news made it to *The Times* front page and the festival organisers, somewhat embarrassed, moved the venue to a 1,000-seat auditorium. Huge crowds gathered at the festival venue. At the after-party, we had to barricade Shah Rukh into a corner, with tables and bouncers guarding him. The Film Festival hadn't quite seen something like this before!

The year we presented Ishara Puppet Theater's *Transposition*, the infamous liquid bomb incident took place at Heathrow as we landed. Having been evacuated from the airport and shipped to Gatwick, we finally arrived in Edinburgh after a 16-hour delay, only to find that 24 of our 30 odd suitcases and outsized puppet boxes and bags had been lost! Each day was spent at the airport and at the airport warehouse (a place where bags are sent in their afterlife), trying to locate something, anything. Five days and three cancelled shows later, the BBC ran a story on our predicament. Hours later, a passenger called Dana Macleod, our coordinator in Edinburgh, rang to say strange-shaped bags were going around the carousel with stickers bearing her name. The show was back on the road!

Sushma Bahl and Edmund Marsden drove British Council's agenda and collaborated with the UK-based Visiting Arts' programme director, Nelson Fernandez, to put together an annual Arts Management Programme where I was invited as a guest lecturer. The aim was to build capacity in India. For three years we worked together, led by course director Rodger McCann, to create offsite weeklong programmes for artists, managers and art administrators. It created a network amongst art groups in India and allowed us to reach out to presenting venues and festival directors in the UK. Much of this resulted in tangible activity: a commission from the Traverse Theatre followed by a UK tour led by Jan Ryan's UK Arts, annual presentations in London's Riverside Studio, ICA and the National Theatre's summer festival.

This in turn culminated in the setting up of the six-month long 'Great Arc Festival' across the UK, a celebration of the 150th anniversary of the scientific measurement of the Earth and the plotting of the Great Himalayan range. Inspired by John Keay's book of the same name, commissioned by India's Department of Science and Technology and steered by an innovative Amitabh Pandey, the then joint secretary, this project virtually brought us to the brink of bankruptcy due to the intransigence of government organisations.

'Reinventing' sounds cool but the process is terrifying! Television paid salaries which the arts could never afford. Investments in shows and festivals in those early days meant that our balance sheets were red, year on year. Setting up or collaborating with existing festivals led to some degree of success, with annual presentations in Singapore, Wellington, Perth and Melbourne. Much of these were a result of networking in Edinburgh and setting out a plan for collaborations, a strategy we adopted for the next few years. As our footprint grew through Asia to include Hong Kong and Indonesia, we began to look westwards.

Prompted by our then Consul General, Navdeep Suri, we set up the Shared History Festival in South Africa, to bring about an awareness of a new India and the many opportunities it offered, amongst the one million strong Indian diaspora. We collaborated with the city of Johannesburg's annual festival Arts Alive, to bring about resurgence in the crime infested, Central Business District (CBD) area of New Town. The city planned to use the arts to re-populate the CBD and reduce crime, bringing back the local populace. With an audience returning to the theatre, New Town has now seen a rise in property prices, new businesses opening and residential blocks being re-built. Though one can still get mugged, as did Indian poet Arvind Krishna Mehrotra, it is by and large a safe zone and a hub of creative activity!

Our accidental business model kicked in as we expanded out of Johannesburg to include Durban, Cape Town, Pretoria and Pietermaritzburg. We were able to amortise costs across the cities and build on revenues in a unique private public partnership model. For a long time I had believed that we needed to build circuits to make festivals pay for themselves and include local communities in the plan. Through CSR initiatives, we reached out to disenfranchised communities in Soweto, Mannenburg and Phoenix, townships that had been created by the former apartheid regime to separate communities. A series of Art Therapy and Theatre workshops run by Puneeta Roy and the Tehelka Foundation, helped reach out to a demographic somewhat different to our average theater-going population.

Governments rarely credit the direct contribution that Arts interventions make to marginalised communities. The arts provide young people an opportunity to express and develop their own views, ideas and confidence.

At Salaam Baalak Trust (SBT), an organisation providing support services for street and working children in Delhi set up in 1988, we laid great emphasis on theatre, music, dance and visual arts as therapeutic tools for homeless children, most often violated and abused. Salim, a four-year old boy, lost his family during a religious procession passing through the city. The police brought him to us and he was beside himself with grief wishing to return home. He had no address and his only action was to draw a house next to a railway line and what appeared to be a church. Our social workers sent out photographs to potential locations and following a six-year search, we were able to reunite Salim with his family. One of eleven children born to a poor family, he returned to the trust to complete his education. He was later cast in an Academy award-nominated short film and went on to become a full time contemporary dancer and actor.

Vicky Roy, an enthusiastic photographer, was inspired by Haran, one of our older kids who had a rare ability to capture incredible imagery and went on to win the All India Photography Award and a commission by the World Photography Association in Amsterdam. Vicky pursued his dream, apprenticing with Benjamin Dix, a volunteer at SBT. He joined leading photographer Anay Mann and thereon was mentored by Anubhav Nath, who provides a platform for artists through the Ramchander Nath Foundation. Nath helped Vicky win an award from the Stuttgart and San Francisco-based Maybach Foundation and the New York-based real estate company, Silverstein Properties, to be one of four young people selected internationally to document the re-building of the World Trade Center in New York. Both Vicky and Haran have had their work shown in galleries and museums across the world, leading to a comment by a famous Indian photographer that: 'a street kid in Salaam Baalak Trust has more opportunities to succeed than other artists'!

Other SBT kids – Kapil, Pawan, Shamshul, Shameem, Viraj and Kumari – trained as puppeteers with Dadi Pudumjee and went on to become independent artists. Shameem joined Miditech as a senior puppeteer, earning an annual salary of Rs 12 lakh ($22,000). Kapil directed and created productions for corporate advertising and stage shows. Pawan, Shameem and Kumari continue to work at the trust creating entertaining productions that included social messages.

Intervention through the Arts creates wealth in a sustained manner, allowing people and their communities to find new ways of overcoming odds and finding unique solutions. Governments, who believe that supporting the arts is about handouts, need to reassess their policies and invest in the future of its people and provide for sustained arts education.

In India, we have 110 million children out of school. Even if the GDP spend on education were to double, it would take 20 years to build the brick and mortar structures to house this population and train teachers required to man these buildings. New ideas and out-of-the-box solutions need to be found, to deliver education to these children. Story-telling forms through the arts could be one way of delivering much needed literacy to those who live outside the system.

Recently we took the Kahani Festival – 'Discover the magic of stories' – to Dantewada, Chattisgarh, an area at the heart of the Maoist insurgency movement. Thousands of kids from a 100km radius were bussed in for the three-day programme of workshops, music, dance, storytelling and art. While many were enrolled in local schools, mainly to access the mid-day meal, none had actually encountered a teacher, few spoke Hindi and most were unfamiliar with the epic texts of the *Mahabharata* or the *Ramayana*. Their day of discovery was to access the wonders that non-verbal forms like puppetry and dance brought to their lives. Transfixed and transformed, they left enriched, even if for a fleeting moment.

Violence-scarred regions should use the arts to anchor the young and old to their tradition and history and allow for a semblance of normalcy. When we cancelled Harud, a literature programme in Srinagar, a distressed author from Kashmir pleaded with us, stating how desperate they were to see a show or share their stories, and have a normal evening out. This was not to pass, as a group of civil society activists drove a campaign against the festival project, saying it would demonstrate that life in Kashmir was normal when it wasn't. Yet another group called for action to stone the authors, the students as well as our team members, should we attempt to host the festival. All because of a misleading article published by one of India's leading national dailies.

As India's economy gained momentum, we began consolidating our position by setting up a slew of platforms: for theater (META), literature (Hay Festival, Kerala) and puppetry (Ishara International Puppet Festival). We sought out new opportunities in Austria, Germany, Italy and Spain, working through agents and driving box office sales to make projects economically viable. We produced *Bollywood Love Story – A Musical*, to reach new audiences. We were amazed to discover how small towns like Einbeck, Stuttgart, Eindhoven and larger ones like Florence and Barcelona had a huge appetite to celebrate and embrace foreign cultures and more specifically Bollywood. Our primarily white audiences came dressed in Indian attire, belting out words of songs they didn't understand. Exporting Bollywood should be the mainstay of our foreign missions in order to capture hearts and souls of people across the world. Stunned by an impossibly large bill for excess baggage, the entire cast and crew of the musical staged an impromptu routine at the check-in counter at Frankfurt airport, cheered along by fellow passengers. The airline staff joined in and waived the excess fees.

Entertainment districts traditionally contribute to a city's economy. Broadway offers up $9–11 billion and London's West End £3–5 billion through its restaurants, nightclubs, theaters, bars and concerts. The Edinburgh festival contributes £225 m of additional spend during the seven weeks of the festival, attracting millions of tourists, artists and art lovers who congregate at this Mecca of the arts world.

At our annual DSC Jaipur Literature Festival, which brings together 250 speakers over five days and attracts over a 100,000 visitors, the additional contribution to the city's economy has been estimated at approximately Rs 15–20 crores ($3-4 m). City hotels see capacity crowds, jewellers, retailers and craft outlets do brisk business, and airlines and transport companies cash in on the annual boom.

In India, where tourism and culture should contribute a greater share to the GDP, we are still stuck in the 5–6 million visitors syndrome. Culture and tourism are still not seen as primary drivers of the economy. Both these represent an opportunity to create jobs locally in a way that is sustainable. We need focused training, development funds for local

Audience at the Jaipur Literature Festival
Courtesy: Teamworks

heritage sites, marketing budgets and basic facilities of toilets, cafes and green transportation. India has a million heritage sites, all waiting to be rediscovered and leveraged. Annual cultural festivals and daily shows against the backdrop of a heritage monument, will allow tourists an opportunity to stay the night, boost local taxes and grow the ancillary food and transport sector. Much of the income can be ploughed back to preserving the built heritage.

Faith and John Singh, in their landmark initiative in Jaipur, showed that built heritage can be preserved with help from the city and local communities. Aman Nath and Francis Wacziarg pioneered the conservation and conversion of crumbling forts, palaces and havelis into boutique hotels, bringing alive little known villages like Neemrana, which have now grown into industrial and tourism hubs. Maharaja Gaj Singh (Bapji) of Jodhpur has demonstrated how investment in the arts builds bonds within communities and creates a platform for development and progress. Dastakar, The Crafts Council of India, Vidhi Singhania's Kota Development Trust, and The Urmul Trust have brought about a revival in the textile and craft handloom industry with innovations in design and marketing skills. Heritage Scotland and England have shown how you can use technology and knowhow to revive historical sites and provide retail and other opportunities to crafts and homegrown businesses.

In today's polarised world, it is imperative that we use the arts as a window into other cultures. The arts know no language and have a universality that allows the viewer to absorb the exotic, within a given context. In the latest commission by the Globe Theater as part of the Cultural Olympiad, an array of exciting productions played out from Afghanistan and India to Romania and Belarus. Each was distinct and brought to the fore cultural differences and yet was bound together by the universal language of theater and performance. Audiences who attended may not have understood the nuances of the languages, but this did not detract from their enjoyment of what they were witnessing. *Pia Behrupiya* by the Company Theater was a brilliant piece of original theatre. Based on Shakespeare's *Twelfth Night,* the ensemble cast, sang, danced and created magic at the Globe Theatre against the backdrop of the Olympic games, much as the Royal Shakespeare Company-British Council production of *The Dream,* based on *A Midsummer Night's*

Buddhist monks perform at the Jaipur Literature Festival
Courtesy: Teamworks

Dream, did some years ago, bringing together diverse actors from the sub-continent.

The Arts were on show at the opening and closing ceremonies of the Olympic Games, which set a new goalpost for creating imagery and cultural specific references, delighting both national and international audiences. What a finale! Almost every newspaper across the world echoed a similar sentiment. The Games had once again made London the centre of the world. If the opening ceremony was quirky quintessential British, the closing was the 'after party' with a song list spanning four decades and boasting a slew of performers, including some thought to have been long dead, resurrected to rouse the crowds and stir memories of Band Aid! Kim Gavin, the artistic director of the closing ceremony, presented it as a tribute to the British pop industry, combined with a subtle message to the Americans: you may have the best athletes, but we have the best bands. British Arts at its best!

India needs to learn from this. Our concept of *jugaad*, which rescues us in the nick of time, is no match for years of diligent planning and preparation. Why can't state governments use lottery money for the arts and sports, much as the UK government does to fund arts infrastructure projects? This is not about priorities but about vision and the will to break the mould, and provide the best opportunities for a billion Indians who have the talent but few platforms to realise them.

While a few first steps have been taken in creating an education policy, which includes the arts as formal coursework in schools, there has been little thought of how this will be delivered in the short term. Theatre must be a part of education and music teachers need to be trained to deliver a syllabus. Organisations like Arts Link in Chennai, which have begun delivering a programme on Indian classical music through schools, need to be expanded to include other cities. Technology is one way of doing this. The MIT driven Indian Raga portal, which has tied in with ITC's Sangeet Research Academy, is a possible way to expand the bandwidth. Rich archive-driven organisations like Sahapedia should be funded to make information on the arts democratically available and accessible to research scholars and artists. Traditional musicians, storytellers and puppeteers should be entrusted with the task of teaching their art form, in state and private school education programmes. This will provide schools with a rich source of knowledge and cultural input, as well as give the artist and artisans a livelihood, whilst preserving their tradition and culture. It is not enough for us to carry on about India's rich cultural heritage, and do precious little to nurture and preserve it. Barring the initiatives of the Indian Council of Cultural Relations (ICCR) and sporadic schemes brought about by the Ministry of Culture and its many institutions, there are few initiatives to realise the needs and aspirations of India's creative class.

This shortcoming needs to be redressed. The government, through its urban development programmes, needs to build sustainable projects which include theatres, museums, rehearsal spaces, experimental studios, galleries, digital labs, ampi-theaters, and do this in a spirit of public partnership. It is sad to see that the capital city of Delhi has not one new public space, with a sense of aesthetics or pride reflecting the national culture. Projects based on the lowest bid will never create excellence and will only lead to further corruption of the nation's soul. Look at how Brazil has created a multitude of neighbourhood cultural centres, funded from taxes and contributions by local traders and business people, co-funded by the city's government. UK's lottery fund is another example of creating a funding mechanism whilst regulating the lottery industry and freeing it from corruption.

Every journalist loves to do a story on the dying art forms or the revival of an art form. In India nothing ever dies, artists like the societies they inhabit, adapt and move on. In a country that has the philosophical breadth and diversity like India, all you need to do is create a ground that is fertile and enrich it with the nutrients of imagination, social and economic inclusion, vision and resources. May a *million fireflies rise*[1] in to the night sky illuminating our hearts and our minds!

Note

1. Fireflies rising is one of the scenarios created for India in a workshop programme led by Arun Maira (Member, Planning Commission, Government of India) for CII in the mid 1990s.

6|

Growing up under the Umbrella of Indian Cinema

Nasreen Munni Kabir

The first film I remember seeing was Mehboob Khan's spectacular fable, *Aan*. I was about twelve at the time and can still picture Nimmi running through a field of swaying mustard flowers, singing '*Aaj mere mann mein sakhi bansuri bajaaye koi*'. The dazzling yellow flowers, the blue open sky, and her bright flowing clothes were all so enchanting. To top it all, far in the distance and astride a beautiful black horse, the splendid Dilip Kumar waited for her. Right then and there, I decided, that when I grew up, I was going to work in films.

One of India's early colour productions, the 1952 film *Aan* had a sumptuous look, the kind you see in old Hollywood movies that are meant to show a fabled exotic East. With fabulous songs by Naushad and Shakeel Badayuni, the film is a love triangle: Mangala, a village belle (Nimmi) loves Jai, a commoner (Dilip Kumar) who loves Rajkumari, an arrogant princess (Nadira). *Aan* showed India as a land of plenty where virtue wins, evil is destroyed and love triumphs. Renamed *Mangala, Daughter of India*, Mehboob's film was a massive hit all over North Africa, and one wonders if the stereotypes about 'exotic' India that spread in Africa in the 1950s have their genesis in *Aan*.

The simple beauty of this lavish fairytale drew me like a magnet into the world of cinema. Though I was born in Hyderabad, Andhra Pradesh, I had no memory of India, as my family had set up home in London when I was a toddler. What was India like? How did people sound? Did they speak in a soft or loud tone? Were roads busy? Were roads quiet? What did a house look like? In those days, even TV documentaries about India were rarely seen on British television. I was young and immature, and was happy to let Hindi films provide me with the images and sounds of a country that I did not really know.

Many of the early films I saw fascinated me. It was probably Hindi film music, even more than the films, that drew me to them. My elder sister had an enviable collection of records, from crackly old 1978s to the 1960s' LPs and EPs. We woke up in the morning and fell asleep at night to the voices of Lata Mangeshkar and Mohammed Rafi. Their wonderful songs provided the soundtrack to our lives, as they did for millions. The poetic lyrics were the reason why many of my generation, immersed in an English-speaking world, wanted to understand Hindustani. Even if we could not express ourselves fluently, it was critical to know what the words in the song meant, as their romantic imagery had such an effect on our hearts. Film music to this day continues to be the glue that binds our deeper sentiments to the Hindi film.

Britain is undoubtedly a culturally enriching and wonderful place to live, but for the first generation of immigrants that came in the 1950s and 1960s, finding acceptance and a confident voice took time. London was not the multicultural society, as we know it today; being different, culturally and racially in those early years, was seen as being the 'other'. Adjusting was a daunting task. Distances were insurmountable and communication difficult and expensive. This was decades before the existence of DVDs, the internet and mobile phones: all the forms of technology that today make the world a mere click away. Travel was also a much bigger deal fifty years ago, and people could not afford a yearly trip to soak in the warmth of India. So, during those years, the impact of Indian cinema on British Asians was particularly potent. I later discovered many millions shared the same lively passion for cinema, whether they had settled beyond India's borders, or had never left the sub-continent.

Watching a Hindi film became a reassuring ritual for people like me who grew up in Britain. What a pleasure to see Dilip Kumar, Nargis or Raj Kapoor on the screen. How gratifying to behold characters that looked and dressed like us, spoke in a language we knew, and expressed familiar emotions. The Scala Theatre on Charlotte Street in central London was the place where my sister and I went on Sundays to see a Hindi film. At midday, we would rush over to Charlotte Street and join the long ticket line. I remember English passers-by looking a little bewildered to see so many brownish faces gathered there. We never knew in advance what would be playing: sometimes it was a new film and sometimes an older one. Our choice was limited then, because Hindi films were not released simultaneously around the world as they are today. Until its closure in 1969, the Scala Theatre continued to draw packed houses on Sundays. A fire later destroyed the building that held so many memories for us. Then the action moved to the Haymarket Theatre near Piccadilly Circus.

By the 1970s, there were about 100 cinemas in the UK that screened Indian movies on a Sunday. Additional shows ran on late nights on weekdays. Catering to the ever-growing Asian population, a few Indian-owned cinemas opened their doors in different places, including Southall and Leicester. But our film-going routine drastically changed when the VHS arrived. Though most tapes were pirated, at least the film selection increased vastly. Video shops and local Asian groceries did brisk business renting out a film for a pound a night. I remember a 1975 newspaper article that claimed the largest groups of VCR buyers were Asians, and we knew exactly why.

The downside of the VHS was that it opened the floodgates of piracy. From a viewer's point, however, it was a complete treat. For the first time, people could watch films in the comfort of their homes, a rare luxury, unless you were rich enough to own a home projector and rent film prints. Thanks to the VHS, viewers could replay or skip scenes or songs, see the film once or several times. The VHS (and all subsequent digital formats) have given the spectator control over the way a film is viewed and experienced. Not a great thing for filmmakers, as the pace of storytelling – once the director's domain – has now fallen forever prey to frisky fingers on the fast-forward and rewind buttons.

Another negative impact of the VHS invasion in Britain was that it gradually put an end to the collective Sunday movie outings. Going to the movies had become a lively social event for the Asian community: families attended in their finery, friends met for a chat and even marriages were discussed during the interval. Today, only a star-studded premiere will bring a vast Asian audience together. The UK Asians (now known as NRIs) continue to see Hindi films, but largely in the seclusion of their homes.

The desire to work in films triggered by my seeing *Aan* never left me. By the early 1970s, I moved to Paris where I did a Masters in Film Studies. I started work on a PhD thesis on the great 1950s directors: Mehboob Khan, Bimal Roy, Raj Kapoor and Guru Dutt. But soon realised that working as an assistant on documentaries and feature films seemed to me a more effective way of learning the craft of filmmaking, so regrettably I gave up the idea of the thesis.

While still in Paris, and struggling to make ends meet, a close friend, Peter Chappell, who later photographed all my documentaries, talked about a fourth terrestrial channel, a public-service broadcaster that was about to go on air in Britain. With the access to countless channels today, it is unimaginable to think that once there were only three British TV channels: BBC1, BBC2 and ITV. The prospect of Channel 4 – that had a remit of making innovative programmes for a diverse community – was a huge boost to many young independent producers. Channel 4 was also keen to attract minority audiences. I thought there was no better way to achieve that, than by broadcasting Hindi films. Peter convinced me to put my ideas forward. So, hesitantly I returned to London in 1981 to meet Sue Woodford, Channel 4's first Multicultural Commissioning Editor.

It was a bleak and rainy day when I set off to their temporary offices on Brompton Road. Sue Woodford was charming and warm and said she did indeed want Indian films in their schedule and asked me to work out a possible Hindi film season. I was so excited that I naively sent her a hundred-page document, outlining the history of Indian cinema, adamant that a first Hindi film season on Channel 4 must have the classics from the 1950s. I could never disguise my bias for the cinema of the 1950s and it has always resurfaced in my work.

Little did I realise that highly pressured TV executives, in the throes of launching a channel, had no time to read even a short letter, let alone a long rambling report. Sue politely said all she needed was a one-page list of ten films that they would buy and air. I think my 100-page report ended up in some trash bin where it probably belonged.

Sue gave me my first contract as Channel 4's Indian cinema consultant and for three years, till 1986, I shuttled between Paris and London by plane, train, bus and hovercraft (no magical Eurostar in those days). I worked for three days a week at Channel 4 and returned to Paris the rest of the week to work with Jean Loup Passek who headed the cinema department at the Georges Pompidou Centre. In 1983 we organised a major festival at the Pompidou Centre with 100 films. The festival included a retrospective of Satyajit Ray who came to Paris to attend. It was a great pleasure to meet this colossus of a man. He was fabulously intelligent and fabulously gifted.

In 1985, we put together a second festival at the Pompidou Centre, this time screening 120 films. French audiences received the selection, made up of Hindi popular cinema, with great enthusiasm. Many top stars came from India for the festival, including Amitabh Bachchan, Smita Patil and Shabana Azmi. I think it was the first time such a large-scale festival of Hindi popular cinema had taken place in the West. Most European festivals had previously favoured Indian art-house cinema rather than pay much attention to the popular cinema, its stars and filmmakers.

Back in London, Channel 4 was nearing their start date and had moved offices from Brompton Road to their new headquarters. What seemed to me a most extraordinary coincidence was that they were now housed in Scala House, in the very building that replaced Scala Theatre on Charlotte Street. Sue asked me which day they should broadcast the Indian film season, and I said it had to be on a Sunday. I couldn't get over the fact that Channel 4 would transmit Indian films that I had selected, from the very spot where thousands of families would enjoy a Sunday outing and where my desire to research Indian cinema had begun. I felt I had come full circle.

When Channel 4 went on air on 2 November 1982, it changed British television programming forever. It was bold, innovative, irreverent and youthful. The channel was really instrumental in holding a mirror to British contemporary life. Britain had become a multi-cultural and multi-racial society and till then this was not sufficiently reflected in mainstream media. Black and Asian faces were rarely seen on television in those days. Even presenters speaking with regional accents from Wales or Scotland were seldom heard. Christmas was traditionally all white too. So imagine the thrill, and perhaps even shock, for Asian viewers to tune into Channel 4 on 26 December 1982, Boxing Day, and see *Sholay* playing at peak time. Nearly a million viewers – a huge number in those days – watched the subtitled film. The next morning, the Channel 4 duty officers' report showed countless phone calls from viewers voicing their appreciation. In the 1980s, many Asians felt that Channel 4 was their channel and thanks to Hindi cinema, it had won hearts that had been largely ignored.

By the mid 1980s, I moved back to London where I have lived ever since. In 1986, Farrukh Dhondy, who had taken Sue Woodford's place, agreed to commission me to produce and direct a 49-part series called *Movie Mahal*. It was the first time I had directed a TV programme, and the heady mix of fear and fearlessness took over.

Aired in both 1987 and 1988, *Movie Mahal* was the first television series on Indian cinema on British TV, and perhaps a world first. At that time even Doordarshan was not keen on programmes about popular cinema. The mushrooming of cable, television and satellite channels in India had yet to happen and the only film-related programme on Doordarshan was a song compilation show called *Chitrahaar*.

I think the most important thing about *Movie Mahal* was that it highlighted the excellent craft of Hindi films. The commercial cinema was by and large regarded as un-cool and lowbrow entertainment in the 1980s. In the *Movie Mahal* interviews, Hindi film practitioners came across as insightful, witty and intelligent. Their comments seemed to surprise viewers who had little experience of hearing them discussing their work and the impact of cinema. There were few books on Indian cinema at that time and film magazines tended to favour gossip. Thankfully, that situation has completely changed. Today there are several serious film books and biographies. Popular cinema now occupies center-stage in India. With the rise of celebrity culture that is synonymous with Hindi movie stars, top actors have never been as popular nor wielded as much power as they do now.

During the months that *Movie Mahal* was broadcast, Channel 4 received many telephone calls of appreciation and hundreds of letters that were really emotional outpourings. Balwant Pande from Harrow wrote saying he and his friends felt the series was the best thing on British TV for Asians. He added that at last a British broadcaster was offering programmes that were for Asians and not about them. Mr Pande became

Dilip Kumar and Nasreen Munni Kabir recording for Movie Mahal
Courtesy: Hyphen Films
Credit: Peter Chappell

a dear friend. We talked to each other on the phone and wrote to one another for over fifteen years. He passed away a few years ago and I still miss his letters and calls. I remember a letter from Mrs D'Souza, another *Movie Mahal* fan, who wrote to say how excited she was to see Tony, her late cousin, among the chorus dancers in Helen's *Mera Naam Chin Chin Choo*. Happy childhood days in Goa came back to her.

There was also a poignant letter from Caroline, an English woman who was born in India and had been raised by an Indian ayah. She said her ayah used to sing her a song every night to put her to sleep till she was four. Caroline returned to England in the late 1950s with her family. In her thirties, Caroline became obsessed with finding out the name of the song her ayah sang for her. Whenever she would meet her Indian friends, she would hum them the tune, hoping that someone would guess the song's name. Years passed and one Sunday morning, Caroline happened to catch a *Movie Mahal* episode on Channel 4. To her utter amazement and joy, she heard the song that had haunted her for decades; the song of her

Lata Mangeshkar and Nasreen Munni Kabir recording for Movie Mahal
Courtesy: Hyphen Films
Credit: Peter Chappell

childhood was none other than Lata Mangeshkar's '*Ayegaa Aanewaala*' from Kamal Amrohi's wonderful film *Mahal* (1949). I found Caroline's letter so moving that I asked her to call me. When she did, we spoke about her childhood in India. All I could do for her was to send her an audio-cassette of the soundtrack of *Mahal*.

When I happened to meet strangers, and they discovered that I had made *Movie Mahal*, I could see their expression turn to delight. They would tell me that they were glued to their television every Sunday and would regularly tape the episodes. Many boasted of having the entire series on VHS, and others would admit reluctantly lending their copies to friends and the copies never came back. Pirated copies were sent all around the world where British Asians had friends and family. I once met an Indian family from Uganda who said they were proud owners of the entire series. Even today, I occasionally get a call from a viewer, asking to buy the whole set of *Movie Mahal*. It was a humbling experience to make something that linked people to their past and meant so much to them, while introducing Indian cinema to many others who knew nothing about it. I am reminded of what Javed Akhtar once told me: 'You never know where, how and when the seeds you plant will flower.'

The emerging economic power of the Asian diaspora in the late 1990s has done a lot to change the role of the Asian community. Indian culture is far more visible today in all walks of British life. That extends to schools and universities. In the early 1990s, I persuaded the South Asian department at the School of Oriental and African Studies (SOAS) to start a course in Hindi cinema. They agreed, and writer and journalist, Asha Richards, taught the first year-long courses there. It is still going from strength to strength. One of the earliest British Film Institute (BFI) publications on Indian cinema was edited by Paul Willemen and Behroze Gandhy. Teachers all round Britain have shown an interest in offering courses on Indian film, and as a result the BFI have produced a teaching pack on the subject.

The year 2002 saw the worldwide culmination of the new interest in Asian culture and proved a particular winner for all things Indian: *Lagaan* was nominated for an Oscar in the Best Foreign Film Category that year,

Sanjay Leela Bhansali's *Devdas* was screened at Cannes with Shah Rukh Khan, Aishwarya Rai and Madhuri Dixit walking the red carpet, Andrew Lloyd Webber produced *Bombay Dreams* with music by A.R. Rahman, Madame Tussaud unveiled the wax figure of Amitabh Bachchan, and chicken tikka was declared Britain's favourite dish. Bollywood dancing too found its way into some schools and gyms. It is now accepted as a mainstream dance-form, eagerly learnt by Asian and non-Asians. Though I have great reservations about the term 'Bollywood', as I think it sounds quite demeaning, I must reluctantly admit it has helped to raise the profile of Hindi films internationally.

This great surge of interest in Indian cinema has decreased ten years on. Although Hindi films are screened in multiplex cinemas throughout the UK (and accessible today on multiple digital platforms), it is still the traditional Indian distributors who are responsible for the films' release. The charm of Hindi films continues to elude British distributors and a wider non-Asian audience. Despite the many changes in British broadcasting, Channel 4 remains the only mainstream terrestrial channel to show Indian films on a regular basis, twenty a year. Channel 4's Tim Highsted and Dan Borgonon in the Film Acquisition department are hopeful to continue showing Indian films, whether or not they are the flavour of the month. Though the demand for documentaries is over, I continue to curate Channel 4's annual Indian film season and produce introductions with stars and directors that precede the films.

I don't believe any other cinema in the world has played as significant a role, as Indian cinema, and perhaps even more so, Indian film songs, in so effectively tying people to their place of origin, emotionally and culturally. There is no denying that Hindi cinema has become the unbreakable thread that has bound many of us, including me, to our roots. I am indebted to Channel 4, Sue Woodford and Farrukh Dhondy for starting me off in a dream job that has lasted for thirty years. It's all about happening to be at the right place at the right time.

7

Geek India

Pradeep Kar

*I*n early September 2012, a bunch of fifty-odd youngsters met at Goa's Majorda Beach Resort. The lush green resort is located on a long strip of clear white sand on the west coast of India. The breeze from the Arabian Sea is salty, strong, and persistent as it blows through thick coconut groves. Goa was the world's top hippie destination in the 1970s and continues to be a major tourist attraction: the sun, sea and feni (local arrack drink), combined with the laid-back nature of the place, always bringing in the punters.

The fifty youngsters puttering around at the Majorda in their shorts and tee-shirts could have easily been mistaken for beach bums. But ever so often, they'd keep popping into a large neatly-organised hall to listen to experts speak on Amazon's Web Services (AWS) and their Elastic Cloud Compute (EC2) infrastructure, to specialists detailing the need for getting patents registered correctly, or even get a quick 101 from veteran venture capitalists on how to structure deals. No one in the room appeared to be over thirty-five. They were all part of technology ideas being incubated by The Morpheus, an Indian start-up accelerator that has funded over fifty companies in the last four years.

Appropriately, The Morpheus itself is founded by thirty-somethings. It calls the three-day event, held regularly for each new batch of ideas being bank-rolled, The Gurukul. In Hindi, 'gurukul' means 'school'. It is a term with roots in ancient India. It draws vivid pictures of sages imparting knowledge, philosophy, ideas and creative thoughts to eager youngsters under open skies and sprawling banyan trees. Gurukuls were traditionally located in isolated environments that had little distraction and encouraged free thinking. But, as one of the youngsters, working on creating a mobile-based solution to alert private bus users as to when to expect their ride, pointed out to a representative of a venture fund: India has changed; the idea of a gurukul has changed; Goa is the best-placed State for infrastructure by the Eleventh Finance Commission and has been ranked at the top for quality of life in India by the National Commission on Population. Could there be a more inspiring location in the country?

Welcome to Geek India, a young nation-within-a-nation, largely concealed from view to outsiders, except in newspaper headlines; a quiet but busy nation connecting the dots to draw new and exciting futures; a nation that understands more than it reveals; a nation that is rising to the challenges of tomorrow but which views them as the opportunities of the future.

Geek India is an idea that has been brewing for over a decade. It is exemplified by enterprising young people like Gurbaksh Chahal, Naveen Selvadurai and Ooshma Garg. Gurbaksh, the 27-year-old founder of Blue Lithium, a global online advertising network, was optimising campaigns deploying data analytics as far back as 2004. In 2007, when the world woke up to Big Data[1], Blue Lithium was acquired by Yahoo! for US$300 million, propelling its founder to be featured on the Oprah Winfrey show as America's most eligible bachelor. Selvadurai founded the mobile social networking site Foursquare with Dennis Crowley. Foursquare is estimated to be valued at US$500 million. At 30-something, Naveen is on AOL's list of World's Young Millionaires and stepped down last March from the day-to-day operations of Foursquare. Ooshma, at 24, created a recruiting and networking platform called Anapata for the legal profession. The normally conservative law community is excited about Anapata and many have called user profiles on the site 'incredible'. Slowly, but surely, Ooshma is also headed for success. But the point is: most of these names are not in the limelight, preferring to beaver away at what they believe they can do best. That's the real character of Geek

India – a nation that is in every corner of the globe – working to make the world a better place.

The astute will pause at this point. How did a nation, best known for exporting spices and precious stones, journey into IT and begin to turn knowledge into wealth? When did the state-led strategy of the nation's founding fathers – stalwarts such as Prime Minister Jawaharlal Nehru – to drive industrialisation, become ineffective and get hijacked by information technology? The government's Green Revolution of the 1960s failed to mimic the industrialisation and skill development roadmap of the West. How did Nehru's powerful 'Temples of Modern India' – factories, research labs, power stations, radio networks, dams and canals – that dominated until the 1980', suddenly give way to information technology as the backbone on which India is consolidating its future? What is driving technology giants like IBM, Google, Microsoft, CISCO and Intel to overlook the bureaucracy and procedural barriers and continue to make massive investments in India's technological capabilities?

The real magnitude of this trend can be visualised in the employment numbers IT has generated. In 2011, the IT sector had generated employment for 2.8 million, and indirectly employed another 8.9 million people.[2] This is more than the population of many nations such as Austria, Switzerland, Israel, Norway, Denmark, Singapore, etc.[3] Incidentally, this number (11.7 million) has far surpassed several forecasts. For example, in 2005, a World Economic Forum report had suggested that India would have created employment for 1 million in the IT sector by 2010.[4]

In the UK, mechanisation and the introduction of technology in the agrarian sector improved labour productivity as a forerunner to the industrial revolution. Skilled and semi-skilled labour from agriculture moved to employment in industry. It was a smooth and natural progression. India's so-called Green Revolution produced no such parallel story. And yet, in the space of a mere twenty five years, the Indian IT industry has clocked in annual revenues of US$76 billion, accounting for approximately 6 per cent of India's GDP, according to the National Association of Software and Service Companies (NASSCOM).[5] Last year, the IT industry grew by a staggering 19 per cent. Indian IT export revenues for 2011 are estimated to be US$59 billion, boasting a contribution of 26 per cent to total Indian exports (merchandise plus services), according to NASSCOM's research report 'IT-BPO Sector in India: Strategic Review 2011'. The report says that the workforce in the Indian IT industry will touch 30 million by 2020 when it will be a US$225 billion industry. Note the numbers. The last time anyone made a forecast, India outran them!

IT has changed the socio-economic face of the nation. It is reshaping India's image. It is influencing people in every corner of the nation. Many of the youngsters at The Morpheus' Gurukul in Goa came from towns and cities like Sangli and Chandigarh, places that many will be hard pressed to pin point on a map. While IT is fuelling growth, it is also powering incredible dreams in small towns like Barmer and Bidar, Mirzapur and Mysore. This is where Geek India is emerging from.

What happened? Where did the new age technology entrepreneur spring up from, practically overnight? How did s/he outrun the long standing textile and manufacturing conglomerates of Indian industry? How did a polity that was based on legislative control cave in to the free spirit of IT dreamers? When did India find the time to sprint out of its comfort zone and evolve into Geek India? Who is now driving this miracle of a modern nation? Where is it headed?

For the last 2.5 decades, I have been lucky to witness first-hand, the changes that IT has brought about in India. By the mid-1990's our company Microland had introduced global IT giants like Compaq, Cisco, Synoptics, Checkpoint and Netscape to India. They could sense the opportunity for growth in the country. In 1997, when we hosted Bill Gates at a CEO event in Mumbai – his first visit to India – he could more than sense what India had to offer. He didn't just whiff the air. He dug deep into the Indian psyche, sharply rising above the obvious conclusions visitors to India reach when they see poor roads and snarl-ups with cows holding up the traffic. I remember him saying that India would emerge as the software superpower of the twenty-first century.

By the end of 1999, we at Microland, were busy setting up internet companies that went beyond networking. With a host of companies

Pradeep Kar and Bill Gates
Courtesy: Pradeep Kar

like Planetasia.com, India's first Internet professional services company, ITspace.com, India's first technology portal, Media2India, India's first internet media company and NetBrahma Technologies, which was busy building IP products for the new generation telecom environment, Microland was developing software tools and Internet portals for global businesses. By 2000, we had launched Indya.com, the definitive online portal of India which subsequently sold to Rupert Murdoch's News Corp. Indya fuelled the internet boom in the country. It wrote out the script for success and began to work as the lodestone for entrepreneurs. In fact, at Indya, we consciously hired people with entrepreneurial skills and ambitions.[6] Thanks to these developments, India was already rushing into the twenty-first century that Bill Gates had predicted. But that period of development and growth was focused around larger cities like Mumbai, Delhi and Bangalore. In the short span of the last decade, much has changed.

I am convinced that the current wave of IT driven by Geek India – yes, young folk in small towns who have understood how to lay their hands on a better life – is the result of shrinking resources. Simple comparisons tell us why this is true. The Indian IT business has never seen large infusion of funds. That is the difference between Geek India and the advanced nations of the West. Freely available funds created technical and technological change in the West. The dearth of funds, on the other hand, drove innovation and efficiency in India. Geek India had no alternative but to adopt the efficiency and innovation change component over the technical change component. This in turn brought into play the elimination of waste, reallocation of resources, the quest for solutions that yield low margins but which impact large underdeveloped markets. Looked at from a strategic point of view, these are approaches that the industry is struggling to adopt globally. These are imperative to sustainability in the long term.

It may be too early to conclude that Geek India is demonstrating how to deploy innovation in a world of constraints and rapidly depleting resources. But surely the hypothesis is not completely flawed. The astute will pause again, this time to applaud Geek India for being ahead of the curve. Geek India is running the four-minute mile in business. It is breaking barriers and demolishing past thinking. It is changing rules to change outcomes. It is using innovation to do so.

India's demographic profile is responsible for the unfolding scenario with 64.9 per cent of the country between the age group of 15 and 64. The median age is 26.2.[7] This means that more than half of India is below the age of 25. This is a young nation with a large working-age population. Combined with the academic infrastructure (389 universities, 14,169 colleges and 1,500 research institutions[8]), it has created an unmatched supply of English-speaking talent. The number of students enrolled for engineering courses increased by 800 per cent from 1998 to 2008.[9] India adds more than one million engineering and science graduates year on year.[10] Admittedly, many are not employable in the traditional sense and need considerable skill improvement. But that's not the point. We are not discussing employability.

What matters is the capability of these graduates to go out there and do things. Many of the youngsters at The Morpheus' Gurukul did not appear to be skilled communicators. But they had figured out how to capture error messages triggered in web browsers by faulty code and how to send it back to the developer in real time[11] and how to create a SaaS-type Point of Sale systems for small restaurants. They may not have been able to order a meal at an Italian restaurant, but they could write killer codes in Pearl, Python, Java, BREW...practically anything.

The fact that IT and ITES firms enjoy a liberal, regulatory environment and minimal policy restrictions has helped. Other nations are trying to emulate this, validating the efficacy of the approach.

If anything, the burden on government and private enterprise to consciously create methods to sustain and power Geek India is substantial. They must map the global megatrends that are shaping jobs and employment scenarios across the world and ensure that these trends in manufacturing, mining, utilities, construction, trade, hospitality, financial intermediation, IT and business service, public administration, education and healthcare, dictate what is taught in schools and universities. Human capital must be tightly aligned with the emerging demand for labour. However, we need to focus on the technology aspects that will impact industries predicted to dominate fifteen years from now. To put it another way, a formal structure to nurture, support and direct Geek India and maximize ROI must be put in place.

Given that IT has grown by leaps and bounds without too much government intervention, this may sound counter intuitive, but must nevertheless be considered. Businesses and government must urgently collaborate to ensure that Geek India continues to grow its contribution to national GDP. It is possible to do this by creating education and relevant curriculum in IT/engineering that is driven by industry requirements, while ensuring that the thrust of the effort should be to prevent over-qualification as well as under-qualification of labour, and instead ensure market-driven employability.

Many nations, such as the UK, are searching for innovative ways to address the challenges of a wobbly economy. They want solutions that result in enhanced productivity and a better focus on sustainability. They want to create jobs that drive consumption. They may do well to seek technical and operational innovation through technology, blending public and private enterprise with an eye on sustainable practices, for the larger good.

The single-biggest lesson in the story of Geek India continues to be smothered by a world fixated on the cultural differences between Geek India and the rest of the world. Frankly, have we made too much of it? The truth appears to be that Geek India is aligning itself to the realities of a globalised economy faster than many others. Our assumption that Geek India will have to vault cultural barriers is true. It has to make a ginormous effort. But, it will learn to overcome them.

Meanwhile, India has been busy focusing its innovations around sustainability, quality, agility and lowered costs that have special relevance to western nations such as the UK. In the UK, for example, the Technology Strategy Board is attempting to apply technology rapidly, effectively and sustainably to drive productivity and growth, create wealth and enhance the quality of life.[12] It may do well to take back some lessons from Geek India: innovations to create low cost mobile technology in areas such as banking for instance. Over 60 per cent of India remains unbanked. Indian mobile banking solutions have resulted in cheap 24×7 anytime, anywhere banking self-services, lowering pressure on physical banks, cutting transaction costs and creating fresh revenue streams for banks through newer services and a lower carbon footprint.

Many Indian realities are powering innovations that have, in today's sustainability context, relevance to the rest of the world. For example, the lack of reliable power in many cities has driven Geek India to create solar powered ATMs that don't need air-conditioning. It's an idea primed for export.

For several decades now India has been searching for ways to rise above its economic condition. There have been a million isolated efforts. Some even spread across the globe. Over the last decade or so, an amazing transformation is taking place. People determined to build a better life, regardless of their political or economic condition, have begun to find each other. Geek India from small towns is finding The Morpheus and hundreds of other such organisations that function as anchors for the vision and passion behind Geek India. The anchors are finding subject matter, experts, mentors, markets, and money (venture capital) that is willing to bet on these minds. When they all meet, the business equivalent of a dopamine factory is set up. I mean it. Dopamine plays a major role in the brain for creating reward-driven learning. Does this sound terribly simple? It is.

Notes

1. 'The amount of data in our world has been exploding, and analyzing large data sets – so-called big data – will become a key basis of competition, underpinning new waves of productivity growth, innovation, and consumer surplus.' McKinsey Global Institute, May 2011, http://www.mckinsey.com/Insights/MGI/Research/Technology_and_Innovation/Big_data_The_next_frontier_for_innovation

2. NASSCOM IT-BPO, Key highlights FY 2012, http://www.nasscom.in/indian-itbpo-industry

3. http://virtualcampuses.eu/index.php/All_countries_by_population

4. India and the World: Scenarios to 2025, World Economic Forum and Confederation of Indian Industries, http://www3.weforum.org/docs/WEF_Scenario_IndiaWorld2025_Report_2010.pdf

5. http://www.ibef.org/industry/informationtechnology.aspx | Report available for purchase at http://www.nasscom.in/itbpo-sector-indiastrategic-review-2011

6. As it happens, an inordinately large number of Indya.com employees have gone on to set up their own businesses and have been highly successful in the last decade.

7. http://www.indexmundi.com/india/demographics_profile.html

8. http://www.d-sector.org/article-det.asp?id=564

9. World of Work Report, 2012, ILO and International Institute for Labour Studies: http://www.ilo.org/public/english/bureau/inst/download/wow2012.pdf

10. http://www.d-sector.org/article-det.asp?id=564

11. Capturing error messages triggered in browsers is not new. The idea of capturing these errors so far has been browser-oriented, not developer

oriented. For example, an error message triggered in Safari can be captured and sent back to Apple for review. This helps improve the browser. But the developer of the page displayed in the browser is unaware that his/ her code was throwing up errors. Returning error messages to the developer within different browsers is a much-needed innovation.

12. Technology Strategy Board, http://www.innovateuk.org/

8 |

Are Books for Keeps?

Sita Brahmachari

At a recent author visit to an inner city London school, I shared the background to my novels – *Artichoke Hearts* and *Jasmine Skies,* and spoke about the inspiration behind both books. I noticed that among a room of gangly teenagers of diverse backgrounds sat a small boy of South Asian origin who had been listening intently throughout my talk. There were the usual questions: 'When did you first think of becoming a writer?', 'What inspires you to write stories?'. Then the teacher signalled that there would be one final question. I scanned the hall full of children, and saw the boy I had noticed earlier tentatively raise his hand. I nodded. His question was this:

'Why do you tell stories?'

His apparently simple question was greeted with boisterous laughter, but I noticed that the boy seemed unruffled. He sat with a composure I never would have had at his age waiting for my answer. As the teacher hushed the hall of children, I had time to think of what was behind his question. As a storyteller, I try to draw readers into the sensory and visual worlds of my novels. Possibly as a result of my background in theatre I think in 'scenes' rather than 'chapters'. Storytelling is a visceral act for me, drawing on all aspects and energies contained within oneself and distilling the story that emerges onto the page. When I go to schools and festivals, I always carry with me a small suitcase with tangible objects, sensory inspiration and images that have in some way inspired my stories. For

Jasmine Skies, I carry the scent of jasmine, photos of a visit to Kolkata, a miniature carving of a jungle and my wedding sari. For *Artichoke Hearts,* I carry with me an artichoke (when in season!), a silver charm, a holey stone, photos of my mother-in-law who inspired the character of Nana Josie, and one of her paintings. These objects are handled with great care by young people without exception. When I handed my silver artichoke charm to one girl, a teacher raised her eyebrows as if I might be taking a risk. She clearly feared that I might never again see the heirloom that is central to the symbolic world of both of my 'Mira' stories. Yet that same suspect girl placed the charm back in my palm with great care.

'Is this the real life charm in the book, Miss?' she asked. 'I'd be careful who you hand it to next time!' she warned me. 'Some people might not know how precious it is!'

I wondered at that point *who* might not know... because if this girl, who her teacher had so little faith in 'knew', then I felt as if there must be something in the power of the story itself that demanded an honest response.

I digress (but these indeed are my experiences relating to young readers and their relationships to the 'Story', and I am sharing with you the uncomfortably yawning moment in which I am scrambling through my mind looking for a succinct answer to my questioner's deceptively simple inquiry). I look back at the young boy's earnest waiting face and without knowing quite how I am going to answer, I take out the sari that was sent to me by my aunt on my wedding day. I ask for a volunteer to help me unfold and fold the sari. A beautiful young woman with a thick plait trailing down her back stands up. 'I know how to fold a sari', she tells me, and holds one end as I unravel the precious silk cloth that connects me not only to an important moment in my own past but to my family in India. When the full length of silk is revealed I find myself clicking through my PowerPoint presentation and bringing up a photograph of my own aunt. The two of us are smiling out at the audience with the same wide, big-toothed inherited grin. I look up at the photograph of my aunt and by way of answer to the boy's question, I begin sharing with the audience one of my own most potent childhood memories....

'I was walking home from school one day from my village school in the Lake District. It was lambing season and I enjoyed watching the young skinny-legged bleating babes skipping around in the fields. My family were living at that time in a converted barn with my maternal grandparents. I walked in to our front room to find, to my astonishment, not the usual tea and scones cooked by my grandmother, but my mum and my aunt – who had arrived from India – folding saris.'

I glance up at my sari-folding volunteer and tell her: 'You are my aunt! And I'm my Mum'. She nods and looks up at the image of my aunt on the screen behind her and grins! We begin what I have come to think of as my sari dance. My volunteer holds the cloth taut and I fold in a concertina movement just as I remembered my aunt folding.

As I watched the two women making tiny folds and communicating mostly in smiles and gestures, because my mother spoke little Bengali and my aunt spoke little English, I began to watch this folding dance as the women from different continents communicated their affection for each other across language, history and culture. When they had finally finished folding the sari, my aunt grabbed hold of my mother's hands in a gesture of great warmth and said:

'You are my sister, the wife of my brother, even we miss him, even with difficult history between us, we are family.'

The hall of children disintegrate into a giggling mass as I grasp my young volunteer's hands warmly in mine. When they have calmed down, I address my questioner.

'When I was your age, I began asking questions about my place in the world. I lived in one landscape but was also historically part of another. My father was from Kolkata and here in our rural living room was his sister, my aunt. Later that evening my aunt danced and sang for the whole family. I was enthralled by this visit that seemed to bring two parts of my identity together. India and my father's family, who I would later visit, were at this stage still part of an imagined world that I had learned about through my father's stories of "back home"... I believe that the love of listening to those stories and imagining the worlds he described, fed into me becoming a storyteller. As a child I wrote letters to my cousin just as Uma writes letters to Anjali in *Jasmine Skies* and these letters were probably my first foray into storytelling because when I read them back, they were a way of presenting myself and my world to an imagined other.'

I ask my hall of students how many of them Facebook or Skype their friends and cousins on different continents. A sea of hands floats in front of my eyes.

'Now I Skype or Facebook my cousins, as Priya and Mira do in *Jasmine Skies*... but I believe that there was a search for an understanding of the wider world in the storytelling place of the letter that I think set me off as a writer', I explain.

'Does that go anywhere near to answering your question?' I ask the boy.

He places his head on one side and shakes his head as if he's only half convinced by my answer.

'So you tell stories to understand what's in the gaps?' He persists.

It's very often easier to negotiate the questioning of adults than the searing demands of young readers.

'I just like it when we meet authors because you can see where the stories come from, and you know it even before you meet them, because you've read it through their book. I knew who you were Miss, before I met you! It makes me think I could write a published story myself,' said my young interrogator.

I share this anecdote with you because I believe that it's something that every storyteller should try to keep in contact with: the question: 'Why do I write stories?' People often ask me if I think I'm in competition with other mediums that young people are so busy multi-platforming on. My instinct is not to be worried. Then I think of the boy who asked me the question. What he was affirming was the unique relationship between himself, the story that he read, and the writer. This relationship appears to me to be different and distinct to anything experienced through any of the mass mediums including the World Wide Web. It is essentially the personal relationship which the reader's imagination creates through any given story that gives the 'book' its unique selling point (USP). The 'Book', in whatever form it is published, is not an antiquated ideal that we are desperately clinging to, but a constantly inventive medium.

J.K. Rowling captured the hearts and minds of every child in us because she told a story that fed into the nature of what it is to grow up in the world. This story crossed backgrounds, histories, cultures and landscapes and yet it spoke (no doubt in different ways) to people across the globe. Of course, from its essential nature as a 'book', it was transformed into film and no doubt a proliferation of games that millions of children play... and yet my own children to whom I read the books, and who have read them several times over themselves, claim that they prefer the experience of the 'book' because it is only here that the story is as *they* 'imagined it'. The best, most applauded film director in the world, with the most wonderful cast of Harrys and Hermiones could not have created what was in mine or my children's minds as we read the thousands of pages of adventure created by one woman writer.

To return to the young boy who asked me the question 'Why do you write stories?', I ended that particular school visit by turning the question back on him... 'Why do you read stories?' There was a shift in the atmosphere in the hall and my question seemed to have placed the young boy on the spot. For a moment, while his pause seemed to stretch out forever, I thought I had made a mistake to place him under the spotlight, but once again he looked steadily back at me.

'You really meet people in books, don't you?'

'You really do', I answered.

In another reading initiative as part of 'The Pop Up Festival', a London based organisation whose aim is to bring books to as many young people as possible, especially those who may not have access to them in the home, I visited a group of young girls who read *Artichoke Hearts* communally in class over the period of a term. Many of the students were from refugee backgrounds and this was the first book that they read in English... for one girl who came from an aural culture, it was the first book that she had *ever* read. It was moving to see how enthusiastic the young readers were about the characters and story and how much they enjoyed the communal nature of experiencing the story together. To return to the work of J.K. Rowling and the wonderful stories of a favourite author of mine, Michael Morpurgo, I believe that once a reader has personally engaged with a story there is great pleasure to be had in talking about the stories and the characters so that their engagement with stories become part of their shared cultural heritage.

Another aspect of this visit that touched me greatly, and this is something I have observed throughout all the interactions I have had with young readers, is that despite the fact that many of them spend a great deal of time on computers, and some will also read books on Kindle, they do seem to still want to build their own bookshelves. There is still, I believe, among young readers a demand for the book as a 'keepsake' once it has been read… especially if it is signed by the author!

The question of how you get young readers to pick up your book in the first place and add it to their bookshelf is an important one. My books have been very well served by their covers. Macmillan Children's Books have taken great care to ensure that young readers will be attracted to the stories through the bright, contemporary covers. My character Mira is a 'doodler' and a 'daydreamer' and draws pictures that speak of her inner life on her school 'Planner' and this is what young readers instantly recognise and identify with in the covers of my books. I often ask young people if they *do* judge a book by its cover, and without exception the unanimous answer is 'Yes'. In this time of multi-media platforms, there is demand for the book among young readers, but young people's engagement across so many different mediums have made them hyper-aware of messages being sent out to them through marketing and advertising. Therefore, although I do feel that there will always be a demand for the story well told, it is *how* the stories come to reach young readers that has changed the nature of publishing. This is where I believe that the 'book' comes into competition with other more visual and communicative mediums such as film, computer games, Apps, Tumbler, Facebook, Twitter, etc., on which young people spend a lot of time. If the 'book' is to survive within this market place, I believe that publishers need to engage with young readers more directly. Macmillan, for example, has a website called MyKindaBook in which all their children's authors are profiled. If readers join the site, they can become part of a 'club' in which they get to review new titles, receive free copies, comment on jacket covers and read 'extra' author articles. All of these activities and added content are designed for the reader to interact with the author and publisher.

When I was completing the editorial process for *Jasmine Skies,* my second novel, my fifteen-year old daughter started asking me when the book trailer was being released! Film trailers I'm used to, but I was unaware that there is a whole industry growing up for promoting books through what is essentially a short, snappy, visual film medium.

'I watch them all the time!' my daughter told me. 'You can pass it around Facebook and tweet it... and you get more of a sense of the book than reading a publicity paragraph... and we pass on the trailers we like...', my daughter explained. I wondered if she was just watching the trailer as she might a short film or whether she actually bought books as a result

Dr Amal Krishna Brahmachari and friends at Trafalgar Square
Courtesy: Sita Brahmachari

of watching the trailer, so she took me through some of the trailers that she's seen and then the books on her shelf that she'd been led to buy through watching the trailer. Of course, like the cover of a book, if a trailer is not well made or representative of the book, this could also have a negative impact. However, I was convinced that a book trailer was a good idea and in fact it has turned out to be an excellent way of leading thousands of people to *Jasmine Skies*. Pan Macmillan India have reported how well the trailer has been received and how effective it is as a means of disseminating information direct to young readers.

In this way, the dissemination of books needs to be viewed in the same light as bands placing their music on YouTube... If an unknown band or solo singer-songwriter can get discovered by publishing their own music on YouTube, then the work of a previously unknown author like myself, can also be found using the same platform! If enough young people 'like' a YouTube clip about a book and then others 'review' the book on such outlets as Macmillan's MyKindaBook or *The Guardian* Review or in a proliferating number of reading blogs, then the way young people engage with reading becomes part of the fast moving contemporary world in which they live and with which they engage. They, like adults, through the use of new technologies, have the opportunity to peer review. The proliferation of blogs by young people reviewing books is a real indication of the power of young people to engage with each other about books in the same way that they might engage with each other about films, music or gaming. There is a real empowerment for young readers in sharing and expressing their views on books, and publishers are aware of the power of these platforms as they watch with interest new trends emerging.

It is possibly because of the proliferation of young people's engagement with multi-media platforms, that 'genre' publishing, such as 'Vampire' stories, has reached such a mass market. I find it interesting too to note that the success of one medium only serves to enhance the other. So, for example, Michael Morpurgo's wonderful novel *War Horse* did not sell to a wide market when it was first published. Some years after publication, it was adapted by The National Theatre in London. Film-maker Steven Spielberg attended the play, which led to the film of the same name. You might have thought that having seen the film or play, people would not then buy the book. The opposite in fact was true. Sales of the novel *War Horse* have been deservedly large. This leads me back to my point. I don't believe that books are at risk of extinction, because there is something 'essential' in the act of one reader opening the page of the book that they hold in their hands and engaging their imagination with the story. However, authors, publishers and booksellers are increasingly aware that they need to be constantly creative in laying down trails for young people to be led to the book, to order it online, or even to go into a book shop and take it off the shelf.

A further positive aspect of the multi-media world in which we all live is the way in which we feel connected to a wider world. For me, personally as an author, this is a key and recurring theme in my work, partly as a result of my own mixed heritage background. My father was from Kokata, India, and my mother from the Lake District in England and my three siblings and I were brought up in Britain in an era before multi-media platforming had even been dreamed of. That makes me sound ancient to my children until I explain to them how fast and furious technology has radically altered our lives. In my first novel *Artichoke Hearts,* readers met my twelve-year-old heroine, Mira Levenson, a contemporary twelve-year-old London girl with a diverse heritage. My editor at Macmillan commented that one of the aspects of my storytelling she enjoyed was that Mira's identity was an 'essential' part of the story but not an 'issue' in it. In *Jasmine Skies,* I have Mira at the age of fourteen travelling to India to see her cousin Priya for the first time. While Mira's mother and aunt used to write letters to each other (letters that Mira steals trying to unveil secrets from the past), Mira and Priya Skype and Facebook each other, swap favourite music, hit the 'like' button on the same things. Yet, even with all this knowledge about her cousin through social media, when Mira arrives in India, her view of Priya is still very much skewed by her own stereotypical notions of India. She imagines that because her cousin is a classical Indian dancer, she will be what Mira has framed in her mind as a 'traditional' Indian girl. Yet the cousin she meets defies all her expectations. Yes, she is a Kathak dancer, but she is also a dubstep DJ working out of derelict houses in old Kolkata!

Rosie Harrison
Courtesy: Sita Brahmachari

What I explore in the story is the nature and depth of our new 'global village' in which young people can hook up with their relations and 'interest groups/clubs' anywhere in the world. But as the reader travels through the story, I invite them to consider how well we can actually know another culture unless we experience it more deeply than the odd exchange on Facebook. For me as a child, if I was not actually travelling somewhere and experiencing a place, the 'book' was my means of a deeper engagement.

A positive aspect for me as a writer in this new multi-media age is that people do feel part of a global network and therefore the increased diversity of characters in stories is simply a part of our reality. Of course my own mixed heritage background was also part of my diversity as a child and yet there were very few stories for me as a young reader in which stories that reflected aspects of my background were represented. When I visit schools and festivals, this 'representation' is an aspect of publishing that young people feel very strongly about. They clearly respond to characters that share and understand their own complex diversity and diaspora connections to the wider world. Living and working in London, the late Noel Greig, playwright and educationalist, once commented to me: 'When you walk into a school here, you find the world in your classroom.'

Before coming to writing these novels I worked in many schools in Britain and America exploring projects with theatres such as The Royal Court and The Royal Shakespeare Company, and theatre-makers such as Kristine Landon-Smith of Tamasha, a British/Asian theatre Company. Primarily, my work in arts-education has been to engage young people's interest in the stories being told through theatre, and to bring their own interests and stories into their dramatic work. As I sit and write at my desk, I imagine that I am writing for these young people that I have met over the years.

The very first question I ask when I go to a school workshop on *Jasmine Skies* is: 'Who has family elsewhere in the world, either in this generation or in the past?'

Every child puts up their hand. This is the complex identity of the young readership for whom I write, and I believe awareness of this audience is also the reason that there is an increasing diversity amongst authors and the stories and characters they scribe. My character Priya seems to have struck a particularly strong chord with young girls of South Asian origin in Britain.

'I love the way she doesn't fit with any of the stereotypes, Miss! I'm sick of all the Asian characters being about arranged marriage or some sort of race issue, or we're a doctor's daughter or some kind of nerdy swot!'

I laugh, because although I am a doctor's daughter, I do know what she means!

9

Science as an Agent of Transformation

K. Vijay Raghavan

On a visit to Cambridge in mid-2010, I was invited to dinner at Trinity College by my American friend who had moved from the California Institute of Technology to help establish the Sainsbury Laboratory of plant sciences. As the dinner progressed, both my host and I began to imbibe the timelessness of the rituals of the evening, juxtaposed with the very weighty contemporary discussions at the table. A lively discussion on whether oysters were ever food for the poor was led by a Fellow who had written a book on the subject and was also an expert on disarmament. Contributing animatedly to the discussion was a mathematician, seated on my right, who I later discovered is a Field's medalist. Only in Cambridge, I said to myself. Connecting Trinity College with the famous Indian mathematician, Srinivasa Ramanujan, I came back to search and found that Ramanujan was the first Indian Fellow of Trinity College. The strange story of Ramanujan and his connection with Cambridge exemplifies the same juxtaposition of tradition and the present, with the added dressing of rebellion and varied interpretations of creativity that link much of the UK and India's scientific interactions. While later in the twentieth century, Indian scientists went in large numbers to train and make a living in the United States, the interactions of the previous generation with the UK were very different in purpose and in the outcome for India.

Srinivasan Ramanujan at Trinity College, Cambridge
Courtesy: K. Vijay Raghavan

The history of science and technology in India goes back many thousands of years. A striking feature of ancient India in this context is that technology developed both from a strong local foundation in basic science and mathematics, and by interactions with societies, both local and global. The strong foundation in science, in turn, came from the value social structures, warts and all, placed on learning: of course interactions with other cultures played a very important part in this value system. Few activities thrive in isolation. Much later, the rise of the British Indian Empire essentially abolished this historical and organic link between science and technology, and the State on one side and society on the other. Science became something the West did and was largely irrelevant to India. Technology became an import in the service of the Empire. Technology had a huge effect on society and became interchangeably associated in the public mind with science. In the public eye, even today, excellence in science and mathematics in India are often seen as activities of the past and the great names remembered are all of dead males, either of ancient times or of the early twentieth century.

The cultural loss that India faced with the colonial and post-colonial period conflating science with technology resulted in a diminished view of science: typically, great discoveries happened elsewhere and role of 'scientists' in India was seen as applying these discoveries to social transformation. The loss that comes from science being culturally absent from – and deeply connected with – society is fortunately not yet complete, nor is this diminished role of science in our society sudden. For both reasons, there is much cause to be positive about the future of learning, scholarship and the quest for understanding nature in the Indian context. This optimism must, as a corollary, naturally extend to two other consequences. First, science-derived ideas when transformed into application through technologies are the hub on the wheel of India's on-going social transformation. It is novel scientific discoveries, as distinct from the mere scaled application of available technologies from elsewhere, that can truly transform India while simultaneously addressing environmental protection and the development, health and feeding of its hundreds of millions. There is a real possibility that this important resurgent role for science will be met by India. A rapid growth of the foundations of science in India, with deep local roots and branching out with close contacts globally, can only be a positive, calming and valuable agent of environmental responsibility in creating a sustainable world. Second, the value of science, as that of music, art and theatre, as part of our cultural heritage is being increasingly appreciated in India. If this assertion is valid, Indian science may have a positive influence globally with regard to the intrinsic value of science in society, particularly in a period when science is increasingly viewed in some circles in the West as irrelevant or as tampering with the laws of nature. Britain continues to be a world-leader in science and innovation with its eccentricity leading to scientific discoveries with extraordinary applications. Even so, there is strong pressure in the UK, strange to the outside, which demands that investment in science see immediate benefit rather than to understand that current benefits are the consequence of much earlier investments in curiosity-driven research. Here too, if India, with its pressing development needs, sees the value of creativity and innovation in science as necessary, it can only strengthen the hands of those in Britain, working for investment in excellence.

Jagadish Chandra Bose is the icon of modern experimental science in India. His pioneering studies on microwaves, wireless signaling and plant physiology are a very short list of the areas of experimental science to which he contributed and excelled. Bose stands out as a pioneer in many other ways. He was one of the first to subvert the principal purpose of the Empire's education system through science. The Presidencies of Calcutta, Bombay and Madras had colleges and then universities designed to train natives in colonial administration. As with the arts, so with science: these and other centres of learning also became institutions where intellectual strings were tied on rebellion's bow. Indians who were successful in philosophy, the law, humanities and science were admired locally not only for their scholarship, but for being able to stand up to the British in their own game. Stirred by a passion to develop the foundations of science in his country, Mahendra Lal Sircar, a medical doctor from Calcutta Medical College, established the Indian Association of Cultivation of Science where Bose later taught. Bose himself established the Bose Institute, a vibrant research laboratory even today. Many of the leading scientists like Bose became institution builders, as India itself trudged towards independence and beyond.

Srinivasa Ramanujan is a household name, but with his life cut tragically short at the young age of 32, it is difficult to know whether he would have taken such practical tasks, as others did. Meghnad Saha's laboratory in Calcutta University became the Saha Institute; P.C. Mahalonobis started the Indian Statistical Institute; Shanti Swarup Bhatnagar set up the Council of Scientific and Industrial Research; C.V. Raman left the Indian Institute of Science to found the Raman Institute in Bangalore; and Homi Bhabha founded the Tata Institute of Fundamental Research. It is stunning that these men excelled and stood their own amongst the best in the world, but what is perhaps equally remarkable is that they also became institution builders. There were many others too, all over the country in colleges and universities, whose teachings and inspiration created a scientific intelligentsia ready to serve the transformation of an independent India. Notable amongst this latter set of teachers were those in colleges started by missionaries, by nationalists or by those seeing western education as a liberating agent from social bondage.

Engineering and medical education institutions too followed science and mathematics but they were fewer, though no less remarkable for the quality of their training. The successes of Indian science are all the more impressive for what they managed to do in extraordinarily difficult conditions. Yet, while India takes great pride in these scientists, and justifiably so, they were working closely with institutions in Britain, the rest of Europe and the United States. Indeed, the absence of a community of peers in India meant very close connections with the best elsewhere. Again, colonial connections resulted in close interactions with Britain, invaluable in unique ways for each of the giants of Indian science to flourish or be recognised.

In the early decades after Independence, there was a burst of institution building. While many new universities were born, a stress on harnessing science and technology for societal change was evident. The Council of Scientific and Industrial Research led by Shanti Swarup Bhatnagar started several new laboratories all over the country as did the Indian Council for Medical Research and the Indian Council for Agricultural Research, the Department of Atomic Energy led by Homi J. Bhabha, and later the Indian Space Research Organisation led by Vikram Sarabhai. These took Indian science and technological efforts in completely new directions. Though investing much less than Europe and America, India began to similarly transform its science to function through organised laboratories and departments in universities and research institutions, rather than only by the periodic appearance of geniuses.

The presence of giants such as Bhabha, Bhatnagar, Raman and Saha in this period of growth and the rapid rise of big projects and research institutions had two effects in the minds of the Indian public. First, that scientists were not excellent unless they were in the same league as Raman or Bose, for example. This was an unnaturally high expectation. The success of these and other giants took place at a time when science was still not the mega-enterprise of today. Intelligence, zeal and genius were 'sufficient' to tackle the most formidable of available problems. An intellectual environment of quality, absent in India, could have allowed these giants to create more geniuses catalytically as happened in Britain and continental Europe in that period. This did not rapidly happen in the Indian environment where the breadth and foundations of science and research were still very modest. After the Second World War, as science became an enterprise, the number of excellent scientists worldwide were no longer a handful. Although there were many excellent Indian scientists in India in this period, they no longer appeared as giants: they were suddenly a smaller fraction of a global pool of excellence. Furthermore, the engines of institution-building had already moved and with the presence of many quality institutions, creating one more did not allow one to stand out as an institution-builder easily either. It was a period, continuing to this day, where excellence is appreciated amongst the peer-group of scientists, but with the public asking why there are no more Ramans or Bhabhas. The second effect on the public with the development of the space, agriculture, health and atomic energy programmes was a somewhat unnatural view that science would very soon transform society and was sufficient to do so. Both these kinds of views were not unique to India alone; they were present in Europe and America too and led to disenchantment with science in some quarters as the subjects were viewed as soulless automatons. The views are clearly misplaced, but it is the lack of effective communication by us as scientists and science-policy makers that is also to blame.

Science in post-independence India has not been barren at all, and has seen several scientists whose achievements are in the league of highest excellence. Interestingly, almost all of them have had close links with the UK in several ways. In mathematics, we have C.S. Seshadri, M.S. Narasimhan and M.S Raghunathan: all from the Tata Institute of Fundamental Research, all Fellows of the Royal Society. From the Tata Institute there is Obaid Siddiqi from the Biology department who is well recognised for his science and institution building. A Fellow of the Royal Society, Siddiqi's hiring at the Tata Institute prompted Homi Bhabha to write to Prime Minister Nehru about what scientific recognition was all about. In Bangalore, C.N.R. Rao and Sivaramakrishna Chandrashekar have done brilliant work in materials and liquid crystals, respectively and are both recipients of the prestigious Royal Medal of the Royal Society; Subrahmanyan Chandrashekar, the astrophysicist;

REF: ᵣ-62.   August 2, 1962.

Earlier this year a well known scientist, Dr. Leo Szilard brought to my attention a young Indian molecular biologist of outstanding ability, Dr. Obaid Siddiqi, who wanted to return to India, through he has many offers of appointment abroad. We have offered him an appointment which he has accepted, and he will be joining us this month. His case was strongly supported by a number of internationally known biologists including Professor G. Pontecarvo of the Department of Genetics of the University of Glasgow. In the course of Professor Pontecarvo's letter to Dr. Szilard the following sentence occurs:

" I think that it would be very important for the progress of
biology in India that he should go back to a job in which
his ability would be fully expressed: in fact, I am really
baffled as to why India seems to promote easily mediocre
scientist-politicians and does nothing to retain their
really good scientists. "

I thought that I should bring this last sentence to your notice because it gives one an indication of the impression that prevails abroad about Indian science and Government's attitude to it, despite the considerable progress that we have made. I am afraid the impression is not entirely ill-founded, and we have not got away from our inheritance of pre-independence days in which whoever spent his time on administration was considered to hold a more important position than someone who was doing work in a laboratory, although the latter might be of greater significance from a world point of view.

Shri Jawaharlal Nehru,
Prime Minister,
NEW DELHI.

HJB:nrr.2.8.62.

Letter to Jawaharlal Nehru from Homi J Bhabha about Obaid Siddiqi
Courtesy: K. Vijay Raghavan

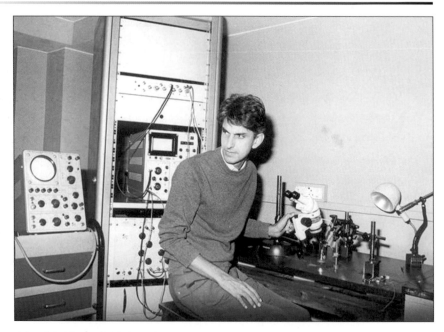

Obaid Siddiqi in his lab in the 1970s
Courtesy: K. Vijay Raghavan

and Abdus Salam from Pakistan being the others with sub-continental origins who have received this honour. Subrahmanyan Chandrashekar and Salam are idolised because of the cachet the Nobel brings, but the achievements of the others surely deserve more popular recognition. This has not happened simply because scientists in India have not pro-actively communicated their work to the society and the political class, an attitude that has been self-destructive. In addition to the small list above, there are at least a dozen more examples of excellence in science coming from post-independence India. Yet few, if any, are well-known outside their peer-group. If Indian scientists are to expect support for science, we need to convey our successes to society in a far better manner.

As for individual excellence, so too for expectations that science can transform society or–when it fails to do so – that science is a soulless automaton. It is true that science and technology can transform society for the better, but only on the shoulder of social change. It is only when the reach of democracy, empowerment and social transformation in

India takes place at a brisk pace that science and technology can be greatly enabling. If the pace of social change is slow, no amount of technology can liberate our people. Technology disconnected with social transformation risks being seen as an agent of exploitation. Social change in India and the attempts to develop a sustainable society, provide great avenues for collaboration between the UK and India. In the areas of ecology, climate change, energy, agriculture and health, the opportunities in India for brilliant minds to aid in the transformation of the world's largest democracy, through science and innovation, is boundless. There is a unique place for collaborating with Britain in this effort, tied together as we are by quirks of history, cricket and language. Here both countries need to make travel, stay and working far easier for each other's citizens. Finally, unlike the smaller and rich countries of the world, India does not have the luxury of defining our science policy choices by the whims or beliefs of the day: evidence must drive our policy choices in how we choose energy and food security. If we as scientists communicate effectively with our society in taking this path, India will have set an example to the West in developing and choosing technologies that enable us to come out of poverty and at the same time create a more sustainable development route. Technology may again become empowering rather than a demon.

10|

How Jamini Roy Found a Home in Baker Street

Nirmalya Kumar

I was educated in India in the 1970s and early 1980s, a time when it was difficult as a teenager to be truly proud of being Indian. The British had left in 1947; and thirty years of post-independence following the socialist model, had left the economy in a shambles. As a result, many educated youngsters escaped the perceived constraints of India to seek their fortunes in the West, especially in the USA. I was no exception.

Gaining a scholarship to study in the USA gave me a powerful immigrant experience of boundless opportunities. But it was also a time of deep personal cultural conflict, trying to escape my 'Indian-ness' to become 'American'. At some stage, realising it was an impossible transformation given my obvious Indian looks and observing the substantial changes taking place in India in the early 1990s, I felt a tug back to India. Unfortunately, India was not yet a place for anyone with an ambition to be a world-class business academic. As a compromise, I moved to Switzerland.

In 1997, on a flight from Geneva to Frankfurt, the inflight magazine contained an advertisement from a gallery in Germany selling a nineteenth century Pichhvai painting. A week later this large, 2 × 1 metre, beautiful painting of Krishna and the gopis arrived at my apartment in Lausanne.

Suddenly, I discovered the transformational power of paintings on my walls and a tangible connection to my Indian heritage. The next few years led to the acquisition of works by a few Bengal school painters from the first half of the twentieth century, artists such as Abanindranath Tagore, Rabindranath Tagore, Nandalal Bose, and Sunyanani Devi. Slowly but surely, I was being sucked into modern Indian visual art. And, then I saw my first painting by Jamini Roy (1887–1972).

It was love at first sight. After that I could not stop, and whenever I considered a Jamini Roy painting versus one by another artist, I always acquired the Jamini Roy. Now more than a decade later, I find myself on Baker Street, the first English street I had heard of courtesy of Sherlock Holmes, with the largest collection of Jamini Roy paintings outside India. Considered to be the father of Indian modern art, the more I learnt about Jamini, the more I was attracted to his work and its 'idea'. And, serendipitously, as a result, I found a resolution to the meaning of my own identity, whilst living in London, the world's most multicultural city.

The British Empire's Judgment on Indian Art

A natural tendency for any academic is to research whatever they are interested in. Besides, all collectors share the common character flaw of being obsessive. Combining these two traits led not only to a unique collection but also an expertise in the artist's work. While initially drawn to the stunning visual appeal of Jamini's art, the research revealed for me the concept of 'modern Indian art' behind his paintings. As a result, my connection to Jamini's paintings moved from purely the visual plane to the deeper emotional and intellectual levels. In order to fully grasp the historical significance of Jamini's art and the idea behind it, it must be understood in the light of India's freedom movement, where the quest for cultural freedom was happening in parallel with the fight for political independence.

By the nineteenth century, in their role of being 'masters' of India, the British had convinced themselves that India had no artistic culture to compare with that of the West. Reflective of this attitude is the quote from the Official Handbook of the Victoria and Albert Museum of 1880:

'The monstrous shapes of the puranic deities are unsuitable for the highest forms of artistic representation and this is possibly why sculpture and painting are unknown as fine arts in India.' This received wisdom was widely shared by the leading British 'India scholars' of the time. For example, Sir Monier Monier-Williams, Boden Professor of Sanskrit at Oxford University, observed in 1885 that: 'As it is, not a single fine large painting nor beautiful statue is to be seen throughout India. Even the images of gods are only remarkable for their utter hideousness.'[1]

The colonial British attitude did, however, also have a more benign aspect. To 'educate' the natives about the superiority of the Western culture and thought, the British took over and managed the first educational institution where Indians could obtain formal training in fine arts. The Government College of Art had a few incarnations before coming under the control of the British government in 1864, with an English principal, in Calcutta. The school exemplified the complex web of good and bad that the British had woven. Before their arrival, not only was there nowhere to study art as a profession, but the concept of creating paintings to be hung on walls of homes simply did not exist in India. However, as with the rest of the colonial education system, the curriculum was entirely western, and its aesthetic principles were alien to the indigenous population. Western art was classically realist, depicting form and volume through illusion, where as Indian art was tonally flat, decorative, and relied more upon the quality of line and expression of colour.[2]

Jamini's Quest for Artistic Freedom

The end of the nineteenth century was a time of great fervent in India for freedom. As Indian artists joined the freedom movement, they questioned what 'Indian modern art' should be. Perhaps, not surprisingly, given their training, the initial answer was Indian subjects painted in the Western academic style. Raja Ravi Varma became the leading exponent of this form in the 1880s. The popularity of his oil paintings led them to being reproduced as posters. In retrospect, his art seems rather old-fashioned even by the standards of his times. Raja Ravi Varma was stuck in the tradition of the artist as a photographer, and Indian modern art was still waiting for the artist as a conceptualiser and as a poet.

It is within this milieu that Jamini Roy entered as a student, and ultimately graduated from the Government School of Art in 1908. He was trained in, and his early paintings were inspired by, western academic style or the Impressionists (e.g., Figure 1: Jamini Roy – *Landscape*). Derivative as these paintings were, this training led him to become a successful portrait painter in Calcutta.

Figure 1: Jamini Roy: *Untitled Landscape*, oil on canvas, 55 × 56.5 cm

In the 1910s, seeking independence from notions of quality grafted on Indian art from a Western perspective, Indian artists turned towards the East. Inspired by visiting Japanese artists, Calcutta painters began adopting pan-Asian techniques and motifs. The result was the 'Bengal revival school' led by Abanindrananth Tagore, Sunayani Devi, and Nandalal Bose. Jamini Roy took part in this movement for a couple of years. His most popular painting from this period is reproduced here (Figure 2: Jamini Roy – *Flower*). One can clearly see the far eastern influences with the wash technique and the tree so evocative of the cherry blossoms! Realising that this approach was too sentimental to be 'Modern Indian Art', Jamini quickly abandoned it.

Figure 2: Jamini Roy: *Untitled Flower*, tempera on card, 73.7 × 47 cm

The second half of the decade of the 1910s was a period in Jamini's career where he was in artistic wilderness. He had achieved competence in painting portraits and landscapes inspired by Western art techniques. These were even signed by him using his English initials 'JR'. However Jamini could not help but feel that depicting Indian scenes using European techniques lacked vitality and an inherent truth. He was faced with the conundrum that all artists must try and resolve at some point: How can I be modern + unique + true to oneself (which in the context of Jamini was being Indian)? What makes Jamini a great artist, beyond merely an accomplished painter, was his signature resolution to this puzzle.

Inspired by Indian folk art, he made a conceptual breakthrough to advance a unique vision of modern Indian art. Starting from the early 1920s, he developed his 'flat technique' and for the next fifty years, we

Figure 3: Kalighat, Early Twentieth Century: *Untitled Cat with Lobster*, watercolour on paper, 46.5 x 27cm

were privileged to watch a perfectionist who single-mindedly pursued his artistic vision to its logical end. The trigger was the traditional Indian Kalighat paintings, where artists sitting by the famous Kalighat temple in Calcutta, produced paintings which were sold for a few paise to visiting pilgrims. Each artist had a distinctive style, and usually a favourite image, which they executed repeatedly. Characteristic of the Kalighat style was to have an unbroken line which was followed by quickly filling the plane with colour. Figure 3 (Kalighat – *Cat with Lobster*) is a rather sophisticated Kalighat painting in terms of the line and complexity, but a popular image of the times.

The early paintings by Jamini after finding his voice (e.g., Figure 4: Jamini Roy – *Musicians*) demonstrate how his 'flat technique' was in opposition to the Western art he was trained in. The Santhals depicted in the painting were a popular subject for Jamini. Being the indigenous people of Bengal, unlike the Calcutta babus, they reflected an India that had supposedly not been 'corrupted' by British rule. As can be observed from the painting, he had now taken a diametrically opposing path from his earlier career as a portrait painter. The medium was watercolour instead of oil; the subjects were the rural rather than wealthy Calcutta patrons; and its technique was Indian in its representation in contrast to the Western realism.

Figure 4: Jamini Roy: *Untitled Musicians*, tempera on paper, 36 × 71 cm

Jamini borrowed but never mimicked. Jamini's line and perspective had the sophistication to transform indigenous folk art into high art. The absorption and transformation is best seen by contrasting the Kalighat cat with Jamini's cats (Figure 5: Jamini Roy – *Cat with Crayfish*). As William Archer explained in his seminal book on Modern Indian Art, Jamini's two cats represent the Hindu priests, who claim they are vegetarians, but behind the scenes are skirmishing for shrimps, a prized Bengali delicacy.[3] Their bodies may be distinct, but their minds have fused together in avarice and greed. The emotion is captured so eloquently in their sly eyes, the bodies puffed up in self-importance, and their tails erect in arrogance. Its impact is multiplied manifold by the blazing yellow dots set off by the black ground. It punches you like a brilliant poster adorned with a master's signature (which is now in the Bengali script).

Figure 5: Jamini Roy: *Untitled Cat with Crayfish*, tempera on paper, 65 × 77 cm

Jamini continued to evolve until his death in 1972 and went through several distinct phases but always remained true to his conceptual flat technique. At times, he did revert to the Western style, but these paintings were few and far in between. Over time, his paintings became more formalised with Figure 6 (Jamini Roy – *Mother and Child*) being an exemplar of his peak and most popular period.

Figure 6: Jamini Roy: *Untitled Mother and Child*, tempera on card, 43 × 28.5 cm

As would be expected, some of Jamini's phases were less successful than others. For example, in the early 1950s, Jamini was in the 'pink period'. Many of his popular paintings were reinterpreted in pink. Thankfully, it was not a brash Barbie pink. Rather, an earthen Indian pink, more reminiscent of the pink sandstone so ubiquitous in Jaipur.

In the late 1950s, Jamini became enamoured by the mosaic Byzantine style and went through what is sometimes referred to as the 'Oyster period'. This was a more successful phase, and again, many of his popular paintings were reworked in this style. The two cats (Figure 5) is from this period. As can be seen, over time, the mosaic had turned into larger dots, almost like crazy paving.

For me, the more artistically successful phase was closer to the end of his career when he became minimalist. Here, the paintings were devoid of the colour that was so characteristic of his most recognisable work (e.g. Figure 6). Now the old man had turned to black, white and all the greys in between. Everything was stripped bare and the linear simplification had the Matisse touch about it. The face displayed in Figure 7 is quintessential of this phase. This is what modern art is all about, condensing experience, emotions, and objects into a few meaningful strokes and gestures.

Figure 7: Jamini Roy: *Untitled Woman's Face*, tempera on card, 33.5 × 25 cm

One of my favourite Jamini paintings is from this minimalist phase. It is a 'mother' (Figure 8: Jamini Roy – *Mother*) that is conceptualised in six strokes. At his peak, Jamini painted the mother and child theme in many different forms, from the cow and the calf to Parvati and Ganesh, to Mary and Jesus. Over time, he realised, and argued, to successfully portray the essence of a mother, one had to capture the somewhat opposing attributes of love and strength. After a lifetime devoted to painting the mother and child comes this tour de force of simplicity. The child is merely suggested and a perfect balance is achieved between the two figures. The work epitomises the revered Chinese philosopher Lao Tzu's observation, roughly translated as: to gain knowledge, add

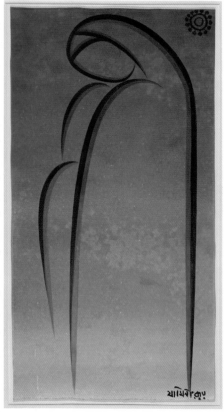

Figure 8: Jamini Roy: *Untitled Mother,* tempera on paper, 66 × 35 cm

something each day; to gain wisdom, remove something each day. The painting is a distillation of a life's work, and we are forced to conclude that, in Jamini, we were privileged to watch a perfectionist who quietly pushed himself to repeatedly prove that 'he has still got it'. Here Jamini shares with the other great artists something that seems so often missing in contemporary art, art that is made by a solitary person out of an intense personal necessity.

Transcending National Identity

Jamini's house was a popular destination for foreigners interested in art, especially visiting Americans and the British who were stationed in pre-independence India. Often they purchased a painting from him which found its way back home. The market for Jamini works outside India is now made up of the descendants of these original buyers selling their inheritances. Jamini's death had provoked the Indian government to declare his paintings a national treasure and ban all further exports in 1974.

While Jamini painted all the religions including Buddhist and Muslim themes, after his paintings of Hindu subjects, the largest output was related to Christianity. An astute marketer, Jamini probably recognised that a substantial base of his clients would be attracted to this theme. Starting in the 1940s, Jamini had a Christian phase.

In Jamini's development as an artist, the 'Christian' phase was important for two reasons. First, Jamini was forced to confront the fact that themes such as the Crucifixion, Flight to Egypt, or The Last Supper had been painted millions of times for almost two thousand years. What could he add to them? Was it possible, for example, to paint 12 people around a table with Christ, stay true to his flat concept, still be unique, and capture the needed emotion? Jamini dips the paintbrush into the imagination of his genius and gives us a masterpiece of a The Last Supper (Figure 9: Jamini Roy – *Last Supper*). The painting appears to scream: compare with those painted by others, more famous than myself. Christ is seated in the middle and all eyes are upon him. The feeling of treachery has been poignantly captured and the anonymity of the disciples makes

Figure 9: Jamini Roy: *Untitled Last Supper*, tempera on card, 25.8 × 74.5 cm

it impossible to know who will turn traitor. You can feel the impeding betrayal as Jamini plays with your mind in a painting that is brilliantly conceptualised.

Second, as explained above, at the start of his career, being Indian was important given the need to free oneself of Western conceptions of art. Part of this quest was searching for subjects and motifs that were truly Indian. The Christian phase allowed Jamini to transcend his Indian identity as he had evolved to painting anything, provided it fit within his vision of Indian modern art. As a result, Jamini became probably the first Indian artist whose power and interest for non-Indian art buyers did not have to depend on Indian subjects and themes. The subject had become secondary to having his paintings look different and uniquely Jamini. Being an artist is all about individuation and difference; finding a voice of your own. To secure his place in the global art history, the final part of the puzzle for Jamini was the reconciliation of nationalism and individuality.

It is here where Jamini speaks so eloquently to my own identity conflict. Unlike the previous need to escape my 'Indian-ness' and become 'American', came the subsequent realisation that my nationality should be a source of pride, not of shame. But as an academic playing on the global stage, I do not want to be a prisoner of being Indian either – this is about independence. As we inhabit a world that is becoming more global, our search for identity becomes more intense. It has been my good fortune to visit more than sixty countries, hold three nationalities, and call four countries home. But, it has taken me fifty years to grasp that you can visit many countries, hold many nationalities, but you can only be from one place, and I am from Calcutta. Jamini has helped me create a mini Calcutta in the middle of London, where I can be simultaneously connected with both my roots and the world.

Jamini Roy and the Indian Art Market

I hope by now I have convinced readers that people usually collect art that features something close to their hearts. As time goes by, a great hobby is one that allows you to grow as an individual. This collection has introduced me to many interesting people in the art world, connected me to my culture, helped me develop a more expanded sense of self, and more recently, aid charities that I wish to support.

As the Indian art community for modern and contemporary paintings is relatively small, I quickly got the reputation for being a collector of Jamini Roy. This led to my being in the 'deal flow'. Whenever a dealer or an auction house had a Jamini for sale, I was often the first port of call. I owe them a debt as they enabled me to become an expert. Now, I am honoured to say, that I am even being approached by some of them to ascertain if the painting is genuine. The resulting self-reinforcing spiral of love, expertise, reputation, hobby, and passion has consumed me for more than a decade.

Buyers from India on the world art market are a new phenomenon. Most Indian art buyers have probably been in the art market for less than ten years. As a result, these collectors are still learning about art and the art market. Many of them believe that it is risky to focus a collection on a single artist and there are two responses to this.[4]

Firstly, it is about one's objectives. If you are a 'speculator,' who buys art as an investment, then the portfolio should be diversified. Similarly, a 'decorator,' who buys what he or she likes to cover the walls and display their taste, or a 'striver,' who buys art as status symbols, will more often be eclectic in their acquisitions. In contrast, a 'collector' is motivated by passion for what they buy. With Jamini Roy, I see myself as a custodian rather than the owner of the works. It is part of India's heritage, and with no plans to sell the paintings, the market value of the works is irrelevant.

Many speculators and investors were attracted by the giddy returns of the ten years that ended with the collapse of the Indian art market in 2008. Now it is mostly the 'collectors' and 'strivers' that remain. For the 'strivers', it is not the art that is important here but what it represents. To them, art is a status symbol like a Bentley car or a Rolex watch. Buyers of contemporary art are insecure and need reassurance. As David Hockney observed, 'people need to look intensely, but they can't. They need to be shown how to'. Most buyers are unwilling to spend the time required to educate themselves to the point of overcoming insecurity. They need the confidence of the most recognisable signature styles. And, the higher price, the more attractive the object is, provided other people are aware of the prices and can immediately recognise the object. This is what drives prices of contemporary art in general, and especially Indian art, given that it is a particularly thin market.

Jamini repeatedly painted his most popular paintings. They differed in terms of size and with small variations in colours. In this, he was being true to the Kalighat tradition, but also anticipating the editions that today's contemporary artists do. He used his two assistants to help make these later works, reportedly assigning them the task of filling the colours after the primary lines were drawn by him. To some Indian art collectors, this negates the value of Jamini as an artist and the commercial value of his work. But, he was in this sense, a true modern conceptual artist. His genius lies, for example, in his concept and his idea of the 'Last Supper', not in the physical act of painting it, no matter how accomplished the execution may be.

Secondly, as has been observed in the past, the big idea in collecting is to limit yourself, only then can your collection become something. Seventy unrelated paintings by different Indian artists would be interesting, but not unique. To be a collection, it must be more than the sum of its parts, and how much more is determined by the quality of the concept behind the collection. Thus, being wealthy is not a prerequisite for becoming a collector, though of course it does not hurt. It is about imagination and vision.

As the collection grows, it becomes more challenging to find a Jamini that will add to it. Now, I will only acquire a Jamini if it will be among the top 12 paintings of my collection. Recently, that led to the acquisition of the widow (Figure 10: Jamini Roy – *Widow*). Here is a woman in the traditional widow's garb of a white sari with a black border. India, and especially Bengal, had a major problem with respect to treatment of widows. Well-off Indians tended to marry multiple times and consequently were often survived by young spouses. Within the structure of the joint family, this was a potential problem. To desexualise widows, they were stripped of all adornments, including their make-up, jewellery, and in extreme cases, by shaving their heads. Jamini's painting is his statement on the emancipation of widows. Can defiance ever be more evocative or attractive? As a collector, this painting had everything one covets: perfect condition, great execution, a strong message and clear provenance. How could I not fall in love?

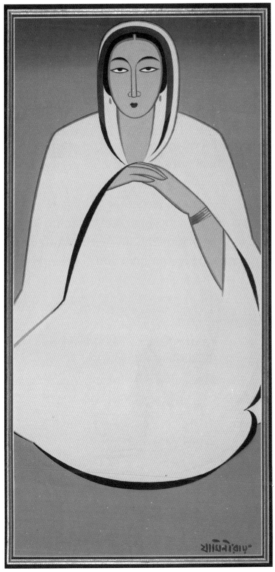

Figure 10: Jamini Roy: *Untitled Widow,* tempera on paper, 77.2 × 36.6 cm

Final Thought

In conclusion, let us recall Sir Howard Hodgkin's comments in the introduction to the catalogue of the *Six Indian Painters* exhibition which he organised at the Tate Gallery, London, in 1982: 'Jamini Roy signifies not just the advent of modern art in India, but the advent of the *modern Indian* artist. There is a special relationship between the identities of "modern" and "Indian" which is uniquely tied to the historical moment. Jamini Roy's painting was modern because he created a new and distinct style, and it was Indian because of its "technique and conception".'[5]

What I have tried to argue in this chapter is that one can limit oneself to appreciating the striking sublime beauty of the Jaminis on my walls and his position in art history can comfortably rest on that. Yet, at another level, they represent the cry of an oppressed nation yearning to break free from a subjugation that went beyond merely the political domain. Today, Indian modern art in Britain has come a long way. The Victoria and Albert Museum has an excellent collection of Jamini Roys, while both the British Museum and the National Galleries in Scotland possess a couple of his paintings, besides other modern and contemporary Indian art.

Notes

1. Monier Monier-Williams, *Brahmanism and Hinduism: Or Religious Thought and Life in India as Based on the Veda and Other Sacred Books of the Hindus.* Reprinted Kessinger Publishing 2005, p. 469.

2. Josephine Rea, 'Bond Philanthropy: Nirmalya Kumar' Bond, 2012, pp. 68-77.

3. William G. Archer, *India and Modern Art*, Macmillan, 1959.

4. Nirmalya Kumar, 'A Collector's Perspective', in *Urban Patua: The Art of Jamini Roy* by Sona Datta (Marg 2010), pp. 11-13.

5. Geeta Alvares Meneses, 'Repository of One Man's Genius', *Libas*, 2012, pp. 148-153.

11

Education and Terrorism

J.E. Spence

The banners hanging from the outer wall of King's College, London, extolling the research achievements of its academic staff include one which simply states: 'How do we understand terrorism?' This is a brave attempt to appear studiously neutral emphasising one important feature of the syllabus of the Department of War Studies. The proposition does at least recognise the obligation the teacher and the researcher have to provide his/her charges with challenging insights and a variety of competing explanations of a particularly contentious topic in both the theory and practice of international relations. This is not to say that – to cite the French maxim – to understand all is to forgive all, but at least an attempt to deconstruct the concept of 'understanding' in an academic context may well be the beginning of wisdom, however partial.

I must stress that I cannot offer the reader any prescription about how to defeat terrorism. I am not involved directly in the so-called 'war against terror' which, incidentally, I think is a misnomer. My role as a teacher in the Department of War Studies involves primary responsibility for a post-graduate MA course in Diplomacy – one of the few non-kinetic modules on offer to students. In my course, I stress that orthodox diplomacy at its best is a liberal enterprise, both civilised and civilising in its role as an informal institution in international relations. It might be best regarded as an instrument of soft power enshrined in Chapter VI of the Charter of the UN which stresses mechanisms for the non-violent settlement of disputes between states. And one major element in this course is whether negotiation with terrorists is possible and morally appropriate, a topic for later discussion in this paper.

Furthermore, I have no direct experience of counter-terror strategy or counter-insurgency in areas where terror is said to flourish. What I am involved in is university education at a variety of levels, both civilian and military: apart from my teaching at King's College, I also have pedagogic responsibility for some 90 senior officers and civil servants (40 British and 50 overseas) at the London-based Royal College of Defence Studies. They spend an intensive year at the College with an unparalleled opportunity to think, read, write and talk to each other and with academics like me, recruited to run inter alia an MA programme in International Security and Strategy sponsored by King's College. Thus, to put a gloss on Edmund Burke's famous comment: better an educated rather than a 'rapacious and licentious soldiery!'[1] This course is part of the UK strategy of defence diplomacy which has acquired greater significance under the impact of globalisation. All the members at the College are potential high-flyers in their military and civil services and most will achieve a 2-star ranking or better in due course. All the governments concerned face – in varying degree – the terrorist threat; all have to plan anti-terrorist strategies which demand inter-state cooperation at a high and enduring level. Many of those on the course have dealt with terrorists at the sharp end and have been involved in discussing appropriate strategies and tactical responses.

My role as a former academic advisor and current teacher on the programme is to engage in intellectual discussion on a wide range of topics including terrorism. I debate with College members, challenging where I can, the orthodox wisdom in the literature. The academic and his military counterpart can, therefore, learn productively from each other. Many graduates of the College will find themselves cooperating on, for example, peacekeeping or peace-making missions and the hope must be that a year's sojourn at the College will make cooperation that much easier and more productive. Indeed, one could reasonably argue that members representing countries in conflict with each other on a variety of issues can and do find the atmosphere of the College conducive to social intercourse and a better understanding of each other's national aspirations.

Thus, for example, the College has, over the years, hosted a significant number of senior officers and officials from both India and Pakistan. Both groups, therefore, have had an invaluable opportunity to learn from each other to their mutual benefit. Thus, what I am involved in is university education at a variety of levels, both military and civilian, but that does not oblige me to convert my intellectual charges to a particular counter-terrorist strategy or to an idiosyncratic view of the structure and process of international relations.

True, some of my King's students have turned out to be efficient captains of war, or, alternatively, able Ministry of Defence (MOD) and Foreign and Commonwealth Office (FCO) civil servants charged with the responsibility of safeguarding the lives and interests of the UK citizenry. But overall, I have an academic responsibility, as I see it, to offer students fresh insights, to refine their thinking and overall provide understanding of the terrorist enterprise to enable them to make independent and, possibly, more sophisticated judgements about its impact.

The emphasis must be on *explaining* the nature of terrorism – old and new – the methods devised for countering terrorist activity and the reasons why alienated groups within societies adopt these means to achieve particular objectives–whether relatively precise or limited, e.g. the African National Congress in South Africa and the Front de Libération Nationale (FLN) in Algeria, or apocalyptic in both means and ends, for example the Baader-Meinhof group in Germany and similar organisations in Italy and Japan during the 1960s. Certainly the Al Qaeda movement, with branches scattered across the globe, seemingly falls into the latter category.

Thus all I can do is to try to equip those I teach with some understanding of terror and, in particular, its manifestation as a so-called new security threat in a raft of such post-cold war threats: international crime; the drugs trade; enforced migration; failing or collapsing states; climate change and latterly the stress and strain of modern democratic states in the

Euro zone facing profound economic difficulties and leading to popular discontent and disillusion with orthodox democratic governments. How governments deal with these threats, what strategies and capabilities are appropriate, is a central feature of both military and civilian education.

In other words, in teaching a university course on terrorism, one must, I believe, try to be reasonably detached in both presentation and argument. Now all this may sound high-minded in the extreme, yet I do believe that one cannot teach controversial topics such as terrorism without one's own personal values and the inarticulate major premise on which those values are based, coming through loud and clear or at least being implicit in the analysis.

So how does the teacher perform his/her duties in a morally responsible way? And in stressing one's implicit moral responsibility, I have probably given the game away. Inevitably, there is a moral dimension – implicit or explicit – in the teacher's role. In these circumstances, one really has no option but to declare where one stands on the issue of terrorism. Thus, one cannot separate one's personal values, prejudices, if you like, from one's attempt at academic analysis, acknowledging that both the teacher and the student must feel free to have their moral and political assumptions and arguments challenged.

One might, for example, argue that some varieties of terrorism have more justification than others: that the killing of innocents (and the notion of 'innocence is in itself a value-laden term which deserves careful deconstruction) either by accident or design is impossible to justify in any morally absolute sense. However, such outcomes might be justified, or at least condoned on the grounds, for example, that a particular repressed or dispossessed group in a particular society, having tried every peaceful means of effecting change, might feel obliged to resort to terrorism, often described as the weapon of the weak. The objective – seemingly laudable and relatively limited – might be to achieve national self-determination, secession from a nasty and corrupt regime or simply recognition and implementation of hitherto grossly abused human rights.

There are such examples, sometimes described as old-style terrorists:

the African National Congress in South Africa, and its counterparts in Algeria, former Rhodesia and Vietnam, also come to mind. One might, therefore, make a pragmatic distinction between varieties of terrorism, analysing as neutrally as one can, the means, objectives and ultimate outcomes, whether achieved or not. One might then ask 'is terrorism being employed as a last resort, all other non-violent means having failed?' Is the objective–freedom from oppression; self-determination; recognition of human rights–on the face of it, a reasonable one? Is the objective of the campaign realisable, worth the costs involved in terms of the production of a more civilised social order? On the other hand, one might, as a teacher trying desperately to be fair, argue that the so-called apocalyptic terrorists who wish to secure the transformation of the structure and process of domestic and international politics have, frankly, scant prospects of achieving that objective. In these circumstances, the death of 'innocents' and destruction of property and state infrastructure is – it could be argued – hardly justified. This would be true of the Baader-Meinhof gang in West Germany, the Red Brigades in Italy and similar organisations elsewhere, together with Al Qaeda in the post-9/11 period, which did spectacular damage to persons and property with little prospect of toppling mature democratic states, let alone the international society of states, however imperfect its raison d'être and responsibility for providing for the welfare of its peoples.

It could also be claimed that a democratic society has the responsibility to find ways and means of deterring, and if deterrence breaks down, defending itself as best it can, against a terrorist attack. This is a straightforward liberal argument and it seems an eminently sensible one in the circumstances. Of course, the critic might invoke the accusation of collective guilt for past and present injustice, but this argument is equally open to a challenge in a well-organised and intellectually hospitable teaching environment.

And in doing so, such defence will have to carefully distinguish and calibrate ways and means for maintaining security and preserving order. At the same time, the state will have an obligation not to pay too high a price in terms of challenges to civil liberty and civil society in general.

In enunciating this view, the teacher is inevitably reflecting a liberal concern with the sanctity of human life, while acknowledging at the same time the state's responsibility for providing protection and security for the citizenry.

But does this set of propositions really undermine the relativist argument that 'one man's terrorist is another man's freedom fighter'? But as academics are wont to say, 'it all depends' how far, for example, does the terrorist in question show some discrimination in choice of targets: the ANC in South Africa tried hard to distinguish between damage and destruction to state infrastructure and the death of civilians caught in the cross-fire. The organisation was not altogether successful in this endeavour, nor could it be given the possibility at the very least of unforeseen and indiscriminate consequences involved in the use of the terrorist weapon. And of course, it could be argued, that the would-be terrorist has to show some degree of discrimination if the campaign is to be successful: too much random killing, kidnapping and sabotage might alienate the uncommitted where hearts and minds are at stake; too little might lead to loss of support and expose the terrorist to easy suppression. Terrorism, to achieve a hearts-and-minds victory, normally has to persist over a long period; if the government can nip it in the bud quickly, then popular support dissipates.

Secondly, in this context, what constitutes the freedom for which the would-be terrorist is fighting? Is there a real prospect of a lasting impact over the long run on the lot of the citizen? Thus the term does require careful analysis in an effort to avoid bland and uncritical acceptance of what seems an incontrovertibly relativist proposition.

This far, I argue, that it is difficult, if not impossible, to be totally objective in teaching topics such as terrorism. The very language one uses reveals something of the teacher's moral position. Hence, any use of terms such as 'innocence', 'old and new-style terrorism', 'the state responsibility to combat terrorism', all these notions have an inescapable moral content. In other words, it is impossible to separate one's own personal moral perspective from the analysis one offers one's charges in the classroom. What one can and must try to do is to inform the analysis with a willingness to consider competing narratives on offer, both in the literature (which is voluminous) and in the ideological assumptions underpinning the behaviour of the terrorist and counter-terrorist in the world beyond the classroom.

Let me end with a personal example of the issue the topic raises in terms of day-to-day classroom pedagogy. The students in my Diplomacy course at King's come from a wide variety of countries and the majority are interested in two topics in particular: one is the role of mediation as a tool of liberal statecraft designed to promote rational and peaceful conflict resolution; the other is the deeply interesting and provocative question of whether one can and should negotiate with terrorists. In this context, what prospect does orthodox diplomacy offer, trying, for example – following the late Hedley Bulls' diplomatic analysis – to see whether an 'overlapping interest' can be perceived and used as a basis for rational negotiation between a state and a terrorist movement.[2] Interestingly, both mediation and orthodox diplomacy have this in common: that negotiation becomes a possibility when a ripe moment appears following mutual recognition that a seemingly unbreakable stalemate exists, usually the result of both sides in a conflict acknowledging that the costs of continuing violence exceeds the costs of stopping, negotiation and reaching a compromise. And here a contact group of disinterested but influential states, putting pressure on protagonists in and out of season, can obviously be helpful in persuading the parties to come to the conference table.

Now, in the course of my teaching, I have encountered those who are willing to challenge the conventional wisdom on the morality and utility of negotiating with terrorists. Several have written superb dissertations on the theme, some of which have been published in learned journals. What one asks students to do in this academic context is to analyse carefully the strengths and weaknesses of the orthodox view on negotiation with terrorism which often seems to preclude any discussion with such groups altogether. The subject has such deep philosophical implications that it does effectively stretch the mind and this is really all that can be asked of both the teacher and the student in their common endeavour.

Finally to conclude: what I believe is that one should strive to get students to think, speak and write critically about the conventional wisdom and to do so with a frank acknowledgement of one's own prejudices. As a teacher, all I can do is to try to demonstrate the need to test one's views and arguments in debate, and acknowledge that there are, in Hamlet's words, 'There are more things in heaven and earth, Horatio, than are dreamt of in your philosophy'.

This, I accept, is the liberal way and I make no apology for it. This involves regular exchange between a teacher and student; a commitment to restraint, scepticism, open-mindedness, courtesy in debate, and above all an acknowledgment of the moral and political complexities of international relations in general, and terrorism in particular. Indeed, if I may be inappropriately dogmatic for a moment, that is the only mode of intellectual enquiry for a respectable and life-enhancing university education. And this is a far cry from indoctrination of a belief system whose adherents – both teacher and student – are consumed by an ideological passion and a refusal to accept the possibility of error in both theory and practice.

The views expressed by the author are entirely his own and not those of King's College or the Royal College of Defence Studies.

This paper is a revised version of a presentation given to a seminar organised by the Democratic Forum at King's College, London on 22 June 2012. The paper commented on the theme of the Role of Education in Countering Terrorism.

Notes

1. Edmund Burke, Speech on Fox's India Bill, House of Commons, London, 1 December 1783.
2. Hedley Bull, *The Anarchical Society – A Study of Order in World Politics*, Basingstoke: Palgrave MacMillan, 4th Edition, 2012, p. 164.

12

The Y Factor: India's Generation Next

Mihir Sharma

One of the things about India most obvious to a visitor is that it is a tremendously young country. You might know that the median age is 25, as opposed to 34 in China, 40 in the United Kingdom or 45 in Germany, but that telling statistic still doesn't prepare you for the overwhelming impression of youth you see on the streets of India. If, at one point, visitors used to be oppressed by the Indian cities' teeming crowds, now they are additionally impressed by how young those crowds are.

India's per capita income has risen sharply every year for over two decades now; social indicators have not improved commensurately, but they have steadily risen too. India's young people are visibly taller and generally healthier than those some decades ago. In addition, they are much more likely to be literate; the overall literacy rate when Manmohan Singh began the reforms process in 1991 was 43 per cent, and it is 74 per cent today. Those under 30 – three-fourths of India's citizens – will barely remember the grey India of Nehruvian socialism, with stagnant real incomes, chronic food shortages and a single television channel. They do not remember an India where the Indian National Congress was the natural party of the government. They do not remember an India suffering from a crippling, post-colonial angst about its place in the world, constantly imagining intervention and humiliation by a powerful West. It is their responses that ensure that Indians, in surveys, reveal themselves as consistently friendlier to the United States, the United Kingdom and Europe than any other country in the developing world.

Yet, as always, looking at this vast country through a single dimension provides a skewed, even warped picture to the observer. Like everything else about India, the fact of its youthful population can lead one to hasty, homogenised, conclusions that would be a serious error. It is important, therefore, at the outset, to try and explain the basic divisions within India's young people, keeping the divisions to three, the minimum required to convey the problem's complexity.

First, there are those who are, in the end, the most important interlocutors for cultural exchanges with the rest of the world. Increasingly global in outlook, enthusiastic mimics, they like to think of themselves as middle-class, using the consumption standards of the West as their benchmark. They are wrong of course: so unequal is India, so poor is its majority, and so tiny is this comfortable upper crust, that it is more appropriate to think of these top few percentiles as the upper class. Of course, that still means that they are larger than the entire population of most European countries. Overwhelmingly from backgrounds that have been privileged in caste and economic terms for generations, it is this elite class of young people that produces and consumes high and middle-brow culture, travels and studies abroad, speaks English habitually and buys global brands.

Then there is India's real middle class. These young people have families that have emerged from poverty in living memory. Mostly, they don't have the benefit of the economic, social or cultural capital that the first group does; but many of them will know people they can identify with, who have grown rich in the past two decades, perhaps through hustling land deals, perhaps through retail, or perhaps through a few lucky deals. They live in small towns and rapidly urbanising clusters that were once rural, where economic relations and consumerism is urban but social mores remain rural. Their main source of entertainment is television and Hindi movies. They believe – if the director Karan Johar shows them so

– that the actress Kareena Kapoor, if playing a British Asian, can indeed have Blenheim Palace as a country home. They know what upscale smartphones look like, and may have played with one or two briefly. They are on the web, perhaps with a Twitter or an Orkut account. They don't know what they will do with their lives, but expect that they will be better off than their parents. If not, someone will pay. There are at least 100 million such young people, probably more. They aren't working class, they aren't middle class; they are young, they have expectations, and they are India's aspirational class.

And, finally, there is the solid core of India, the one that economic growth and the government policy has being trying to chip away at for decades. India's upper class speaks unselfconsciously for that vast part of India that is still unconnected with global markets, trends and attitudes, but the two classes are almost irretrievably alien to each other. For these young people, whether or not they will do noticeably better than their parents, isn't a certainty at all. Yes, many have mobile phones and, increasingly, access to television programming. Most of them are better fed and better clothed than they were a generation ago. But, for them, the quest for minimal economic security remains the major task of their lives. Even those not strictly poor by government definitions perch precariously over official poverty lines, their families and their dreams ready for consignment to the depths at the first catastrophic event: dispossession by the powerful, say, or a lingering and expensive illness of a family member. They live in India's villages and on the margins of its ever-increasing towns, their lives an incomplete escape from the fears of caste-based domination, sexual violence and state power that ruled those of their parents and grandparents before them. Their numbers shape Indian politics; their purchasing power sparks happy fantasies at India's low-end consumer companies; but their impact on cultural production, their imprint on the face India turns to the world, remains minimal. The great task for India over the next generation is to see how that can change.

Yet, in the meantime, generalisation across these three groups is difficult and dangerous. They have starkly different expectations of the future, the

Indian state, of their parents' generation and of the outside world. The interplay of these various dynamics will shape India's politics, its society and the economy for decades to come.

Politics

India is a gerontocracy. Of the major countries surveyed by *The Economist* in 2012, it has the biggest gap – forty years – between the median ages of its Cabinet ministers and of the population as a whole. Not only are Indians young, but their leaders are old. Prime Minister Manmohan Singh is 80; his former deputy in the Cabinet, now India's president, Pranab Mukherjee, is 77. In the last general elections, Singh's main rival for the prime minister's post was five years older than him. Rahul Gandhi, the Congress party's general secretary, is rather oddly talked of as a 'youth leader' when he is over 40.

This gap has effects on Indian politics that are often excruciating to watch. It means, first of all, that many young members of the Indian elite are contemptuous of the inclusive nature of democratic politics enhanced by the clumsiness on display by policymakers or party leaders when they attempt to address matters relatively more important to younger Indians. The current technology minister, for example, is a regular butt of jokes because of his feeble attempts to control the content of social networks like Twitter and Facebook, which he clearly does not understand too well. Fifty million Indians are on Facebook. That number grows by an astonishing 50 per cent every year; if this trend continues, there will be 150 million such users – more than in the US – by 2015. Three-fourths of these will be under 35. The Indian state's obvious bumbling online will be the cause of ever greater contempt for it and its out-of-touch leaders among younger citizens.

The mass mobilisations of urban Indians, mostly young and relatively well-educated, that marked the years 2011 and 2012, should be seen partly in this light. In 2011, the social activist 'Anna' Hazare – Anna means 'elder brother' – went on a series of fasts to demand the immediate passage of a strong anti-corruption law. The law itself was justly criticised as being half unworkable and the other half draconian, but the fasts became the spark for enormous demonstrations in which public fury against corruption at all levels of government was given expression. Yes, there were families there, and people from villages and older members of the working class. But, overwhelmingly, the image that most observers took away was of members of the elite or aspirational class of young people, zipping around in cars or two-wheeled vehicles, wearing the white cotton cap, once associated with Mahatma Gandhi, but also worn by Hazare, and carrying the Indian flag. Angry expressions of disdain for elected representatives and for the political process were heard everywhere. The government's reaction – the reaction of the entire political class, in fact – revealed its inability to come to terms with this estrangement. Myopic commentators declared that it was a battle between the State and its People; but, in fact, the problems were partly born of an elderly political class that finds itself unable to communicate so as to effectively assuage younger people's grievances, a familial generation gap played out on sub-continental scale.

In December 2012, an even more stark demonstration of this problem became evident. News broke in the middle of that month of a particularly brutal sexual assault by a group of six young men of a 23-year old paramedic student who had gone with her friend to watch a movie in an upscale South Delhi mall. Delhi has long suffered from a reputation, backed up by crime statistics, of being the most unsafe large city for women in India, already thought of as the worst place in the world to be born female. Harassment and intimidation are daily events for most female residents of Delhi; the ever-present possibility of abduction and rape turns public spaces into locations of constant threat. The horrific nature of this particular assault – the victim was forcibly penetrated with a rusty iron rod, leaving her with internal injuries that caused her to lose her intestines – served to help coagulate years of anger at Delhi's callousness towards women. Young men and women thronged the streets at the centre of power, India Gate, and began walking towards Rashtrapati Bhavan, the imperial palace on a hill where India's President lives. Once television got involved, and the word spread over BlackBerry messenger and social networks, similar gatherings sprung up in a flash across other Indian cities and towns. No political or government leader felt able to respond to them in a language that they understood. Eventually the protests turned violent; many of the protesters had come away from the experience feeling their state was a stranger. Political leaders spoke a language of gradual reform, of shared familial concern, several mentioning that they had daughters, and so naturally they too were concerned. The younger people on the street had the shorter time-horizons and the impatience that paradoxically characterise those with their whole lives ahead of them. They demanded protection of the sort available in the rest of the world as a right; the sexagenarian state, with its bone-deep belief that India is a second-class country with second-class capabilities, felt itself unable to meet their demands.

The victim's tragic death, thirteen days later, in a hospital in Singapore, only increased the anger amongst the youth, and the protests continued into the New Year. A call went up for 'young leaders', but all that India could provide was the children of older leaders. Many of them are sensible, ethical individuals. Many would make excellent policymakers. But they owe their positions not to their youth or attitudes or energy, but because they have inherited their parents' constituencies and voters. For that reason, they cannot adequately meet the expectations of the young. No matter how young and dynamic the hereditary politician, she cannot represent the people she was not chosen to. The structural features of Indian politics – the large constituencies, the difficulty in making a name for yourself in anything less than a decade, the money and connections required to progress – mean that there are no easy solutions to this problem of representation, which is most acute for the aspirational and elite classes of young Indians, with their rapidly altering expectations.

Efforts have been made to bridge the gap. The Congress party's youth wing, for example, has been pushed by Rahul Gandhi into holding extensive internal elections in various states in the hope that they will throw up younger leaders. This experiment ended in failure because the hierarchical structure of the Congress, in which policy decisions are taken at the highest level and communicated to those below, meant that the internal elections were devoid of any real content. They became pure exercises in patronage, popularity and connections, and, as such, were won by the children of politicians best placed to do so.

Where Indian politics is going, there are no maps. The stresses on even a stable political system in a uniform society, caused by sustained high growth, are strong enough; just look at the internal dissension brewing even in the oppressive People's Republic of China. But when it is accompanied by a major demographic shift, then there are neither guides nor precedents. All we know is 'Here Be Dragons'. Very likely, some form of political radicalism will rise in India's future.

Never before in history has a large country undergone a demographic transition while being a vibrant, open democracy. So predictions are hard. Yet, it is certain that, if the Indian state moves at its usual glacial pace, while its citizens grow ever younger, the estrangement between the two will grow ever deeper. It is not the recipe for a stable polity.

Society

Demographic transitions are tricky things. In any society, when restless young people begin to dominate its numbers–its jobseekers, its voters, its mobs – then destabilisation of some sort or another inevitably follows. Consider, for example, the decade-long social upheaval that accompanied the coming of age of the post-War baby boomer generation in the United States. India is beginning to see some of these effects, too.

The political estrangement between India's young people and its state doesn't just reflect; it also slightly deflects estrangement between its generations. Statements by older politicians that betray their illiberal social values are greeted by many members of the young urban elite with an anger that could more effectively be directed at their own families, at their teachers and at their cultural heritage. During the anti-corruption protests of 2011, as well those in 2012 that followed the Delhi rape, the young people on the streets demanded, in essence, that a state that they saw as out of touch with their values, change itself. Like the protests of May 1968 France, which were nominally against the closure of universities but actually against the reactionary social order exemplified by the Charles de Gaulle government, or those in West Germany in the same year, which were actually against the incomplete de-Nazification of that country's institutions, the state acted as a lightning rod for the energies sparked by the tension between generations. Yet, unlike those societies, India has a certain degree of post-colonial insecurity, even among younger people, that causes criticism of its own culture to be muted. Thus the transmission from anger at outdated social norms to action on social reform is very incomplete.

During the protests following the Delhi rape, voices largely blamed government incompetence in implementing women's rights. Its action in clamping down on the protestors who had broken through to the heart of the government district in central New Delhi was seen as an inability to speak to young people properly, a parent who seems unable to communicate with their child and replaces understanding with discipline. Yet that wasn't the only dynamic on display, and to imagine it was, is folly. There was also the very real fact that divisions in culture and norms between groups of young people lie at the root of India's entrenched misogyny. Vernacular pop culture, pandering to the young of India's aspirational class – in which boys, not girls, have disposable income – has turned increasingly misogynistic. In Mumbai's Hindi films, girls fall in love with the boys that harass them. In lower-budget movies popular across North India and made in local dialects of Hindi, women who go out with male escorts are crassly commodified. I remember being shocked when, ten years ago, a neighbour of mine in a graduate-school hostel – a gentle boy who read Milan Kundera at lunchtime, but who had never before left the small town he grew up in – returned from his first trip to a South Delhi cinema. 'There were girls smoking, wearing lipstick, without anyone with them', he said quietly. 'Are they all prostitutes?' He was serious. These are the norms which, unchallenged, many younger people have inherited from their parents. Nor will a focus on state incompetence and the veneration of India's past that paradoxically characterises many of the country's most outward-looking young people lead them to be seriously challenged.

Instead of a social reform movement or escalating tensions between state and citizenry, what is more likely is that divisions in India's cohort of young people will be exacerbated. Chetan Bhagat, India's best-selling author, when asked at the 2012 launch of a collection of his essays entitled *What Young India Wants* about what young India did in fact want, replied *naukri* and *chokri*: a job and a girl. Young people were tired, he said, of norms that required them to woo each other clandestinely, or to avoid emotional or physical closeness in public. Bhagat is right, but only partly so. The sad truth is that the thugs who go around attacking card shops before Valentine's Day or raid hostels where the sexes are mingling freely at parties, are also, after all, young people. They believe too, that their state and their parents' generations have betrayed them, but that they have done this by abandoning, too easily, the essence of 'Indian culture', usually defined in a narrow Hindu revivalist way. The new India might well be made in their image, not that of Bhagat's readers.

This emphasis on India's glorious past co-exists comfortably with economic modernisation and even a friendly attitude to the West. This isn't schizophrenic at all. In some ways, the benchmark for the Indian elite and aspirational classes is the Indian diaspora in the West, particularly in the United States and the United Kingdom. Freed of the constraints of the reformist, interfering, and bureaucratic Indian state, the diaspora has prospered, and also developed a sternly uncritical view of India's heritage. In this worldview, the values of the modern West are reduced to conformity with economic structures and the accumulation of capital, with the institutionalisation of liberal norms assumed to be something of significance purely to whichever regional culture is hosting them. Lee Kuan Yew of Singapore and China's aggressive and prickly party leaders would recognise this combination of beliefs, and declare it authentically Asian. Many among India's aspirational and elite youth might therefore appear comfortable with the West, as long as 'Western values' know their place, far away from India.

To this must be added the facts that the Indian educational system places little or no emphasis on critical thinking, and that mainstream parenting techniques devalue the humanities and the social sciences as irrelevant to the achievement of professional security. This has created young people who are simultaneously hyper-respectful of 'qualifications' and who find questioning received wisdom difficult. To return to Chetan Bhagat, one major source of his popularity is the fact that he, himself, went to the Indian Institute of Technology and then to an Indian Institute of

Management. These are 'qualifications' relevant to his career as an author, and as such they are always trotted out on the back covers of his books. There is a small cottage industry of such authors now, trying to edge in on the apparently lucrative market for books aimed at young Indians, and they all announce their qualifications in full. And the Indian internet is full of young engineers, astrophysicists or pathologists, often trained in the UK or US, who believe that their 'qualifications' provide them with unparalleled expertise with which to come to conclusions about, say, the exact history of the Turkic and Afghan invasions of India in the medieval period, conclusions which rarely match what professional historians would say, but do sound suspiciously like the simpler bigotry of their parents' generation.

Thus, Indian young people are split down the middle, even more than their parents before them, on what we would call liberal values. Both liberals and conservatives can agree to hate the Indian state, if for different reasons, and thus effective social mobilisation always has an anti-state element to it. But it is impossible to see the enormous influence of younger Indians, over the next few decades, as leading uncomplicatedly to the sort of transition in social values that marked the 1960s in the West. Instead, we stand on the brink of the culture war that threatened India in the 1990s and then was held in abeyance by the right-wing Prime Minister, Atal Bihari Vajpayee's, Urdu-quoting, America-embracing urbanity, and subsequently by the double electoral triumphs of the woolly and inclusive Congress party. And, given India's violent public culture, there is no reason to suppose that this conflict will be played out only on blogs or in the Parliament. The mobs that ransack art exhibits, threaten to shut down showings of movies or plays deemed offensive to one religion or another, are not composed of the elderly or the middle-aged. They are young, and they have agency. For the young, pride is important; and for many young Indians, pride in India, in caste and community, is increasingly valuable and easily threatened.

Indeed, it is important to note that consciousness of caste is not necessarily decreasing with time. Many liberal thinkers blame this on the policy of the Indian state that recognises caste in order to right historical wrongs through positive discrimination. Of course, it is not as easy as all that. For the poorest of young Indians, overwhelmingly members of the castes that the Brahminical system classified as the 'lowest', the patronage opportunities afforded by close identification with their caste is pretty much the only method open to them for advancement. Several studies have shown that the private sector systematically discriminates against lower-caste and Muslim individuals; they find it, additionally, more difficult to go through the bureaucratic rigmarole associated with formal finance and the other red tape associated with entrepreneurship, given that bankers and petty bureaucrats are overwhelmingly upper-caste. Meanwhile, for many members of the comfortable upper castes, the concept of 'merit' – which unsurprisingly superimposes itself neatly on the caste hierarchy – seems debased by lower-caste activism and state action. Young people from the urban elite proudly claim that they do not even know what caste they are, not knowing that if they weren't upper-caste, the world would have told them so repeatedly. The fissures of caste and community are not being closed by time and prosperity; they are being concealed and disguised, even as they widen. The anger with which some politicians, especially regional leaders from North India, are viewed by young elite Indians, has more than a trace of caste contempt in it.

Social change and reform is thus, not impossible in India over the coming decades. The process of urbanisation and of greater aspiration will make some of it inevitable. But it is not going to happen without more pain and violence than is currently expected. The anti-corruption movement, of which young people were the drivers, was supposedly led by a 'Gandhian', Anna Hazare, but had little or no awareness that corruption was not led by the state, but those who evaded taxes or paid bribes for their own comfort. The protests against the Delhi rape squandered their energy in flailing at an unpopular Central government instead of wondering what form of social reform would destroy the edifice of misogyny and oppression that supports North Indian society. Such lost opportunities will be the hallmark of the years to come, as India's elite and aspirational youth – impatient, arrogant, aggressive and self-assured – are not likely to spend much effort on introspection about the values they have taken for their own.

The Economy

Much of the hope surrounding what Wall Street analysts and Delhi headline-writers call the Indian Growth Story, depends on young people. That the age composition of India's population is heavily slanted towards younger people is often cited as the reason that its economy will inevitably overtake China's, which, it is feared, will 'grow old before it grows rich', thanks to the one-child policy the People's Republic introduced to curb overpopulation. The demographic transition will yield a 'demographic dividend', in which a population, with higher than normal levels of those of an age to work, will have correspondingly higher average productivity, and save and invest more.

It is slowly coming home to even inveterate boosters of the India Growth Story that the demographic dividend can as easily become a curse. India has moved too slowly to reform its economy and open up jobs for the enormous number of young people joining the workforce. Thirteen million of them enter the job market every year; India will have created only eight million new jobs in that same year. This imbalance is filled by those who live off parental subsidies, in the elite; by those who take on low-paying service jobs that power India's 'service revolution', in the aspirational class; and, for the rest, through disguised unemployment or backbreaking manual labour.

Two things need to be done, yet India's sclerotic decision-making process has delayed them. First, the young need to be given greater human capital. India's education system, traditionally top-heavy and elitist, has been supplemented with an intensive focus on primary education that has pushed up literacy numbers. But only under Prime Minister Manmohan Singh has it been recognised that the real need is to create avenues for these young people to acquire marketable skills. The state higher-education system, rife with inefficiency and interest-groups unwilling to change, has resisted a change in government support from subsidising traditional universities to creating a wider, industrial-training architecture.

Even if this first problem was solved, the second would still be a hurdle:

that India's manufacturing sector just does not have the scale or the competitiveness to absorb enough aspirational young people to create a sizeable middle class. Throughout history, that is how it has happened: increasing the size of the manufacturing sector, employing more workers and consequently increasing productivity, gives the employees a higher and more stable standard of living. This is happening in China and across Southeast Asia, as it happened in Japan and Korea and in the United Kingdom, the first industrial nation. But it isn't happening in India, because socialist-era controls on manufacturing prevent it from growing and becoming internationally competitive. Most importantly, you can't fire anyone; and so no factory owner hires anyone either, except on contract, and therefore outside the law, and for a pittance. Yet relaxation of labour laws, long seen to be essential to growing manufacturing and creating employment, run up against a coalition of interests: left-leaning influence-peddlers and NGOs; pusillanimous politicians in both the Congress and the current political opposition; and those already employed, relatively comfortably, in 'permanent' jobs in industry.

The Singh government, which is stocked by reformers who have been unable to proceed because they owe their political power to those in the Congress party unwilling to change the status quo, has finally broken free from the shackles and announced a manufacturing policy that, it claims, will create a hundred million jobs by 2025. That is to be achieved through policies to boost export competitiveness, China-style manufacturing hubs, and a great deal of hope that infrastructure such as power and roads can be upgraded soon enough to make factories an investable option. This will not be easy, but at least it is a start. The question is whether it has been left too late for many of India's aspirational young people. The Singh government has also hinted that labour laws will finally be relaxed; such is the promise in the document that contains the Twelfth Five-Year Plan, which is to govern India's economy to 2017 and which all the country's chief ministers signed on to in December 2012.

It is important to note that the search for a manufacturing sector that can employ India's young people is not necessary just because that is how living standards have always been raised in the past. It is necessary because it is clear that that is what younger people in the aspirational and working classes want. The service sector can provide employment, but it is chancy and the income you earn is not steady. Farm work is backbreaking, and most young people in rural areas do not want to work on un-mechanised farms unless they have to; and who would blame them? Ideally, everyone wants a government job, because that represents stable employment with a secure income and a pension on retirement. But the government cannot employ thirteen million people a year. A vibrant manufacturing sector in a growing economy is the only thing that can provide steady jobs on that scale. Recognition of this truth has come late in India's reform process – the 'shining India' narrative of the early part of the 2000s, touted India's 'services-led growth model' as a feature, not a bug – but that it has finally been recognised and provides some hope that India's economy can change fast enough to ensure that the demographic dividend doesn't backfire. A millions-strong army of unemployed and unemployable young men wandering a stagnant economy is the stuff of dystopian nightmares.

India is a young country, but an old civilisation, it is sometimes said. This is nonsense. A civilisation is only as old as the memories of its people, and those don't go back very far. In India's case, they go back even less than elsewhere. Like all brash young civilisations, it will destabilise itself and look on a more staid and elderly world with adolescent resentment. It will exhibit the brilliance of the young, attracting the world's best minds and instincts away from the greying problems of older societies. But you never know how the young will turn out, and that's the case with this terrifyingly young country, too. Independence from Britain is 66 years old; Midnight's Children have hit retirement age. They leave their country to the world's largest group of young people. I'm not sure that we know what to do with it.

13 |

Young Brittannia: Living on the Edge

Kapil Komireddi

On a cold December evening in 2010, Prince Charles took his wife to see a performance in a West End theatre. London had been smouldering for weeks with angry protests by young students. That day, the police corralled thousands of young men and women demonstrating against the government's decision to hike university tuition fees into suffocatingly tiny spaces. Those who escaped the cordons vented their rage by setting fire to the Christmas tree in Trafalgar Square, smashing shop windows on Oxford Street and defacing a statue of Winston Churchill in Parliament Square. Finally, they spotted Charles's car, its royal occupants moving in splendid detachment as their kingdom burned around them. 'It's Camilla', someone shouted, recognising Charles's wife. They approached the vehicle, doused it with white paint and cracked one of the windows. Charles and his wife looked on in silence, defenceless, jaws frozen in mid-collapse, their startled faces captured on camera.

The young men who attacked the royal couple and rampaged through London that day were relatively better off than the many millions of youngsters who languish in abject poverty in Britain today. But the momentousness of the event, exposing established order to the frenzied passions of the young, lay in the possibilities it implied for the future. And that future looks increasingly grim.

To get a sense of the deteriorating position of the young in Britain, consider the results of the most recent European Social Survey, conducted a year before the Olympics. Of the 29 countries surveyed across Europe, some of the most hostile views about the young were recorded in Britain. If you are British and in your 20s, you're more likely than any other Europeans in your age bracket to be treated with contempt by your elders. What about respect? British youth are considered least deserving of it. They are also presumed to have low moral standards, and are viewed as unfriendly, incompetent and unworthy of admiration. On the question of negativity, they are at the very bottom of the pile: 29th among the 29 countries surveyed.[1]

This is a dangerous trend – not least because the crystallisation of these prejudices among the grown-ups has been accompanied by an almost unprecedented degree of erosion of opportunity for the young. Nearly a million people between the ages of sixteen and twenty-four are out of work in Britain today[2]. The unemployment rate for people in this age group hovers above 20 per cent; long-term unemployment among the youth, at 7 to 9 per cent in some parts of the country, is twice the national average.[3]

The reigning attitudes towards the young, however, seem to persist in complete isolation from the actual experiences of the youth. This explains why the government, committed religiously to a programme of spending cuts, evinced no unease as it set out its proposal in 2012 to abolish housing benefits for people under the age of 25. David Cameron described the benefit as part of an 'entitlement culture' that 'discourages' young people from working, an unfair burden on hardworking taxpayers, before alighting on the maxim that supposedly governed the thinking of its recipients: 'Get housing benefit, get a flat, and then don't ever get a job or you'll lose a load of housing benefit.'[4] Given that out of the five million people who claim housing benefits, only about 385,000 are under the age of 25, it's a measure of the prevailing hostility towards the young that Cameron could so easily single them out for censure.[5] In reality, as of 2010, only one in eight claimants of housing benefits was out of work.[6] Besides, in many cases housing benefit is the only route to a safe and dignified future for young people who have grown up in abusive family homes.[7] The government's suggestion that young people should simply move back into their parents' houses overlooks those tens of thousands who do not have a family home to return to, or have been displaced as a result of currents beyond their control. An estimated 80,000 youngsters are forced to endure homelessness each year.[8] Who is responsible for them? Where should they go?

These questions assumed great urgency in the aftermath of the riots that erupted across the country in 2011. They were sparked by the killing of Mark Duggan, a 29-year-old man from north London, by armed police. Mark was a father of three children, and he was black. He grew up in Broadwater Farm, a sprawling housing estate near the site of his death, whose residents – overwhelmingly black and unexceptionally poor – nurse a deep distrust of the police. A day after Mark's death, about three hundred people from the Farm gathered outside the local police station in Tottenham to begin a peaceful protest demanding 'justice' for the Duggan family. At some point, a scuffle broke out between a teenaged protester and a police officer. A short while later, young men from the area hurled bottles at two police patrol cars near the police station. By 11.00 pm, the two police cars, along with a double-decker bus and a local supermarket and a carpet shop, had been set on fire. The chaos inaugurated by this sudden flare-up of violent rage generated tantalising opportunities for plunder. Young men and women ferried out trolley-loads of stolen goods from ransacked department stores and sports shops that night. This was the beginning.

The royal wedding of Prince William to Catherine Middleton, broadcast live on television networks around the world only months before, showcased a sedately cheerful nation bound by tradition. Now, as rioting and looting engulfed major cities, an altogether different country clamoured for attention: a Britain where too many young people seemed to find a triumphant consolation, a kind of release, in the breakdown of order. The violence claimed five lives.

It seemed difficult at the time to determine the causes of the riots, the reasons that prompted people to participate in them. A pattern, to the extent that one could be stitched together, was discernible in the areas that first ignited–traditionally deprived–and the people pillaging them: overwhelmingly young. But what explained the spontaneity of the riots? Among the causes tossed about by the pundits hastily assembled by news networks to make sense of the tumult were: multiculturalism, family breakdown, unemployment, BlackBerry Messenger, spending cuts and excess spending. The influential Tudor historian David Starkey, bemoaning the transformation of Britain into 'literally a foreign country', placed the blame on 'black culture'.[9] To many it looked as if a subterranean world of savages, having organised on some inscrutable Internet network, was intimating its presence in an extended moment of organised terror.

On a recent afternoon in Broadwater Farm, I met a small group of young people gathered around a shrine to Mark Duggan: a slab of concrete on the pavement, inlaid with epitaphs crudely carved into it. The Duggans had moved out of the Farm some years ago. But all the youngsters at the shrine knew Mark, a figure of awe, respected, admired. On the evening that he was shot, Mark was on his way to the Farm to meet his brother, Marlon. Armed police brought Mark's taxi to a halt just as it reached Ferry Lane. At 6.13 pm, moments after he stepped out of the taxi, Mark was shot dead by a police marksman: one bullet in the chest, another in the right bicep, fired from an MP5 submachine gun.[10] The Met Police did not inform Mark's parents about their son's death. They learnt about it on the television news later that evening.[11] The Independent Police Complaints Commission (IPCC), which monitors complaints made against the police, told journalists that there had been an exchange of fire between the police and Mark Duggan. Some even claimed that Mark opened fire on the police first. The IPCC revised its initial account and admitted that it made a 'serious error'.[12] But a profile of Mark was swiftly constructed from the contested accounts of his death and the information passed on to reporters by police sources. Mark emerged in this as a drug dealer and a dreaded gangster, a gathering threat being trailed by a specialist police operation.[13]

This sinister figure many on the Farm could not recognise. 'This is a tough place', one of the youngsters told me. 'You got to earn respect here, but

Mark didn't hurt nobody. If the police are gonna shoot people for selling drugs, this place is gonna turn into a graveyard.' 'And who buys the drugs?' he asked. 'Rich white boys and girls', his friends echoed. Had Mark been white, they all believed, he would have lived. Every one of these young men had either been to prison or knew someone who was serving time. Almost all of them claimed to have been stopped and searched by the police at least once before they turned 18. They hated the police, and they were open about it.

Later that day I talked to Abdul,[14] a former resident of the Farm who now runs a grocery store there. He grew up with Mark, and in those years, he said, the Farm was a hotbed of criminality. One of the largest housing estates in the country, the Farm was a utopian act of social engineering. Its architects, inspired by Le Corbusier, built elevated walkways between the grey brutalist buildings. They imagined communities walking in the air, always connected. Instead, in the unlit spaces beneath those bridges, crime flourished. Drug peddling, prostitution, muggings, thefts and burglaries became part of the experience of growing up on the Farm. In 1985, a resident of the Farm died after being pushed about by a policeman in her own flat. A riot broke out the following day. A policeman was stabbed to death by some of the protesters. The memory of that death still haunts the Farm. 'The police won't forget it', Abdul said. Abdul converted to Islam and stayed away from trouble, but many of his friends have drifted in and out of prison since then. Abdul saw Mark as a casualty of the enduring rivalry between the police and the Farm's youth.

Abdul and the others told me they weren't surprised by the riots that followed Mark's killing. They believed that the police, anxious about cuts to their own forces, instigated the riots only to spotlight their indispensability. Theirs was a conspiratorial vocabulary, but it was forged during long years of exposure to the roughest edges of police power.

The subsequent looting and arson was to be expected. What have the politicians and businessmen been doing over the last decade, they asked. Weren't MPs fiddling their expenses and bankers running the economy to the ground? Why shouldn't the young have had a go at it? One youngster, from Clapham in south London, put forth an analogy. The riots were like a slaughterhouse, he told me. There's blood everywhere, guts are lying on the floor, it's ugly, and it stinks. The sight of it shocks us. The politicians and 'bankers' – and this was an all-encompassing epithet – are feeding on the same meat, but their feasts take place in the enclosed elegance of restaurants. Their meat is cleaned and cooked and served on expensive plates; and the violence that goes into procuring it is hidden from the public eye. He was 17 and fiercely articulate. And yet he felt he had no prospects for a decent future in what David Cameron insists is 'still the greatest country on earth'.[15]

An independent commission set up by the government to investigate the causes of the riots drew attention to what it called the 'forgotten families who bump along the bottom of society'. It urged the government to commit itself to a 'youth job promise' in order to create a stake for young people in the society.[16] The report makes for uncomfortable reading. This is not because of any inherent deficiencies in it, but because it exposes the entire exercise as a futile ritual, part of the lesson-learning pretence that follows all public disasters.

Many of the participants in the riots emanated from neglected families and communities. A sincere effort to create a stake for them in the society would start with a dialogue. Instead, it started with the language of persecution. Public opinion wanted blood, and Cameron was eager to deliver it. In the days following the riots, the Prime Minister, determined to appear tough, refused to indulge any explanation that was not excruciatingly simplistic. Turning into a blow-horn for the most reactionary sentiments in the country, he put the riots down to 'criminality, pure and simple'.[17] His idea of expressing justice did not stop at trying the rioters in specially convened courts. Where families of convicted offenders lived in social housing, he wanted them evicted. It was his way of 'enforcing responsibility in our society'. Where, he was asked, would the displaced go? They 'should have thought of that before they started burgling',[18] he answered. Cameron's Communities Secretary, Eric Pickles, declared that the rioters had 'wilfully made themselves homeless'. 'That may sound a little harsh', he conceded, 'but I don't think this is a time to pussyfoot around'.[19]

Analysis carried out by *The Guardian* showed that more than half of the people brought before magistrates for involvement in the riots in London were under the age of 18. Many of those who pleaded guilty were either sentenced to serve time or remanded to custody. [20] One 23-year-old was sentenced to six months in jail for the crime of stealing a bottle of water. [21] The result is that hundreds, maybe even thousands, of young people will grow up with criminal records, returning to a life shattered by humiliation, homelessness and displacement: the very conditions that breed criminality and encourage recidivism. After being condemned in this manner, it is difficult to fault the young for reflexively recoiling from the lofty ambitions outlined by government commissioned reports.

An extreme but instructive example of the dismal plight of those young people who not only have not breached the government's very thin limits of tolerance, but have actually tried to follow Cameron's advice to 'work hard, go to college, get a job, live at home, save up for a flat', [22] is Victoria Harrison. Vicky was 21, and had 10 good GCSEs and 3 A-levels. She dreamt of becoming a teacher, but paid work was impossible to come by. She signed on to claim £51.00 per week on Jobseeker's Allowance (JSA), another welfare scheme that has acquired a thick coat of stigma through years of denunciations by politicians. In the popular imagination, beneficiaries of this allowance are lazy, work-shy scroungers.

Vicky was nothing if not industrious. She searched for secretarial work. She knocked on the doors of local schools for work as a dinner lady. She visited supermarkets to ask for a job stacking shelves. By the time she wrote out her suicide note, in 2010, Vicky had made 200 job applications. 'I am sure that the latest rejection letter combined with the fact that she had to go and sign on [for JSA] the next day was too much for her', Vicky's mother later told a reporter. 'She never wanted any charity and that is why she was so desperate for work. What upsets us so much is that there are obviously so many other people in a similar position.' [23]

In the absence of meaningful work, the government has resorted to supplying young labour to private businesses on a conveyor belt of dubious workfare schemes. The Mandatory Work Activity (MWA) programme places JSA claimants on four-week placements with local organisations, under the threat of terminating their benefits for up to three years if they do not comply. This may seem reasonable–except that the government's own research, conducted a year after the programme was launched – found that 'an MWA referral had no impact on the likelihood of being employed compared to non-referrals'.[24] Bafflingly, on the very day that these results were published, the government announced its decision to spend an additional £5milion to extend the programme to a further 70,000 JSA claimants.[25] 'People need to be aware that for those who are fit enough to work it is simply not an option to sit on benefits and do nothing', the employment minister, Chris Grayling, said.[26] It was as if Grayling was operating in another world: extolling a scheme he knew to be useless, while amplifying the falsehood that laziness, and not lack of jobs, is the principal driver of benefit claims. A succession of reputable charities, alarmed by the government's clandestine efforts to subject sick and disabled benefit claimants to the MWA, withdrew from the project in 2012.

The Apprenticeships Scheme, the other idea heralded with great vigour by the government, rapidly descended into an exploitative racket. Through the National Apprenticeship Service, the government invested £1.4bn to help businesses recruit apprentices. Recruiters are not obliged to pay apprentices the national minimum wage.[27] The government bears the full cost of training for apprentices aged 18 and half the cost for recruits over the age of 19. Small and medium enterprises can claim £1,500 against every apprentice they draft. But as a BBC investigation soon discovered, far from preparing young people for employment, many apprenticeship positions were being fabricated on paper in order to mulct the government.[28] A scheme powered by the presumption that jobless young people were fleecing the state created abundant opportunities for private businesses actually to do just that. And they made creative use of them. The BBC investigation revealed that nearly four in ten workers at Morrisons, one of the nation's largest supermarket chains, were classed as 'apprentices'.[29]

Then in June 2012, a night before the thousand-boat flotilla costing £12 million sailed down the Thames to celebrate the diamond jubilee year of the Queen's coronation, about eighty people were bussed into London to steward the pageant.[30] They were made to sleep under London Bridge, in the rain and cold, and the following day worked 14-hour shifts in rain for no pay. They were a mixture of jobseekers and apprentices, contracted out to private companies under the government's workfare schemes. It was a vivid display of the remoteness of the nation's governing elite from the people condemned to labour under their policies.

There is hardly any evidence to indicate that their fortunes will recover in the years ahead.[31] If anything, the transition to adulthood for a generation of young people seems to have been postponed. The defining stabilities of adult life – job security, economic independence, family, parenthood, property ownership[32] – that a generation ago were accessible to people in their twenties are today largely beyond the reach of people in that age group. The result is that some of the most disabling features of youth – debt, dependency, drift – have prolonged their lifespan.[33] If and when the economy recovers, and permanent jobs become more available, a substantial portion of a generation of young people will enter the workforce with pyramids of personal debt. This, as the Bank of England warned in March 2012, will mean that people will have to work longer to pay for their retirement. In other words: it's tough being young in today's Britain, but the worst is yet to come.

Notes

1. 'The Poor Perception of Younger People in the UK: A Research Report from the Intergenerational Foundation', Intergenerational Foundation, London, August 2011: http://www.if.org.uk/archives/960/if-analyses-ess-research-of-56000-people-across-29-countries

2. David Hough, 'Youth Unemployment Statistics', 13 December 2012, House of Commons Library: http://www.parliament.uk/briefing-papers/sn05871

3. For a detailed analysis of youth unemployment, see the ACEVO report published in 2012: 'Youth Unemployment: The Crisis We cannot Afford'.

4. The Prime Minister's speech to the Conservative Party conference, 10 October 2012.

5. The relevant statistics, from the Department of Work and Pensions, are available at: http://statistics.dwp.gov.uk/asd/asd1/adhoc_analysis/2012/hb_under25_passported_status.xls

6. 'Housing benefit warning', Shelter, 22 June 2010: http://england.shelter.org.uk/news/previous_years/2010/june_2010/housing_benefit_warning

7. Leslie Morphy, 'Why We Must Defend Housing Benefit for the Under 25s', New Statesman, 12 November 2012: http://www.newstatesman.com/politics/2012/11/why-we-must-defend-housing-benefit-under-25s

8. According to the charity Centre Point: http://www.centrepoint.org.uk/media/205237/12-04_consequences_of_scrapping_housing_benefit_mw.pdf

9. 'England riots: "The whites have become black" says David Starkey', BBC News Online (August 2011): http://www.bbc.co.uk/news/uk-14513517

10. 'Police marksman was "absolutely certain" Mark Duggan was holding gun', The Guardian, 26 September 2012.

11. IPCC Report, reference: 2011/016449.

12. 'Leveson Inquiry: IPCC "error" over Mark Duggan shooting', BBC News Online (March 2012): http://www.bbc.co.uk/news/uk-17537293

13. A number of journalists later criticised the reliance by reporters on 'official' sources. 'One of the worst parts of the post-riots coverage', the President of the National Union of Journalists later said, 'was where the content of newspapers came directly from the police'. See Roy Greenslade, 'What the media did wrong in the riots – and how to put it right': http://www.guardian.co.uk/media/greenslade/2012/jul/31/london-riots-universityofleicester

14. Not his real name.

15. Speech to the Conservative Party Conference, 2012.

16. The Riots Communities and Victims Panel, 'After the Riots': http://riotspanel.independent.gov.uk/wp-content/uploads/2012/03/Riots-Panel-Final-Report1.pdf

17. Hansard, HC Deb. 11 August 2011, Col 1051: http://www.publications.parliament.uk/pa/cm201011/cmhansrd/cm110811/debtext/110811-0001.htm

18. 'David Cameron back councils planning to evict rioters' [sic], BBC News Online (August 2011): http://www.bbc.co.uk/news/uk-politics-14509779

19. 'Police out in force to deter riots', Reuters UK (August 2011): http://uk.reuters.com/article/2011/08/12/uk-britain-disorder-idUKTRE7752QX20110812

20. 'UK riots: The demographics of magistrate cases and convictions': http://www.guardian.co.uk/news/datablog/2011/aug/11/uk-riots-magistrates-court-list

21. 'England riots: What is the impact of a criminal record?', BBC News Online: http://www.bbc.co.uk/news/uk-14556347

22. Speech to the Conservative Party conference, 2012.

23. 'Job seeker, 21, with 3 A-levels and 10 GCSEs, kills herself after she was rejected for 200 jobs', *The Daily Mail*, 23 April 2010: http://www.dailymail. co.uk/news/article-1267953/Job-seeker-Vicky-Harrison-commits-suicide-rejected-200-jobs.html

24. 'Mandatory work scheme does not improve job chances, research finds', *The Guardian*, 13 June 2012: http://www.guardian.co.uk/society/2012/jun/13/ mandatory-work-scheme-government-research

25. 'Mandatory work activity scheme extended', Department of Work and Pensions, 12 June 2012: http://www.dwp.gov.uk/newsroom/press-releases/2012/jun-2012/dwp061-12.shtml

26. Ibid.

27. The national minimum wage is £6.08 per hour; apprentices are paid £2.60 per hour.

28. BBC News Channel, Panorama: The Great Apprentice Scandal, 8 April 2012

29. 'Morrisons "undervaluing" apprentice scheme', *The Scotsman*, 2 April 2012: http://www.scotsman.com/news/uk/morrisons-undervaluing-apprentice-scheme-1-2211036

30. 'Unemployed bussed in to steward river pageant', *The Guardian*, 4 June 2012: http://www.guardian.co.uk/uk/2012/jun/04/jubilee-pageant-unemployed

31. For a detailed (and depressing) account of the government's economic policies and their consequences, see John Lanchester, 'Let's Call It Failure', *London Review of Books*, 3 January 2012, Vol. 35, No. 1.

32. Gill Jones, 'The Youth Divide: Divergent Paths to Adulthood', Joseph Rowntree Foundation, 2002, p. 2.

33. For a brilliant and detailed guide to the progressively worsening condition of Britain's young, see Ed Howker and Shiv Malik, *Jilted Generation: How Britain Has Bankrupted its Youth*, (London, Icon, 2010). Also see, David Willets, *The Pinch: How the Baby Boomers Took Their Children's Future – And Why They Should Give it Back* (London, Atlantic, 2010).

14 |

The BBC and India in the Twenty-first Century

William Crawley and David Page

When the BBC World Service left Bush House in July 2012, the move had been planned for many years. But it was an emotional moment for both past and present staff to part company with a building which had been synonymous with the World Service for the greater part of its eighty-year history. For former BBC staff like us who had had a chance to say farewell to the building a few weeks before, there were vivid associations with the labyrinthine corridors and cramped offices, the studios where programmes had been recorded in over forty languages, and the BBC club and canteen where many different nationalities came together in the nearest thing one could imagine to the United Nations on British soil. Bush House was not only broadcasting to countries across the globe, it was also receiving visitors from many nations: politicians, poets, musicians and authors, who came to be interviewed for programmes, and many listeners too, who came just to see Bush House and to meet the broadcasters whose voices were so familiar to them in their homes, thousands of miles away.

During our time in the BBC Eastern Service, we remember visits by leading South Asian politicians to Bush House, including President J.R. Jayawardene of Sri Lanka, the veteran Nepalese Congress leader, B.P. Koirala, and the Indian BJP leader and later Prime Minister, Atal Bihari

Vajpayee. We remember one extraordinary occasion when General Zia-ul-Haq rang the Eastern Service very late in the evening to comment on a programme. But perhaps the most enduring image is of the Tamil Nadu Chief Minister, M.G. Ramachandran (MGR), coming to Bush House with a large and glamorous retinue, and sitting with the BBC Tamil Service senior producer, Shankar Shankamurthi, in his small office on the fifth floor, before being ushered to a studio to record an interview. MGR was both a powerful politician and a legend of the Tamil film and media world. Shankar ran one of the smallest BBC language services. MGR's presence in Bush House–frail with age, with glossy dyed black hair, dark glasses and his trademark fur cap–seemed a striking testimony to the power of radio, the impact of BBC Tamil broadcasts, and the regard in which Shankar and a small group of broadcasting colleagues were held.

In the 1970s and 1980s, the BBC's Indian language services, broadcasting on medium wave or short wave in Hindi, Urdu, Bengali and Tamil, were being heard by millions of listeners across South Asia, who regarded them as a lifeline at times of crisis because their own electronic media were almost entirely state controlled. It is a very different situation today. There are now over two hundred television channels available to the urban Indian viewer, and twenty-four hour news channels in most major Indian languages. A satellite and digital revolution has transformed the choices and the information available to Indian viewers and listeners and led the BBC to redefine its own relationship with India. The BBC, which celebrated its ninetieth anniversary in 2012, can point to a long tradition as an autonomous British national broadcaster, as a pioneer and trusted international broadcaster, and as an upholder of a particular tradition of public service or public interest broadcasting. But today, a realistic view of the BBC is that of one player in a highly competitive commercial global market place.

The BBC, in its operations in India, and its relations with Indian audiences, governments and broadcasters is subject to these current realities. But more than any foreign broadcasting institution in India, the BBC–for good or ill–carries its history with it. The baggage includes its record of involvement with the beginnings of Indian broadcasting and a close association with the former British colonial power, which controlled the Indian broadcasters. It is a long history in which the BBC has often been admired, sometimes vilified, but generally heard. It has a reputation which in many respects has served it well, but which has also magnified the causes and consequences of disputes when they have arisen.

In response to the globalising trends of the past twenty years, the BBC has developed its international role as a global news provider. In a speech to the Commonwealth Broadcasting Association in 2010, Peter Horrocks, the director of BBC Global News[1], described a practice of forging partnerships by supplying news and other programmes to stations around the world. It is a key strategy in the BBC's new relationship with India. In the same mould, BBC Media Action (formerly the BBC World Service Trust), the BBC's international development charity, has built partnerships with the donor community and national radio and TV stations, to make programmes on issues like AIDS and Malaria, which have found very wide audiences in India and elsewhere.[2]

The BBC's present policies also reflect the increasing fragmentation of audiences produced by the proliferation of new media. 'Opinion formers', however defined, have long been seen as a prime target audience for BBC services in Hindi and other Indian languages. Now the BBC aims to reach 'people who need and want the news we bring'.[3] They are not necessarily part of a civil service, political or business elite. But BBC experience is that they are people who look for independent reporting on global and regional news. They value an input from international sources and a global perspective on issues relating to India's rise as an economic power. They are opinion formers in their own towns and rural areas of the Hindi-speaking heartlands. They form a part of what is often referred to as 'civil society'.

The BBC is recasting its relations with India at a time of economic resurgence in India and severe financial constraints in the UK. The British Foreign and Commonwealth Office (FCO), which currently funds the BBC World Service through a parliamentary grant-in-aid, required cuts of 16 per cent as part of a government-wide austerity package in

2011–12, which led to the discontinuation of many language services.[4] From 2014, as part of a deal to avoid even deeper cuts, the BBC has agreed to fund the entire World Service budget out of the domestic TV licence fee, which currently provides the corporation with a £ 3.6 billion annual budget.[5] The FCO has insisted on a future role in the strategy of the World Service and the prescription of languages, though its influence will very likely wane once it ceases to pay the piper. Whether the BBC, as a publicly funded domestic broadcaster, will have the same commitment to overseas audiences as it had under the old arrangements, seems highly questionable. All this makes the re-imagining of relations between the BBC and India much more unpredictable than it might have been five or ten years ago. But it is a very good time to review a long and complex history and to set new directions.

Early History

The BBC's relationship with India goes back to the very early days of the corporation's own history. Sir John Reith, the founding father of the BBC, was keenly interested in India and in the mid-1920s even contemplated going out there himself. However, in the mid-1920s, the Government of India was not in listening mode. Broadcasting in India had started on an experimental basis in 1921 and in the early years was left to the radio manufacturers, radio clubs and gifted amateurs, a highly decentralised process. The Government of India collected the licence fee but left the rest to the market. In 1930, when the Indian Broadcasting Company, the country's first commercial broadcasting venture, went bankrupt, the government was only persuaded with difficulty to step in. As Reith put it in his diary, there was 'neither vision nor recognition of the immense potentialities of broadcasting...just commercialism'.[6]

By the mid-1930s, however, the situation had changed both technically and politically. With full provincial autonomy in prospect under the terms of the new Government of India Act (1935), officials began to realise that radio had a potentially powerful role to play and Reith found himself pushing at a more open door. He convinced the Viceroy, Lord Willingdon, that India needed to have a centralised national broadcasting service

Recording session for the poetry magazine 'Voice' the monthly radio magazine programme which broadcast modern poetry to English-speaking India in the Eastern Service of the BBC. l-r, sitting Venu Chitale, a member of the BBC Indian Section, M.J. Tambimuttu, a Tamil from Ceylon, editor of Poetry (London) T.S. Eliot; Una Marson, BBC West Indian Programme Organiser, Mulk Raj Anand, Indian novelist, Christopher Pemberton, a member of the BBC staff, Narayana Menon, Indian writer. l-r, standing George Orwell, author and producer of the programme, Nancy Parratt, secretary to George Orwell, William Empson, poet and critic
© BBC

and he set out his vision for 'a British corporation...in India...to cover the greater part of the continent'. It was not a vision shared by the emerging provincial governments, who had initially been allocated responsibility for broadcasting under the new constitution, but over the next few years, All India Radio (AIR) came into being, very much according to Reith's own prescription and at the hands of a man he nominated for the task, its first controller of programmes, Lionel Fielden.

The creation of AIR served an important imperial purpose. It was a powerful voice for the government of India at a time when nationalist forces were coming to power in the Indian provinces. It became even

Princess Indira of Kapurthala broadcasting on the BBC World Service
© BBC

more so during the Second World War, when the Congress opposed the war effort and radio became a propaganda tool.[7] But Fielden was far from being an imperial bureaucrat. He was a creative BBC producer with a somewhat volatile temperament, who was much more interested in developing broadcasting as an art form than in its political potential.[8] He would have liked AIR to be more inclusive but he was constrained by the political circumstances of the day. The Congress regarded it as a mouthpiece of the Raj and despite Fielden's encouragement, Gandhi politely refused his invitation to broadcast. But Fielden did succeed in creating a lively and professional broadcasting culture. He recruited and empowered a number of very talented broadcasters, who established ways of broadcasting which drew on the best of BBC practice and Indian culture and experience.[9] One of Fielden's young disciples, Syed Rashid Ahmed, later spoke of his 'dynamic and non-conformist personality' and his ability to gather round him 'a band of idealistic and imaginative young Indians, who were attracted by the romance of broadcasting'.[10]

Two of the young Indians who worked with Fielden to develop the creative ethos of broadcasting in India were the famous Bokhari brothers: A.S. Bokhari, who became the first Director-General of All India Radio, and his brother, Zulfiqar Ali Bokhari, an equally successful station director in Bombay. Their prominent role in the formation of AIR led to it being dubbed 'the Indian BBC' or 'Bokhari Brothers' Corporation'. But of the two, it was Zulfiqar who had the greatest influence on the BBC and its relations with India. In 1939, as war clouds gathered, he was invited to London to take up the post of Indian Programme Organiser, with a brief to develop services for India in English and in Hindustani to counter the propaganda of the Axis powers.

Zulfiqar Bokhari was a man of many parts: a teacher, writer, poet and actor as well as a broadcaster and administrator. He was both a servant of the Raj and a confident, even arrogant, critic of its shortcomings. He was clear from the start that his fellow Indians would not be won over by mere propaganda and that it would be more effective to engage them intellectually. As a result, the roll call of the English programme's broadcast to India during the war years reads like a guide to the best of contemporary British poetry and prose. Such figures as George Orwell, E.M. Forster, J.B. Priestley, Louis MacNeice and T.S. Eliot were regular visitors to the BBC studios, as well as leading journalists and economists.

John Arlott, who began his career as a poetry producer in the Eastern Service, working with some of these literary figures, later became one of the BBC's most celebrated cricket commentators. In May 1946, when the Indian touring team was playing its first match at Worcester, his boss, who knew him to be a cricket lover, asked him to provide a commentary for India. The BBC representative in Delhi sent a telegram: 'Cricket broadcasts greatest success yet East Service stop must be continued at all costs stop'. Arlott was asked to keep up the commentaries throughout the Indian tour. Modestly, he said that he had known nothing about commentating, and that probably all the listeners wanted was the score. But those Indian listeners opened up a new career for him, in which he became an iconic radio voice of the British game.[11]

Zulfiqar Ali Bokhari was also responsible for setting up the BBC Hindustani service, which began broadcasting to India in May 1940. The team that he hastily assembled in London was made up mainly of Indian Muslims, who had either Punjabi or Urdu as their mother tongue, and these were later reinforced with professionals from AIR. Bokhari's aim was to broadcast in simple, intelligible Hindustani and to reach out to as wide an audience as possible, 'from the highest nationalist politician to the lowest peripatetic advertisement salesman'.[12] Radio was growing fast in India but was still a largely urban middle class phenomenon and the Hindustani service, like the English service, beyond the regular news bulletins, concentrated on building a cultural bridge between Britain and India, with a strong emphasis on drama, poetry and literature. Among the early Indian broadcasters was Princess Indira of Kapurthala, who broadcast in both English and Hindustani, on political affairs. Balraj Sahni, who went on to become a famous film actor, spent much of the war, broadcasting from London. Bokhari himself was a regular broadcaster of talks and loved to act in the dramas. Even after Partition, when Bokhari became the first director general of Pakistan Radio, on visits to London he would from time to time participate in plays, including once as Othello to

Atia Habibullah's Desdemona. Atia Habibullah, who later wrote *Sunlight on a Broken Column*, a wonderfully evocative novel about Lucknow in the pre-Partition period, was a regular participant in Eastern Service dramas in the 1950s.

After 1947, the Hindustani service was replaced by two separate services for India and Pakistan in Hindi and Urdu. The commitment to simple language remained but the BBC recognised that it had to respond to the emergence of the newly independent states and their language policies. Links with AIR and Radio Pakistan were cemented by a system of secondments, which brought training opportunities for their staff and provided a trade-off for the national broadcasters, which continued to relay some BBC programmes. The two services were based first at 200 Oxford Street, and from 1957 in Bush House in the Aldwych. They attracted a stream of visitors from the subcontinent and many Indian students eager to earn a few guineas to supplement their grants. In those days, news was the prerogative of the newsroom, which had to be translated accurately by the programme staff. But with only one broadcast a day and generous budgets, many producers, following in the footsteps of Bokhari, relished the opportunity to produce weekly dramas and other specialist programmes. For Yavar Abbas, who began a sixty-year association with the BBC World Service at this time, 'news and news-talks were an appendage to the real business of broadcasting–the reflection of the best of British drama and literature to audiences in the subcontinent'.[13]

All this began to change in the 1960s, a period of dramatic social transformation in Britain, which was gradually reflected in new styles of broadcasting, more space for popular music and culture, less deference to politicians and a wave of satire and plays on social themes, which targeted the class system and traditional values. BBC services for India changed more slowly but by the end of the decade, thanks largely to the spread of the transistor radio, a new era of mass listening in South Asia was in the offing. BBC services to the region benefited from a far-sighted programme of transmitter construction – in Cyprus, Oman and Malaysia – which improved short wave reception and provided medium wave coverage of north western India up to New Delhi in the early morning and late evening. But it was the Indo-Pakistan war of 1965 which provided the spur to the growth of new audiences, putting information at a premium on both sides of the border. The BBC Hindi and Urdu services responded by introducing longer current affairs programmes, a new journalistic thrust which persisted in the aftermath of the twenty-three day war. *Aajkal* and *Sairbeen*, the Hindi and Urdu service, current affairs and analysis programmes, emerged at this time and became a daily date for millions of Indians and Pakistanis in the turbulent political years ahead. The period between the 1965 Indo-Pakistan war and the Gulf war of 1991 was the heyday of these services, with South Asian audiences increasing in response to BBC coverage of a series of cataclysmic events: the Bangladesh war of independence of 1971, the Indian Emergency of 1975–77, the Pakistan National Alliance movement against Zulfiqar Ali Bhutto in 1977, the Punjab crisis and the assassination of Indira Gandhi in 1984, the Kashmir disturbances of the late 1980s and destruction of the Ayodhya Mosque in 1992 by the forces of resurgent Hindu nationalism.

This was a period of heightened Indo-Pakistan tension and war. It was also a time of improved communication, rising public expectations, political populism and growing authoritarianism. By the mid-1980s, according to professional surveys conducted at the time, the BBC Hindi, Urdu and Bengali services had an audience of some fifty million adults in the three countries.[14] It was an extraordinary achievement and one which owed a great deal to some remarkable BBC broadcasters and correspondents, of whom Mark Tully became the most famous, supported by a network of outstanding journalistic contacts across the region. BBC stringers in India, like Yusuf Jameel in Srinagar, Ram Dutt Tripathi in Lucknow, Subhir Bhaumik in Calcutta and Sam Rajappa in Chennai, played their part in developing the BBC's reputation for speed and accuracy, and once the technology improved in the 1990s, many of them also became regular broadcasters for the Hindi and Urdu services. More widely, the voices and personalities of BBC Hindi broadcasters such as Aley Hassan, Purshottam Lal Pahwa, Gauri Shankar Joshi, Ratnakar Bhartiya, Mahendra and Rajni Kaul, Kailash Budhwar and Achala Sharma did much to foster the loyalty of the BBC audience. But the governments of

Rajiv Gandhi in Calcutta on the morning of his mother's assassination, listening to the news on the BBC

Courtesy: Mark Tully
Credit: The Telegraph, Calcutta

India and Pakistan played an equally important role by allowing the BBC to report openly on these extraordinary events while maintaining a strict monopoly of broadcasting themselves.

The Correspondents

Of the BBC staff who represented the BBC in India in the first fifteen years after Independence, Donald Edwards and Gerald Priestland later wrote about their experiences in autobiographies. Donald Edwards arrived in India in 1946, one of the first corps of foreign correspondents sent by the BBC's then director general, Sir William Haley, to key postings after the war. Edwards reported on the tumultuous year that led to Partition and the post-Partition riots and mass displacement that accompanied Independence for India and Pakistan. His account of a meeting with Gandhi is a still-fresh vignette of that remarkable man. Edwards had observed that poverty in India was worse than he had seen anywhere in the world. 'Who do you blame?' Gandhi asked. 'Some blame the British and some blame religion', he replied. 'Both are guilty' Gandhi had said.[15] It was another BBC correspondent, Robert Stimson, standing a few yards from Gandhi when he was shot on 30th January 1948, who broadcast an eyewitness account of the assassination. Stimson's farewell despatch when he left India fourteen months later, drew on his twelve years of working as a journalist in India, first for the *Times of India,* before he was recruited by the BBC in 1947. His verdict as he left was that India was a 'happier place (for a British person) to live in' since Independence, memorable for a thousand things but 'especially the quality of an Indian friendship, which once given is given unconditionally and for life'.

William Ash, BBC representative in Delhi from 1950, and his successor Derek Holroyde described themselves as 'India freaks' and were deemed by British diplomats in Delhi to have crossed the line in 'going native'. Ash wrote a semi-autobiographical novel – *The Lotus and the Sky* – in which he described the uneasy social communication between British expatriates and the professional and bureaucratic elite of Indian's capital. Derek Holroyde and his wife Peggy immersed themselves deeply in Indian culture. Before he went to India, a senior BBC colleague said to him: 'You will find, Holroyde, that the Indians have Third Programme minds' (a reference to the high-brow BBC cultural radio channel that later became Radio 3). On his return to England, he was proud to be told by his BBC boss that it was 'arguable whether he had been a good representative of the BBC in India but it was certain that he had been a good representative of India in the BBC'.[16] Peggy Holroyde wrote a popular and accessible introduction to Indian music – *The Music of India* (1972) – with a foreword by Ravi Shankar, which played a part in educating both the Beatles generation and the new audiences for World Music. The Holroydes later settled in Western Australia where they actively championed the celebration of South and South East Asian cultures.

Gerald Priestland's time as BBC correspondent coincided with Holroyde's as BBC representative. In his book *Something Understood* (1986), a graphic account of his life as a correspondent, he reaches some different conclusions to his predecessor, Donald Edwards. In Priestland's view, 'contrary to the belief of many westerners, India is not a profoundly spiritual country but a profoundly materialistic one'. Several other former correspondents have written engaging books, either about their time in India or about wider social issues in a fast changing country. Mark Tully, after twenty years as the BBC's principal correspondent, established himself as a widely read author and observer of Indian society. His earlier

Mark Tully and Satish Jacob with Swaran the dog during the writing of the book *Amritsar: Mrs Gandhi's Last Battle*
Courtesy: Mark Tully
Credit: Sophie Baker

work with Satish Jacob – *Amritsar, Mrs Gandhi's Last Battle* (1985) – was based on their reporting of the events leading up to 'Operation Bluestar' by the Indian army against Sikh militants in the Golden Temple in Amritsar, and the subsequent assassination of Indira Gandhi. The book was a real contribution to public understanding of the complex politics and history of the time, one of the best examples of collaboration between an Indian and a British journalist in reporting India. More recently, former BBC correspondents have written books on aspects of contemporary India. For example, Daniel Lak has written *India Express* (2008) on India as a 'future superpower' and Sam Miller's *Delhi: Adventures in a Megacity* (2009), reflects on India's massively expanding capital city. This illustrates an obvious truth that being a BBC correspondent in India was never 'just a job' but an experience that often amounted to a long term engagement with India, Indian culture and Indian friends, a critical engagement but a lasting one.

The Louis Malle Affair

With the rapid spread of transistor radios in the 1960s and the emergence for the first time of BBC radio services with a mass audience, it was to be expected that the sensitivities of the Indian government to reporting by the BBC would increase. But the issue that triggered the first serious crisis in BBC relations with the Indian government was the broadcasting of a series of documentary films by the well-known French director, Louis Malle, in 1970. These films had been shown on French television without protest from the Indian government. So the fact that their screening on BBC TV in the UK became a major cause of dispute, leading to the closure of the BBC Delhi office and the expulsion of its correspondent from India, requires some explanation. The dispute and subsequent negotiations have been described in personal accounts by those involved and by reference to the BBC archives and records.[17] More recently, they have been analysed in the broader context of post-colonial sensitivities and cold war politics.[18]

The principal Indian official involved was the spokesman of the Ministry of External Affairs, S.K. Singh, who was responsible for the decision to

expel the BBC correspondent, Ronald Robson. It was believed at the
time that there was a strong personal antipathy between S.K. Singh and
Robson.[19] Singh denied this, saying that he hardly knew Robson, though
he believed that Robson's Indian army background had shaped his
attitudes to India in a negative way. In contrast, the veteran *Times of India*
journalist and long-time highly respected BBC contributor, Subhash
Chakravarti, described Robson 'as a very honest and straightforward
man'.[20] Speaking to the academic, Alasdair Pinkerton, some fourteen
years later, Singh did not deny that he disliked Robson and his style of
journalism. But explaining the Indian government's acquiescence in
the French TV screening of the Malle films and the angry response to
the BBC's showing of the same films, S.K. Singh stressed that Indian
sensitivities over the affair had been enhanced by the frequency of
business, diplomatic and journalistic traffic between India and London
and, it may be added, a vociferous Indian community in the UK. The
French government, by contrast, was 'totally helpless', Singh argued, and
'their organisation (ORTF) was not as tightly knit with the government
setup and the foreign policy establishment as the BBC was'.

As between France and Britain, this was perhaps the opposite of the
truth, but it illustrates a long-standing and still persistent belief in
Indian government circles that the BBC's editorial independence is not as
real as is claimed. The perspective on the affair set out by Pinkerton, as a
younger scholar much influenced by post-colonial theory, reveals a longer
history of Indian government exasperation at what officials had seen as
an unbalanced representation of independent India, often featuring
pictures of snake-charmers and starving children, rarely recognising
the progress that India had made as a modern industrialising state, a
narrative that has now taken over as arguably the dominant, though
equally lop-sided, representation of the country.

The expulsion of the BBC correspondent was more than the outcome
of a conflict of personalities and the pretext was questioned at the time
in the Indian media. A year later, when the Bangladesh war broke out
and millions of refugees flooded over the border into West Bengal, BBC
correspondents were allowed back into India to report on the human

tragedy which was unfolding. The Indian government appears to have recognised that that BBC reporting of the 1971 war with Pakistan, which established Bangladesh as a separate state, had not been unfavourable to India. With this background, negotiations led by Oliver Whitley, managing director of the BBC External Services, and Mark Dodd, head of the Eastern Service, led to the re-opening of the BBC office in 1972 and the return of Mark Tully as the BBC representative 'with a news watching brief', in effect as a correspondent by another name. Over the next twenty-five years in this role, which was new to him when he first took it up, Mark Tully became the voice of the BBC in India.

The BBC and the Emergency

In many ways the crisis that arose in relations between India and the BBC at the time of the Emergency was a direct development of the issues exposed by the Louis Malle affair five years earlier. The same push by the Indian government for state control in the field of information, which had emerged as the subtext in the standoff in 1970, was asserted in 1975 in a more generalised form against the Indian and foreign media as a whole. The key decision for the BBC was whether to accept the comprehensive censorship of news copy required by the Indian government of all media outlets both Indian and foreign. The Indian government was not alone in demanding such enhanced media control, either then or since. This coincided with UNESCO moves in the 1970s to establish a 'new world information order' and to make reporting an issue of national sovereignty. China had been virtually exempt from the expectation of free reporting by the foreign media, and in Indian official eyes, this was a double standard applied by western governments to those governments they thought would comply. The BBC had, after all, accepted military censorship both during the Second World War and at other times, for example in South Africa and Israel. To more farsighted Indian opinion, China was the exception that demonstrated to the world at large, India's greater regard for media freedoms. The decision by Rupert Murdoch twenty years later to bow to Chinese pressure in restricting the access of BBC World TV, which was then on the Murdoch-owned Asiasat platform, provided another telling example of China's continuing indifference to press freedom and the pull of its huge commercial market on a leading western news provider.

In the event, the international news and financial data agency, Reuters, was the only leading foreign news organisation to accept the Indian censorship regulations. Mark Tully, who had been the first to report news of the arrests which heralded the Emergency, was told that he would have to leave and the BBC withdrew him as its correspondent. Prakash Mirchandani, who was Mark Tully's assistant, thought this was the wrong decision. He remained in India and was able to continue building useful contacts, although the BBC Delhi office was closed. Mark Tully believes that the Indian government wanted to impose censorship without anyone being aware of it; that if the BBC had stayed, it would have devoted much energy to circumventing the censorship; and that probably the Indian government would have thrown the BBC out anyway.

Despite the withdrawal of its correspondent, the BBC continued to access and publicise Indian opposition voices which were critical of the Emergency. The BBC Hindi service, live news transmissions on medium and short wave, provided the BBC with some of its biggest mass audiences. The service was also listened to and appreciated by some of the prominent opposition politicians, including the veteran socialist, George Fernandes, and the right-wing free marketer, Subramaniam Swamy, who were jailed during the Emergency. Though the Indian print media were forced to comply, there was vocal opposition from leading press magnates, especially Cushrow Irani, managing director and later in effect, the owner of the Calcutta *Statesman*. The last British editor of the Delhi *Statesman*, Evan Charlton, had joined the BBC staff after he returned to the UK and was managing the Hindi Service. Charlton was very critical of Irani's management of *The Statesman*, though he recognised his courage in standing up to censorship and government controls. Irani was awarded the prestigious Magsaysay Prize for his contribution to press freedom at this time.

In Britain, Indira Gandhi's trusted adviser and leading industrialist, Swraj Paul (now Lord Paul), was active in mediating between the British media and the Indian government. He organised meetings with the minister of information, V.C. Shukla, who was celebrated for his reported statement 'Bring me all rumours and I will deny them'. The BBC director general, Sir Charles Curran, met Shukla at a lunch organised by Swraj Paul. It was not that the BBC was the only organisation being penalised, but as Mark Tully observed, it was 'far and away the most high profile foreign news organisation in India'. Compared to ITN or other news organisations, the BBC had 'a completely different relationship'.[21]

In the end, the BBC's stand against censorship served its reputation well. After Indira Gandhi's election defeat in 1977, the incoming Janata government acknowledged the mistakes of the Emergency. Although Indira Gandhi herself was bitter at the way she felt she had been treated by the press, opposition to press censorship had become more firmly engrained in India's constitutional and governmental priorities. Though there have since been real government concerns about some aspects of Indian TV coverage (especially in Mumbai in 2008), and there have been other ways in which the Indian media have been restricted, no Indian government has advocated statutory censorship seriously in the past twenty-five years. The Emergency proved a test for the shared journalistic values which the Indian print media had upheld strongly, and the BBC emerged on the right side.

The BBC and All India Radio

From the very early days, there was a close relationship between the BBC and AIR, which reflected the shared history, common aspirations and the many friendships among the staff. Iqbal Singh, who joined AIR in 1941, when Fielden was still in Delhi, was involved in producing one of the first BBC-AIR programme collaborations: a discussion programme involving Rajkumari Amrit Kaur, then a member of the Viceroy's council in Delhi, and Lady Violet Bonham Carter in London.[22] Iqbal Singh became friends with early BBC broadcasters such as Wynford Vaughan Thomas and BBC producers such as Reginald Smith and his more famous wife, the novelist Olivia Manning. Like many other AIR broadcasters, he maintained his contacts with the BBC and was a frequent visitor to London until well into the 1980s.

For broadcasters like Iqbal Singh and for many Indians of a liberal persuasion, the BBC model of public service broadcasting, independent of government, underwritten by parliament and financed by a licence fee, became an ideal, which Indian politicians from time to time considered, particularly when in opposition, but never actually implemented when in power. When Indira Gandhi, then India's information minister, appointed the Chanda Committee in 1965 to make recommendations on the structure of Indian broadcasting, Leonard Miall, a senior BBC executive was appointed an adviser, specifically on the expansion of Indian television, and Dr L. M. Singhvi, who was to become High Commissioner in London in the 1990s, was a member. In its enquiries, the committee looked at many broadcasting systems – including the Soviet, Egyptian, American and Italian systems – but according to Singhvi, 'most of all we concentrated on the British system', and the report contains 'a very clear declaration of respect and affection for the British model'. In a visit to London, the committee met Lord Reith who spoke 'with great authority and clarity,' emphasising the value of independence over mere functional autonomy. Singhvi, as a much younger man, was impressed by this 'man of heroic proportions to my eyes at the time'.[23]

Indira Gandhi did not follow the recommendations of the Chanda Committee and Indian broadcasting remained firmly in the hands of government. After the Emergency, the Janata government, many of whose members had been jailed during the previous three years, appointed the Verghese Committee to decide on the details of an autonomy bill. But once the Janata Party had lost the 1980 election and Indira Gandhi was returned to power, the idea was shelved again. Indian broadcasting remained a department of government, subject to complex bureaucratic protocols and scrutiny and a poor match for nimbler news agencies.[24] In 1984, when Indira Gandhi was assassinated by her own bodyguards, an event of enormous magnitude for the Indian people, the BBC was able to broadcast the news several hours ahead of AIR, which had to seek official confirmation before being able to do so. A photograph of Rajiv Gandhi on his way back to Delhi, listening to the BBC on a transistor radio for the latest developments, told its own graphic story at that time.

The Role of the Indian High Commission

The Indian High Commission in the Aldwych, just a stone's throw from Bush House itself, played a pivotal role in monitoring British media coverage of India and vetting applications for filming in India. In the 1980s, Surendra Kumar, then the Indian press counsellor, was a channel for complaints about a number of BBC television programmes. *The Turban and the Sword,* a documentary which carried interviews with some hardline Sikh militants, triggered furious protests from the Indian government – which since the storming of the Golden Temple and the subsequent assassination of Indira Gandhi – had been highly sensitive to extremist Sikh activity and to diaspora Sikh opinion both in India and the UK. Surendra Kumar later voiced the anger felt in Indian political circles at a BBC Panorama programme *Rajiv Gandhi – India's Pilot Prime Minister.* But if offence was taken by the occasional programme, Surendra Kumar asked rhetorically: 'Who but the BBC would have decided to telecast fifty-two episodes of Indian television's *Mahabharata*.'[25] To which one might add: how was it that the quintessentially British comedy *Yes Minister,* satirising British bureaucracy, went down so well in India and even numbered Indira Gandhi among its fans?

Adam Clapham, a BBC television producer, who began making documentaries in India in the 1970s, remembers 'the distrust of foreign broadcasters' and 'draconian restrictions' in force at that time.[26] All foreign film crews were required to obtain permission to film in India from the Ministry of External Affairs, to provide detailed treatment of locations and interviews, and to be accompanied by a government representative. Adam was once reported to Delhi for recording '*Baa Baa Black Sheep*' at a music school in Chennai on the grounds that it was a racist song! All films also had to be shown before broadcast to the Indian High Commission, which reserved the right to require anything objectionable to be removed. Under the terms of its charter, the BBC could not cede control of a programme to a foreign government, but it did agree, by way of a compromise, 'to entertain their comments on the film's factual accuracy'. The trick, as Adam recalls, was not to place Indian diplomats in a position where they felt they had to object, as both sides knew that would have produced a new crisis in BBC-India relations.[27]

The Indian government still imposes strict conditions on foreign film crews, but the sensitivity to BBC coverage of India is much reduced, and the Indian community in Britain, which now has access to many Indian TV channels via satellite, is less focussed on what the BBC is saying. According to Ashis Ray, a former president of the Indian Journalists Association in the UK, when BBC reporting on Indian affairs clashes with Indian perceptions, there is still sometimes a sense of betrayal, which prompts strong criticism and even anger, but it 'does not occur so much or on the same scale today'. Indian diplomats in the UK still harbour sensitivities about the activities of Sikh separatists and the expression of opinion hostile to India among the Sikh diaspora. But in recent years, specific issues have been dealt with quietly by behind the scenes negotiation rather than through a press campaign.[28]

The Satellite Revolution and its Impact

If the transistor revolution of the 1960s provided the BBC with a new mass audience, the satellite TV revolution of the 1990s ushered in an extraordinary transformation of the South Asian electronic media which gradually undermined the BBC's dominance of the airwaves. The Indian state monopoly of broadcasting, which had been maintained since the 1930s, gave way with remarkable speed to a new multi-channel television universe, in which news, sports and entertainment are provided twenty-four hours a day in most of the country's main languages. The urban Indian viewer now has access to a multitude of channels and the TV advertising market has grown phenomenally in the past twenty years, becoming a major motor of Indian economic growth. The importance of mobile phones in the dissemination of news and information has also grown massively. The number of mobile phones in India now exceeds that of landlines, radio and television and internet access combined.

Despite the fact that technological developments are opening up more and more space for cultural autonomy and personal choice, the government of India has attempted to maintain a centralised approach to media management and control. It permitted, or failed to act to prevent, the transformation of the TV landscape but it has not relaxed its control of Doordarshan, though the state TV channel has lost much of its urban audience and is losing rural audiences as well. Advocates of a BBC model for state broadcasters in South Asia still argue that real autonomy would enable these highly bureaucratic organisations to transform themselves into more competitive and more effective public broadcasters. But the argument falls increasingly on deaf ears. Governments can now argue with some justification that in a multi-channel universe, the state has a right to its own voice, even if it is being drowned out by others.

Government attitudes to the expansion of radio have also been restrictive for security and other reasons. Many commercial FM stations have been licensed but they are mainly for entertainment. Restrictions remain on news and current affairs programmes – an amazing contrast to the toleration of twenty-four hour TV news. For similar reasons, community radio struggled for years to achieve recognition, which has only come in grudging instalments. Despite the considerable advantages of radio in terms of speed, versatility and economy, the Indian government has not licensed any national commercial radio station and has been unwilling to allow much experimentation in this field.

For all these reasons, the new Indian media universe has proved a challenging one for the BBC, which now has to communicate with Indian audiences using many platforms. As more Indians have transferred their allegiances to satellite TV, which provides wall to wall coverage of any major national story, BBC radio services have found their audiences dropping, despite a growing investment in local news coverage. BBC World Service Television, now known as BBC World, which was started in 1991 without the benefit of government funding, attracts a significant educated audience of some 2.5 million regular viewers for its international news coverage in English. It also produces some special programmes for India, such as Question Time India, which has introduced a winning British programme format to Indian audiences and enriched the media's role in the process of political accountability. Efforts to launch a Hindi TV service have been less successful. In 1996, the BBC Hindi service entered into a partnership with Home TV and an Indian news agency, Asian News

International, to provide an hour of TV news and current affairs every evening. But Home TV and the partnership foundered within a year. In 2012, the Hindi service returned to the Indian TV market with a half-hour weekly programme entitled 'Global India', featuring international stories of Indian interest, which is broadcast on ETV's regional channels. But the impact so far is limited.

In the radio field, the BBC Hindi Service moved almost all its staff from London to Delhi in 2009, with a view to competing more effectively and more economically with Indian news outlets. But it has proved difficult to reverse the gradual decline in short wave audiences. Efforts to develop partnerships with India's many FM stations have been more successful. The BBC is now available on FM in over fifty Indian cities through partnerships with a number of commercial radio consortia, though there has been some loss of identity in the process and the ban on news has limited cooperation to more general features.

In 2011, faced with deep cuts in World Service funding, the BBC management decided to end Hindi short wave broadcasts, which then had an estimated regular audience of over nine million listeners. This provoked strong protests both in Britain and in India. The UK Parliamentary Foreign Affairs Select Committee lent its weight to the protests [29], the government relented, at least to some extent, and the broadcasts were reprieved but at a reduced level for one more year. The latest audience research gives a figure of 3.7 million regular listeners for the service. But staff numbers have already been cut back and many see the writing on the wall.

BBC Hindi Online, which was started in 2001, is now a higher priority. It plays to the growing internet market and it serves the Indian diaspora as well. But the Indian online market has its own compulsions, which have brought different editorial approaches to news and a different style of language. The BBC, like many online platforms, encourages interactivity and provides a space for citizen journalism but its contribution to verifiable news content is in practice limited. Frequently the more sensational or trivial human interest stories involving film stars and other celebrities, or even purely bizarre stories, are avidly read online, while significant news stories or current affairs assessments are ignored. To some extent, this has influenced editorial judgments towards a more marketable tabloid style. The service currently attracts 350,000 unique weekly users.

Some argue that in its efforts to compete on different platforms, the BBC is losing its unique selling point: fast and accurate news, authoritative comment and distinctive programmes. Such concerns increased in 2013 when the BBC decided to dismantle its last remaining regional news bureaux, making several experienced staff reporters redundant, and to concentrate on reporting India from Delhi. There are also concerns that by concentrating on new media, the BBC is serving the urban middle class at the expense of the rural areas, where sizeable short wave audiences still exist and the need is arguably greater. Everyone agrees that change is necessary. As one audience research specialist put it: 'You can't trade on legacy. They won't go out of their way to find you because they respect you. You have to be where they are.'[30] The question is whether the right choices are being made.

Until the mid-1990s, the BBC was monitored closely in India, in tacit acceptance of its influence as an international broadcaster, and of the role of its Indian language services as virtually an Indian domestic broadcaster. The reporting of the BBC Urdu service on Kashmir was particularly carefully tracked. But with the growing dominance of the local TV channels over the past fifteen years, there have been fewer contentious issues over BBC reporting. The BBC has a good reputation and there is still a generally positive attitude and broad goodwill towards it. Listeners tend to return to the BBC during a crisis. But it does not have the impact that it once had. The cycle of love and hate that used to characterise BBC-India relations has been broken.

That may be a source of regret to some but in the broader context of BBC-India relations, it is to be welcomed as a sign of a new equality. The heyday of the BBC Indian language services was a time of severe media restrictions in India. Their relative decline reflects a new vibrancy in the Indian media scene. In the new globalised media world, audiences in the UK are watching Indian TV programmes, while Indians with an interest in

Britain, can access BBC online, one of the world's most popular websites. The BBC is unlikely to attract such massive Indian audiences again, but as one of the world's most influential public service broadcasters, it still has much to offer if the right kind of partnerships can be developed. In this new media world, the pursuit of excellence will probably be more important than the pursuit of audiences, in a spirit of collaboration, not competition, and in the best traditions of the BBC's long-standing commitment to India and its people.

Notes

1. See http://www.bbc.co.uk/mediacentre/speeches/2010/horrocks_peter_cba.html

2. See http://www.bbc.co.uk/mediaaction/

3. Interview, Nikki Clarke, Head of BBC Journalism for South Asia, 3 December 2012.

4. See http://www.bbc.co.uk/pressoffice/pressreleases/stories/2011/01_january/26/worldservice.shtml

5. See http://downloads.bbc.co.uk/annualreport/pdf/bbc_ar_online_2011_12.pdf

6. Quoted in H.R.Luthra, *Indian Broadcasting* (1986), p. 3.

7. In an article on Transmitters and Culture: the colonial roots of Indian Broadcasting, David Lelyveld explores the implications for broadcasting in independent India of the centralising trends established at this time. See South Asia Research, vol. 10, no. 1, May 1990.

8. Fielden's autobiography, *The Natural Bent* (1960), provides a first-hand account of his Indian experiences.

9. For a brief history of the BBC's role in the early days of Indian broadcasting, see David Page and William Crawley, *Satellites over South Asia: Broadcasting, culture and the public interest* (2001), chapter 2.

10. Syed Rashid Ahmed, first Manager of the Lahore Radio Station, interviewed, Karachi, March 1998, quoted in Page and Crawley (2001), p. 41.

11. *A Broadcasting Partnership – India and the BBC 1932-1994*, Indo-British Review, vol xx, no. 2 (1995), pp. 111–112. This special edition of the Indo-British Review, edited by William Crawley, examined the BBC's relations with India and included many interviews and reminiscences of historical interest.

12. Indo-British Review (1995), p. 108, reproduced from *The World In your Language* (1990), a BBC publication to make the fiftieth anniversary of the Hindi Service.

13. Yavar Abbas, Interview, 9 September 2009.

14. This account of the early history of BBC services to India draws on contributions to *The World in Your language* (1990, and an article on Language, Nationhood and Diaspora at the BBC Urdu Service (1940-2010) by David Page, published in *Diasporas and Diplomacy, Cosmopolitan Contact Zones at the BBC World Service 1932-2012*, edited by Marie Gillespie and Alban Webb (2012).

15. *The Two Worlds of Donald Edwards* (1970), cited in Indo-British Review (1995), p. 115.

16. William Crawley, The BBC in India Indo-British Review, vol xiv, no. 1 (1988), pp. 41–51.

17. See, for example, Indo-British Review (1995), pp 30–40 (Prakash Mirchandani); pp. 41–47 (Subhash Chakravarti); pp. 56–57 (Mark Tully); pp. 80–81 (S.K. Singh); pp. 151–61 (Leonard Miall).

18. See Alasdair Pinkerton: A new kind of imperialism? The BBC, cold war broadcasting and the contested geopolitics of South Asia, Historical Journal of Film, Radio and Television, Volume 28, Issue 4, October 2008, pp. 537–555.

19. Indo-British Review (1995), pp. 80–81.

20. Indo-British Review (1995), p. 41.

21. Indo-British Review (1995), p. 60.

22. Indo-British Review (1995), p. 88.

23. Dr L.M. Singhvi, former Indian High Commissioner in London, quote in the Indo-British Review (1995), pp. 162–168.

24. See Page and Crawley, *Satellites over South Asia* (2001), p. 63.

25. Interview with Surendra Kumar, Indo-British Review (1995), pp. 71–76.

26. Adam Clapham has written amusingly about his experiences as a TV producer in India in *Beware of Falling Coconuts* (2006), chapter 4.

27. Interview, Adam Clapham, 3 December 2012.

28. Interview, Ashis Ray, 8 December 2012.

29. http://www.parliament.uk/business/committees/committees-a-z/commons-select/foreign-affairs-committee/news/implications-of-cuts-to-the-bbc-world-service

30. Interview, Colin Wilding, 5 December 2012.

15

Engaging India: Reconnecting through Trade and Investment

Jo Johnson

*I*n late July 2010, within three months of taking office, all the pivotal figures in the newly-formed coalition government were to be found several thousand miles away, scattered across the Indian subcontinent.

To an upmarket audience of business leaders assembled at the Taj Mahal Hotel in Mumbai, George Osborne, the newly-minted Chancellor of the Exchequer, was to be found underlining the personal investment the key figures in the British Government were making in the UK-India relationship.

He explained how, in opposition in 2006, he and David Cameron – the Conservative leader – had made India their first major foreign port of call; and how, in the wake of a General Election that had left the Conservatives in alliance with the Liberal Democrats, they were now both back.

Planning for a follow-up visit – involving what the Chancellor described as 'the strongest and most high-profile British delegation to visit India in modern times' – had started practically the day the new team took office.

'While it took one of my predecessors as Chancellor ten years to visit India, I have made it a priority to come here in my first ten weeks', Osborne told his audience at the Taj that afternoon, underlining the new urgency attached to developing closer relations with the big powers of the future.

Other big beasts of the coalition – the Business Secretary, Vince Cable; the Foreign Secretary, William Hague; the Minister for the Environment and Climate Change, Greg Barker; and the Culture Secretary, Jeremy Hunt – scattered themselves across the Indian subcontinent.

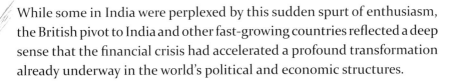 While some in India were perplexed by this sudden spurt of enthusiasm, the British pivot to India and other fast-growing countries reflected a deep sense that the financial crisis had accelerated a profound transformation already underway in the world's political and economic structures.

Although more government ministers have visited India since May 2010 than any other country (excluding Belgium), the intense engagement with New Delhi is merely emblematic of a broader ambition to develop stronger relations with countries fast emerging as regional and global players.

As one of the Atlantic powers that had seen its influence dwindle, Britain either adapted to the new world order or would see its relevance decline, with consequences for its role in international affairs, for national security and for the British economy.

This paper will focus on the trade and investment relationship with India, in the context of the UK's need for export and business investment-led growth and the on-going negotiations for an EU-India Free Trade Agreement. It will not dwell on the broader political, military and diplomatic relationship.

The first section, 'Achieving Growth', discusses how the UK needs to orient itself in the global economy, dealing with slow or potentially negative growth in the Eurozone, and examining the success of other EU members, such as Germany, in repositioning themselves towards high growth markets.

The second section, 'India as a case study of UK engagement with the BRICS', looks at the way UK policy has developed in relation to India and compares it with the approaches of other EU members such as France and Germany.

The third section, 'Getting the EU-India Free Trade Agreement right', discusses the need for an ambitious deal that goes beyond goods to include real liberalisation of services, arguing that this offers the best chance the UK will have for some time to make progress towards longstanding goals of British commercial diplomacy.

The fourth section, 'Problem areas in the EU-India FTA negotiations', is an overview of some of the issues where negotiators are likely to focus their attention over the coming months, such as Mode 4 and the liberalisation of services.

The fifth section sets out 'Six ways to expand UK-India trade and investment'. It offers suggestions for ways in which the UK can strengthen an already strong relationship by focusing on a few core areas where it needs revitalising.

Achieving Growth

Coming into office in 2010, David Cameron noted in his first speech on the economy as Prime Minister that Britain had long suffered from twin deficits: a structural budget deficit and a longstanding trade deficit.

On the first of these, progress has been rapid and effective and is underpinning the UK's ability to borrow ten-year money in the capital markets at well under 2 per cent. The UK's budget deficit has been reduced by one third in three years of this government.

The current structural budget deficit is forecast by the independent Office for Budget Responsibility to fall to 2.9 per cent by March 2015.[1]

The backdrop to the second of these goals, reversing the trade deficit, is even more challenging. A trade deficit is a symptom of a lack of international competitiveness and the UK has run one every year since 1984, and in all but six years since 1900.

A surplus in its trade in services (seen in every year since 1966) has traditionally failed to compensate for a deficit shown in the UK's trade in goods. The last time the UK registered a fleeting surplus on its trade in goods was in 1982, but only thanks to North Sea oil. In 2010, the current account deficit was £48.6 billion, equivalent to –3.3 per cent of GDP, not far off the 1989 record of –4.9 per cent. In 2011, it shrank a little, to £29 billion, or 1.9 per cent of GDP.

The UK has steadily lost share in global exports over the past sixty years. This is partly due to the emergence of competitive low-cost exporters from the developing world, epitomised by China, which has been pursuing an aggressively mercantilist approach and keeping its exchange rate down through huge foreign currency intervention. But it is also due to ferocious competition from developed, world structural surplus countries, such as Germany and Japan.

While developed economies' share of global goods exports has fallen from about 75 per cent in 1950 to just under 60 per cent, the decline in the UK's share has been sharper, from 10 per cent to under 3 per cent.[2] The same trend is manifesting itself in the post-recession recovery. The fall in the external value of sterling has had less of a positive impact on exports than anticipated.

In a two-speed world, there is nothing to dictate that Britain must stay in the slow lane of economic recovery, but it must recognise that it is facing the wrong way and must better position itself to take full advantage of the booming emerging markets that will account for the bulk of global growth over the next few years. (The IMF forecast in October 2010 that the world economy would expand by $20,000 billion during the following five years, with advanced economies contributing around $8,500 billion and faster-growing emerging and developing economies adding $11,500 billion.[3])

The Prime Minister has repeatedly urged British business to take advantage of growth in the world economy that was 'not in the Eurozone, but in huge modern cities from Bogotá to Istanbul', where 'people [were] hungry for the skills and services Britain is best at'.[4]

Other senior ministers have also repeatedly urged businesses to lift their horizons. George Osborne, has said that 'an enterprising Britain is one that sees a world with a resurgent China, a booming India, a thriving Brazil and understands that it is an opportunity not a threat'.[5]

Although by instinct suspicious of the Heseltinian tradition of herding businessmen onto aeroplanes bound for faraway countries, Messrs. Cameron and Osborne have consistently led from the front what has been a concerted cross-government effort to boost Britain's commercial diplomacy. The creation of a new UK Trade and Investment (UKTI) cabinet sub-committee, chaired by Lord Green, previously Group Chairman of HSBC, was an early and welcome indication of resolve in this respect.

The urgency of this reorientation has if anything increased over the last two years. With the Eurozone economy yet to emerge convincingly from recession, UK exporters are likely to struggle in a market that accounts for 45 per cent of all external trade. Overall UK export performance is still to a great extent determined by demand in the Eurozone (and in other OECD markets accounting for a further quarter of the UK's trade).

No one is suggesting UK businesses should seek to export less to the rich European countries that form the world's most important trading area, with a GDP of about €12, 000bn and a population of 500 million. Indeed, the UK has to continue pushing for the completion for the single market. Eliminating significant, non-tariff trade barriers could increase our trade with other EU members by up to 45 per cent, according to the Department for Business, Innovation and Skills, and boost per capita incomes by 7 per cent.[6]

The UK and Europe have to work on boosting internal and external trade in tandem. In order to re-invigorate domestic European demand, countries such as Spain and Italy will have to continue in their efforts to reform their public and private sectors, and EU members will have to genuinely commit to liberalising the single market. At the same time, in order to take full advantage of growth in developing countries, the EU has to push for the Free Trade Agreement (FTA) with countries outside the EU that will help unlock their markets to European firms.

Ultimately, while it is demand in emerging countries that has the greatest potential to drive forward UK, European and global growth, re-orienting existing UK trade towards higher growth markets will take longer than a political cycle. Our trading relationships have been shaped by distance, market size and cultural, linguistic and historical ties and the EU will continue to be the UK's biggest market (albeit a slow-growth one) for at least a decade.

Over the last decade, the rate of growth of exports to EU countries has been roughly half than that to non-EU countries over the last decade. A breakdown of goods exports by destination shows that the fastest growth has been to Australasia and parts of South East Asia, such as South Korea and Indonesia. Even though annual growth in exports to some countries has at times exceeded 100 per cent, the fact that the export share was initially so low means that many countries remain relatively trivial trade partners in absolute terms.

These new emerging markets are therefore unlikely to be any quick fix for growth within the term of this parliament because the base of our economic engagement is still too small to make any noticeable difference to the overall picture. There are some striking figures that illustrate this point. India's share of UK exports, for example, remains well under 2 per cent, notwithstanding volume growth of around 40 per cent in 2011. In total, the four BRICs (Brazil, Russia, India, China) accounted for current account credits worth £31.3 billion in 2010 or 5.1 per cent of the £615 billion total.

China accounted for about 1.9 per cent of total UK current account credits in 2010, India and Russia for between 1.2–1.3 per cent each, and Brazil for 0.75 per cent. Exports to Ireland of £20 billion in 2010 exceeded the combined value of exports to India and China (£19.4 billion). That is an improvement on the previous year, when the UK notched up more credits on the current account with Ireland (£28.7 billion) than it did with the four BRICs, Indonesia and Mexico combined.

It is noteworthy that other developed countries have re-oriented their export profiles more effectively than Britain has done. The proportion of Germany's goods exports going to the BRIC countries, which are showing strong demand for its capital goods at this stage in their development, is more than twice ours, having more than doubled from 4.5 per cent in 2000 to 10.6 per cent in 2009.

Furthermore, it is worth noting that the UK ran a big current account deficit with the BRICs of about £21 billion in 2010 (up from £17 billion in 2009), which represents an increasing drag on UK growth. This is principally because of the UK's current account deficit with China, which, at £20.9 billion (up from £17 billion in 2009), is the largest of any individual country. The UK ran a small current account deficit of £1.3 billion with India (down from £1.5 billion in 2009), and modest surpluses with Brazil and Russia.

It is of course essential that the UK becomes more engaged with these markets, as they will be the principal sources of global growth over the next five years, with China and India likely, notwithstanding slowing growth rates, to develop into economies that eventually are the size of those of the US and EU today. But it will also be important to change the terms of trade, so that the UK ceases to run substantial current account deficits with China and India.

This will not be easy. Penetrating difficult and distant markets will be a marathon, not a sprint. But the government can have an important part to play in encouraging new firms to export, in facilitating the re-orientation of existing exporters towards emerging markets, and in breaking down non-tariff barriers and other regulatory hurdles to trade. There is much to be done, but the work undertaken in the first three years of the coalition government has been impressive.

The organisational overhaul of UKTI, the restructuring of the Export Credit Guarantee Department and the Foreign and Commonwealth Office's decision to create thirty new posts in India and fifty new positions in China, roughly a 7 per cent increase in each mission's manpower, at a time of severe budgetary restraint, all underline the seriousness of the coalition's intent to boost its commercial diplomacy in BRIC countries.

India as a Case Study of UK Engagement with the BRICs

India and the UK are re-connecting at an unprecedented rate, forging a partnership of equals that is no longer overshadowed by their colonial history. The coalition has stated its determination to forge a 'new special relationship', an ambition that is finding an echo in India as it prepares to play a bigger role on the global stage.

With respect to India, the urgency underlying the new approach is more than justified. The UK has been rapidly slipping down the rankings of India's trading partners over the last decade. In 1999, Britain was India's fourth most important source of imports, according to official figures collected by India's commerce ministry. By 2011, it was its twenty-first.[7]

Many of the countries that have overtaken the UK in the rankings of India's trade partners are energy-rich ones, in a position to supply India with oil and coal. But that is not the whole picture. Germany has made phenomenal progress in penetrating the Indian market and is now easily the largest goods exporter to India among the EU27. It is meeting a massive demand for the capital goods needed to plug India's various infrastructural deficits. It is not alone in outstripping the UK: even Belgium exported more goods to India than Britain in 2011.

That is not to say the absolute growth in UK-India trade is unimpressive: UK goods exports jumped 40 per cent and services exports by 23 per cent in 2011, taking the total value of UK exports in goods and services to £8.06 billion, up from £6.25 billion in 2010.

At this rate of growth, Britain is on track to meet its target of doubling 2010 levels of trade with India by 2015, a significant achievement. But there is no doubt that other countries are out-trading the UK and that we are losing market share in many sectors.

While the volume growth has improved, the quality of UK exports to India remains questionable. Non-ferrous metals, non-metallic mineral manufactures, metalliferous ores and metal scrap, seem to account for a considerable proportion of the export basket. Such commodities are hardly high value-added or particularly reflective of the areas in which the UK economy is potentially competitive. This is an area of concern.

Part of the explanation for this relative under-performance vis-à-vis Germany and others is that the Indian market has been relatively closed in the areas where the UK economy is competitive and open in others where Britain is weaker. Although there are encouraging signs that this might change, following a long-awaited announcement of liberalising measures made in September 2012, Britain's services exporters have historically encountered major obstacles to effective market entry in India.[8]

India's near $500bn retail sector, for example, has been completely closed to investment by foreign supermarket groups, even though allowing in the likes of Tesco and Sainsbury's (not to mention Wal-Mart and Carrefour) would simultaneously raise farmer incomes and lower food prices for consumers. Food price inflation has been running at high levels for many years to the extent that a kilo of onions in Tesco is now cheaper than a kilo of onions in Bombay.[9]

Financial services liberalisation has also proceeded at a glacial pace. Foreign banks continue to find it difficult to open up branches across India and their cause has not been aided by the financial crisis, which left India largely unscathed and reinforced what was already a very conservative mindset at the Reserve Bank of India.

The UK's hopes of achieving its market access goals in financial services have also suffered with respect to the insurance sector, where Foreign Direct Investment (FDI) in the insurance sector remains capped at 26 per cent. Even though the Indian Government first promised, nearly a decade ago, to lift this ownership restriction, the legislative logjam in the Indian parliament, paralysed by a spate of corruption scandals, has been a longstanding obstacle to reform.

The Indian economy is much more open in sectors where the UK's competitive advantage is less obvious, notably in infrastructure, capital goods, project engineering and manufactured products. This pattern has played particularly favourably to the strengths of countries such as Germany that have larger and more competitive manufacturing sectors. Machinery and vehicles and other manufactured goods account for almost 80 per cent of EU27 exports to India.

That said, the UK has also let some opportunities to increase its market share of Indian merchandise goods imports slip. Potentially game changing deals have been lost, with the Eurofighter consortium's failure to secure the Indian Ministry of Defence order for one hundred and twenty-six multi-role combat aircraft, the most noteworthy recent example. Valued at over $10 billion, this would at a stroke have embedded British firms in key supply chains in India.

Getting the EU-India Free Trade Agreement Right

The Eurofighter example shows the tension between the EU as a union of competitors on the one hand and as a union of countries with a common interest in gaining more favourable market access to rapidly developing markets on the other. It is in the latter capacity that the EU launched FTA negotiations with India in June 2007.

After eleven full rounds, they are now in a phase where negotiators meet in smaller, more targeted clusters, rather than full rounds. This entails expert level intercessionals, chief negotiator meetings and exchanges at Director General level. Following the EU-India Summit on 10th February in Delhi, negotiations are at an intense phase but there is a limited political window of opportunity and a formidable amount of work still to be done on important issues, particularly with respect to the overall ambition of the services package.

If an agreement can be reached, the prize is great. An extended FTA, according to an analysis conducted for the European Commission in May 2009, could see India gain €4.9 billion in the short run and €17.7 billion in the long run, and the EU gains €4.4 billion in the short run and €1.6 billion in the long run. It would, therefore, bolster further what is an already strong EU-India trade relationship.[10]

The EU is already India's largest trading partner accounting for just over €100 billion in trade in goods and services in 2011, up sharply from approximately €86 billion in 2010. The EU accounted for 19 per cent of India's total exports and 14 per cent of India's total imports in 2010. Although the EU is still a more important trading partner for India than India is for the EU, this dynamic is changing.

India ranked eighth in the list of the EU's main trading partners in 2010, up from fifteenth in 2002. India accounts for 2.6 per cent of EU's total exports and 2.2 per cent of the EU's total imports. There is still much potential for trade growth on both sides, and the completion of an ambitious FTA–unlike the modest FTA that Japan concluded with India in February 2011–would be a significant enabling factor.

Estimates vary as to the value potentially to be created from such an FTA. Britain alone believes the UK could see a trade boost of upwards of £300m a year, and potentially more, depending on how ambitious the deal is and on the time-frame adopted for the phasing in of the most important liberalising measures. But the overall picture is that an FTA would help underpin the EU's position as the number one supplier of goods and services to India at a time when its grip on that position is under considerable competitive pressure from countries such as China, South Korea and the UAE.

The FTA is a way to give the EU an advantage against the competition by providing its businesses with access to the Indian market on a preferential basis (as WTO rules provide for a carve-out from requirements to multilateralise for bilateral FTAs that cover substantially all trade).

The EU-India Summit reaffirmed both sides' commitment to the early conclusion of an 'ambitious and balanced package'. From the UK perspective, negotiations for an FTA are an ideal opportunity for Britain to improve the terms of its trade relations with the subcontinent. The UK remains committed to the multilateral trading system, but in the absence of progress on Doha, it is also supportive of broad and ambitious FTAs that open markets and boost trade and jobs.

Concluding the EU-India FTA is a priority for Britain, but certainly not at any price. While it is helpful to aim to have a final text ready for ratification (a process which will itself take at least a further fifteen to eighteen months) by the end of 2012, it is essential that the opportunity for an ambitious agreement, covering not just goods, but also services and investment, is not wasted.

The leverage that the negotiation of an FTA provides, offers the best chance that the UK will have for some time to make progress towards longstanding goals of British commercial diplomacy.

On the goods side of the negotiation, most of the pieces are now in place, even if the EU still expects India to show some movement on cars and wines and spirits, which attract import duties of 150 per cent, in return for concessions on the export of garments and textiles from India to the EU.

On the services side, however, there is little to show for six years of talks. The EU only received an Indian offer of any sort in March 2012. This exchange of offers on services was of course a welcome development, as it was a sign of progress and gave member states a chance to comment for the first time. As much of the services offer fell short of UK expectations, however, it in fact raised many more questions than it answered.

The unsatisfactory nature of the negotiation should not have been surprising, given India's general defensive posture in the WTO and track-record of crafting 'trade light' FTAs, pursued more for foreign-policy than commercial reasons. Indeed, India is reckoned to have the worst-quality FTAs among major Asian FTA players.[11]

It is unlikely that the negotiation will succeed in meeting the timetable envisaged as, in a number of important specific respects, the UK, and it is far from alone in this respect, clearly needs India to move much further than may be politically deliverable in New Delhi. Although the recent announcement of unilateral liberalisation in the retail, aviation and insurance sectors is encouraging, significant obstacles remain.

There is still a significant risk that the EU-India FTA will be taken hostage by domestic Indian coalition politics and that, like the Doha Round of multilateral trade talks, it will die a lingering death.

The announcement of a new wave of reforms made in September 2012 is a recognition that India was failing to put in place the conditions to allow the economy to regain and sustain the near double digit growth rates of the 2005–2008 period. It also reflected concern that India could lose the confidence of international investors, demonstrated by Standard & Poor's decision in April 2012 to announce a 'negative outlook' on the country's BBB-investment rating and criticism that the global economic crisis has thus far 'induced marginal protectionist backsliding rather than further liberalisation'.[12]

The proposed reforms represent the UPA government's perhaps last attempt to salvage its reputation as a steward of the 'India story' and to make the most of the very limited political space it had available to it, following disappointing setbacks in battleground state elections in Uttar Pradesh in March 2012 and ahead of national elections in 2014.

P. Chidambaram's return to the finance ministry in 2012 has been well received by international investors and by members of the Indian strategic community, to some extent allaying concerns that India risked falling into a 'middle income trap', like a number of former emerging market darlings which failed to sustain turbo-charged growth-rates for more than a few years.[13]

Crucial Issues in the EU-India FTA Negotiations

There are seven areas in the EU-India FTA negotiation which will decide its future. These are set out as under.

Mode 4

London is reluctant to make further concessions in relation to India's most important request in the services negotiation, which relates to the 'temporary movement' of services professionals under the so-called Mode 4 provisions of the General Agreement on Trade in Services. This covers the movement of natural persons. The size of the UK's services sector means that London's stance in relation to Mode 4 is of critical importance and will be a key factor in whether an ambitious trade deal can be concluded this year.

Given the need to balance Mode 4 offers with the annual limit on non-EU immigration sought by the coalition government, however, the UK is expected to be unlikely to offer a more generous settlement in any bilateral trade negotiation than it has already made as part of the Doha negotiations. It will not be possible for the UK to make commitments in the FTA which are incompatible with the government's efforts to reform the immigration system. The first major change to reduce immigration into the UK took effect in April 2012, when the UK government's new annual immigration limit came into force.

This, along with radical changes introduced to the student route and plans to tackle permanent settlement, is intended to cause net migration to fall back down to the tens of thousands. Under the annual limit, employers will be able to bring only twenty thousand seven hundred people from outside the EU to work in skilled professions under Tier 2 (General) of the points-based system. A further one thousand visas will be made available to people of 'exceptional talent', to ensure that Britain remains open to the brightest and the best. Those earning a salary of £150,000 or more will not be subject to the limit.

The Intra Company Transfer route (ICT), which is not part of the annual limit and is of particular importance to Indian information technology service providers, will also be changed in three ways:

- the job will have to be in an occupation on the graduate occupation list;

- only those earning £40,000 or more will be able to stay for more than a year; they will be given permission to stay for three years, with the possibility of extending for a further two years, and

- those earning between £24,000 and £40,000 will be allowed to come to the UK for no longer than twelve months, at which point they must leave the UK and will not be able to re-apply for twelve months.

Banking

Little progress has been made on the Reserve Bank of India's roadmap for liberalisation since the onset of the financial crisis. This undoubtedly made financial sector reforms less easy to achieve politically, strengthened the hand of conservatives within the Indian regulatory establishment and provided a pretext for a continuation of a variety of protectionist practices.

There is, in particular, an urgent need for clarity over the RBI's subsidiarisation plans for foreign banks. UK banks such as Standard Chartered, HSBC, Barclays and RBS need to have it confirmed that foreign banks converting to subsidiaries will receive 'national treatment', just as Indian banks such as ICICI do in the UK, which is now home to nearly thirty Indian financial services firms.

Branch licensing restrictions prevent UK and other foreign banks from expanding in wealthier areas unless they meet quotas for lending to priority sectors and open branches in rural areas. The UK is pushing for these lending restrictions to be eased as and when banks convert to subsidiaries (at present they operate as branches of their UK operations).

The UK accounts for half of all foreign bank branches in India, but that is in large part because British banks have been in the country longer than many others and have in some cases stuck with a difficult market through thick and thin. For example, the Chartered Bank, a forerunner of what would become Standard Chartered, opened its first overseas branch in Kolkata in 1858.

A financial sector which is dominated by state-owned banks and Indian private sector banks – foreign banks account for about 2 per cent of the Indian market – is struggling to provide the capital required to meet India's massive infrastructure requirements. Poor physical infrastructure – particularly in roads, ports, and power – is one of the principal bottlenecks for continued Indian growth.

Financial liberalisation would significantly help India meet its infrastructure needs, which exceed the capacity of the domestic banking system. The government estimates a financing gap of over $310 billion over the next five years alone. India's savings rate is high, at over 30 per cent of GDP, but is not harnessed effectively into productive investments because the banking system is repressed and capital markets are under-developed.

Pensions and Insurance

Lifting of the caps on FDIs in the insurance sector would provide a further source of funds for investment in Indian infrastructure. British institutions such as the Prudential and Standard Life, which are minority partners in market-leading private sector insurers, are potential sources of long-term funds for investment in infrastructure.

The UK, along with a number of other countries, notably the US, has been pushing successive Indian governments to honour a commitment made to lift the FDI cap in the insurance sector to 49 per cent from the present level of 26 per cent. Progress with the Pensions Bill is similarly slow-moving as these liberalising steps are dependent on legislative changes that are controversial in India.

Although the government said last month that it would move the Insurance Laws (Amendment) Bill, 2008 and The Pension Fund Regulatory and Development Authority (PFRDA) Bill, 2011 during the budget session, few are betting on rapid progress in a political environment in which the Indian government is hunkering down ahead of a general election in 2014 and unlikely to expend political capital on liberalising reforms.

Legal and Professional Services

Foreign lawyers in India are banned outright from setting up offices in India, and even domestic firms are heavily restricted. They cannot grow in size to beyond twenty partners each and they cannot incorporate, advertise or tie up with companies outside their profession.

Numerous studies have recommended that India's legal profession be opened if only to rebalance the market, which derives 90 per cent of its revenue from litigation and is small compared with the size of the economy. But many Indian lawyers, a good number of whom also sit in parliament, have fiercely opposed the entry of their foreign rivals, arguing they are not prepared for competition from global firms and that corporatisation will destroy the values of the local industry.

Britain is the EU country keenest on deregulation, although it is certainly not alone, because London is home to some of the world's largest and most international law firms, including Clifford Chance, Linklaters, Freshfields Bruckhaus Deringer and Allen & Overy.

The passage of the Limited Liabilities Partnership (LLP) Act should make it easier to pass the legislation needed to open up the sector. It is estimated that liberalisation of the sector could boost the Indian economy by $2–3 billion a year.

The LLP Act also marked an important step forward for the international accountancy profession, which has faced similar obstacles in opening up the Indian market. Firms such as KPMG are not allowed to use their own brands in the Indian market. There is a need also for independent regulation of the sector. Indian Chartered Accountant (CA) firms are regulated by the Institute of Chartered Accountants of India (ICAI) under provisions of the Chartered Accountants Act (1949). The requirement for the rotation of corporate auditors in the Companies Act (2011) and pressure from international investors for higher standards of corporate governance and for the adoption of international accounting standards, have reinforced pressure from the EU for the liberalisation of the accountancy industry in India.

Retail

Failure to open up the retail sector to multi-brand retailers such as Tesco, Wal-Mart and Carrefour had long been emblematic of the government's waning energy. Steps to move ahead with the liberalisation announced in September 2012 are therefore highly significant, underlining the extent to which Prime Minister Manmohan Singh had seen the opening of this sector as a way to cement his legacy and continue the economic reforms he supervised as finance minister in the 1990s. A more efficient retail sector is likely to boost employment and better connect farmers to urban markets.

Indian critics of FDI, however, fear the loss of neighbourhood stores and a restriction in consumer choice. The decision to press ahead with the reform, which had been put on hold after it was initially floated as a proposal in November 2011, has encountered stiff opposition from the BJP, which has a strong Poujadiste tradition and considerable support from small traders. It has also imperilled the electoral arithmetic of the UPA coalition, with the defection of its second largest constituent party, the All India Trinamool Congress, led by Mamata Banerjee.

Investor Protection

The investment chapter of the EU-India FTA negotiations has barely been opened. The delay reflects in part the fact that the European Commission only in January 2011 requested the expansion of its negotiating mandate to include investor protections. EU member states have Bilateral Investment Treaties (BITs) with very high levels of investor protection, which India wants to repeal in the event that there is an over-arching investment chapter in the FTA.

This reflects less a desire to avoid duplication than the wish to tighten up bilateral treaties that India regards as excessively open-ended. India is concerned by the trend for companies to have recourse to international arbitration under these bilateral treaties, which were signed in the 1980s and 1990s at a time when India was a largely closed economy and attracted little FDI. The UK-India Agreement for the Promotion and Protection of Investments, for example, dates to March 1994. BITs contain important protections against state interference with investments of investors from the other state. These include the obligation to provide full compensation in the event of expropriation, but also other protections, including protection against arbitrary, discriminatory and unfair treatment.

The retrospective changes to Indian tax law announced in the March 2012 Budget, which affect Vodafone and many other companies, makes it likely that the investment chapter of the negotiation will be one of the hardest to close as such arbitrary action reinforces the demand for strong investor protection. There would appear to be good grounds for arguing that the imposition of a retrospective tax would constitute unfair treatment in breach of a BIT. Given that work has not even started, this is a considerable hurdle to the signature of an FTA by the end of the year.

Clearly, there must be a balance between not exposing a resource-constrained Indian state to costly arbitration and India's need, as a country running a substantial and widening current account deficit, now equal to around 4 per cent of GDP, to attract healthy flows of FDI. The two-way flow of investment between India and the UK has been strong. There have been some sizeable mergers and acquisitions, notably the Tata Group's acquisitions of Corus and Jaguar Land Rover, which, strikingly, has made Tata the largest single employer in the UK manufacturing sector.

There is more Indian investment in the UK than in all other EU countries combined. In the other direction, Vodafone's purchase of Hutch Essar, the mobile operator, and BP's partnership with Reliance Industries, India's foremost oil, gas and petrochemicals group, were major ventures in the other direction. But, in general, notwithstanding the significance of these big tie-ups, both countries acknowledge that the potential for more intensive economic cooperation remains to a great extent untapped and will remain so until key liberalising reforms are undertaken by the Indian government.

Human Rights and Democracy

Indian objections to the inclusion of a standard 'human rights and democracy' clause in the proposed FTA, have the potential to re-emerge as a stumbling block. This clause, which is likely to be discussed in the end-game of the negotiations, could be a deal-breaker for India.

Making human rights observance an 'essential element' and a condition of trade terms and development aid gives the EU the ultimate right to suspend all or part of an agreement if a partner country does not fulfil its human rights obligations. New Delhi argues that the 'essential elements' clause conflicts with India's longstanding position that economic agreements should not be 'contaminated' by political riders. It suspects that such clauses provide protectionist cover and is unlikely to give ground.

Since a decision by the EU Council in 1995, which was re-affirmed in 2008, the European Commission has systematically included this 'essential elements' clause in bilateral trade and co-operation agreements. It now applies to agreements with more than one hundred and twenty countries. The FTA is therefore caught between an irresistible force and an immoveable object.

The Commission has triggered an intense debate among the EU's member states by pushing for an apparent exception for India, on the grounds that a 1994 EU-India co-operation agreement covers human rights questions.[14]

Given how much both countries can potentially gain from the FTA, the Commission argues that the FTA should leave more political considerations for other agreements. Feeling is equally strong in sections of the European Parliament on the need for consistency across FTAs. India is a member of the United Nations Human Rights Council, but ranks low, according to the Asian Human Rights Commission, among the international community in terms of the ratification of international conventions and covenants.

Ways to Expand UK-India Trade and Investment

The UK can strengthen an already strong economic relationship by focusing on a few core areas where it needs revitalising.

Commission must Reflect British Interests

First, as trade is an exclusive EU competence, it is vital that the Commission reflects UK interests to the greatest extent possible in the negotiations over the long-awaited EU India Free Trade Agreement. A comprehensive FTA that addresses considerable remaining tariff and non-tariff barriers, particularly on the services side, could deliver significant economic benefits as well as helping to reduce poverty in India. The coalition, on a bilateral basis, through the ongoing economic and financial dialogue and other mechanisms, must also continue to encourage further liberalisation of Indian markets, particularly for financial and professional services and for goods, including wines and spirits, defence, chemicals and automotive parts. The conclusion of an ambitious FTA (and, of course, of the Doha Round, in which India is a key player) would make it more likely that the UK will achieve its objective of doubling trade with India by 2015.

Business First

Second, the coalition must encourage businesses to rise to the challenge of exporting to a country rightly seen as 'difficult'. India never scores highly in surveys measuring the ease of doing business. In the World Bank's 2011 survey of one hundred and eighty-three countries, India ranked one hundred and thirty-fourth, behind Brazil (one hundred and twenty-seventh), Russia (one hundred and twenty-third) and China (seventy-ninth).

In terms of enforcing contracts through the court system – a critical attribute of any market economy – India scores appallingly, coming one hundred and eighty-second. The World Bank estimates going to court to enforce a contract involves forty-six procedures, takes an average of one thousand four hundred and twenty days and consumes 40 per cent of the value of any claim. Obstacles such as this explain why surveys consistently show that UK firms are wary of pro-actively seeking out business opportunities in these priority markets.

Smaller and innovative firms have in the past experienced disproportionate barriers to exporting to India. Recent surveys show that only 23 per cent of UK SMEs export, compared to an EU average of 25 per cent, a shortfall of a hundred thousand firms that could deliver a potential £30 billion to the UK economy if they rise to the challenge. This is a legitimate area for vigorous government intervention, and the drive to reform both UKTI and the Export Credits Guarantee Department, renamed UK Export Finance, is welcome.

The take up of UK Export Finance (formerly ECGD) products aimed at SMEs has in the past been disappointing, with the UK's official export financing arm underperforming comparable bodies such as France's Coface and Germany's Hermes. The UKEF is now explicitly targeting 'small exporters' and it will be important for that organisation to be held to account for its progress in this respect.

Connectivity

Third, we must overhaul connectivity to the big emerging markets. While London has excellent direct connections to its traditional business partners, it lags behind European competitors in serving the BRICs.

It has two hundred and fifteen departures a week to New York, for example, but only thirty a week to two destinations in mainland China (compared to sixty-four to three such cities from Paris Charles de Gaulle and fifty-six to four such cities from Frankfurt). UK-India air traffic has trebled in the last five years, due to the liberalisation of the UK-India market, but this rate of growth will be hard to sustain given the UK's historic failure to make long-term provision for runway capacity in the south-east. This will be a major brake on our ability to capitalise on the commercial opportunities presented by growth in India, as well as other fast-growing emerging markets, and is expected to cost the UK economy up to £14 billion over the next decade.

Runway utilisation at Heathrow is operating at 98.5 per cent, compared to 70 per cent to 75 per cent at other big European airports, such as Paris Charles de Gaulle, Amsterdam and Frankfurt. This is causing delays and reliability problems that are damaging Britain's attractiveness, and restricts London's ability to expand to new markets without sacrificing existing ones. Jakarta, Osaka, Caracas and Bogotá have all been removed from Heathrow's destination boards in recent years, while Lima, Manila, Panama City and Guangzhou have never been available. They are all served by London's three main rivals. All options for expanding hub capacity for London are controversial but all options need to be urgently considered.

Aid

Fourth, we need to overhaul an anachronistic donor-recipient aid relationship, which risks trapping Britain in some outdated attitudes towards its former colony. After a decade, in which the UK sharply increased its aid to India to make it the Department for International Development (DfID)'s single largest country programme, the tide is now turning. DfID is effectively freezing aid to India, while shifting resources in the existing programme towards investment in private enterprise, focusing funding on states that need it most and measuring its impact more systematically.

A new era of partnership in international development is emerging and Britain and India have an opportunity to be in the vanguard of this process.

India is now emerging as an aid power in its own right, as demonstrated in July 2011 by New Delhi's announcement that it intended to set up its own $11 billion development agency. This has yet to materialise, however. As and when it does, it will find DfID to be a willing potential partner. In February 2011, Andrew Mitchell, then Secretary of State for International Development, described a future in which the UK and India could work together, as equal partners, to reduce poverty in other developing countries.

Talent

Fifth, we must embrace global talent, which is in super abundance in India. Britain has a strong base on which to build. It is the preferred launch-pad for Indian firms hoping to conquer European markets, with more companies headquartered here than in all other EU member states combined. London has an unrivalled place in the hearts of the Indian wealth-generating class. Le tout Delhi is in London in June, drawn by the mild climate, Wimbledon and the cultural activities the British capital has to offer. It still remains the preferred place for the affluent to buy their first home outside India.

These ties form a powerful emotional connection between the two countries that should not be underestimated. Of the roughly twenty-nine million people in the UK labour force, two and a half million were born overseas. Of that figure, more than six hundred thousand originate from the Indian subcontinent. That is almost as many as both the six hundred and thirty-one thousand from the fourteen pre-enlargement members of the European Union and the six hundred twenty-five thousand from the enlarged EU-10 that began to arrive after 2004.

But links between students, especially through universities, are not as strong as they could be. Indeed, British universities attract more people from China than they do from India, despite our stronger historical and cultural links with the subcontinent. A 2010 British Council report based on market research confirmed a widely-held belief that 'students tend to choose a country first before choosing a university, meaning that it is crucial to build a national brand showing the UK as a safe and exciting place to study, offering a rich life experience and enhanced career prospects'.

Tapping top-flight student talent globally will not just mean the UK gains in terms of innovation, research and a broader science and skills base. Greater exchange of students now will mean stronger relationships later. The UK cannot afford to lose touch with the next generation of opinion-formers, let 'Britishness' become a currency of depreciating value for a more Americanised elite or allow Britain to recede further as a cultural reference point.

The launch of the British Council's Re-Imagine: India-UK Cultural Relations in the twenty-first century project, the announcement of a new Chevening Science and Innovation Leadership Programme and plans to help top UK universities partner with the new Innovation universities that India plans to create, are all steps in the right direction.

Conclusion

The emergence of new powers in the east and south has led to a sensible shift in the UK's focus from the Euro-Atlantic world towards a more multi-polar world. Progress in forging an 'enhanced partnership' with

India over the last two years has been significant and welcome. The 40 per cent growth in trade in 2011 is emblematic of this renewed vigour in the relationship, but there is much more to be done. It is a concern that the UK is in some quarters seen as a country of diminishing relevance in India, as indicated by a leading research institute in Delhi recently ranking India's strategic partnership with Britain as less significant than the one with France in terms of its historical significance and potential for the future.[15]

This reflects a worrying disconnect between perceptions of what Britain offers and the reality of the UK as a friendly country with relevant capabilities, not just in financial services, but across a wide spectrum of India's needs as a developing economy and emerging global power. It also mirrors a broader disenchantment in New Delhi with the idea that the EU, as a plural, composite and democratic polity of twenty-seven nations and five hundred million people, can provide any kind of positive reference point for India as it builds up its own national power as a huge multi-lingual, multicultural state with a federal form of government and constructs its own continent-sized internal market. Mired in the Eurozone crisis, the EU as a whole is at risk of being seen as an agglomeration of declining countries rendered rudderless by baroque decision-making processes, a deepening democratic deficit and lack of political solidarity between member states.[16]

Unless Europe puts itself back on a growth path, by undertaking structural reforms and completing the single market, it will lose its appeal as a strategic partner for India and the UK will lose its value as a bridgehead to Europe. Equally, there is awareness among reformers in New Delhi that India still faces a broad range of potential futures, not all of them happy, and that further economic reform is the key to prosperity for many tens of millions. Over the twenty years since the onset of the reform era, India has benefited hugely from liberalisation, but a second wave of reforms, whether linked to an EU-India FTA or not, is long overdue. The choices India makes in the coming years, while it still has a chance of reaping a demographic dividend from its young and growing workforce, will set the parameters of its potential for decades to come.

Acknowledgments

The author would like to thank Business for New Europe for making possible a research trip to New Delhi in April 2012 for the preparation of an earlier version of this essay, which also draws in places on the introduction to 'Reconnecting Britain and India: Ideas for an Enhanced Partnership' (edited by Jo Johnson and Dr Rajiv Kumar, Academic Foundation, 2011).

Notes

1. Office of Budget Responsibility, Economic and Fiscal Outlook, March 2012, p. 13.

2. Ernst & Young, *The outlook for UK exports*: ITEM Club Special Report, February 2011 (see p. 2) (refers to IMF, Direction of Trade Statistics database).

3. IMF World Economic Outlook: *Recovery, Risk and Rebalancing,* October 2010 quoted in Department for Business Innovation and Skills: Trade and Investment for Growth, p. 27, February 2011.

4. David Cameron, Speech at BFI, 10 November 2011.

5. George Osborne, Speech at British Business Leaders' Lunch, in Davos, 28 January 2011.

6. Department for Business, Innovation and Skills; BIS Economics Paper No. 11; *The economic consequences for the UK and the EU of completing the Single Market*; February 2011.

7. Source: Ministry of Commerce, Government of India.

8. Finance Minister Palaniappan Chidambaram announced on September 14, 2012 a range of liberalising measures that included federal-level approval of foreign direct investment (upto 51 per cent ownership) in multi-brand retail; permission for foreign companies to purchase stakes of upto 49 per cent in Indian airlines; and a repetition of promises to raise the FDI-ceiling in the insurance sector to 49 per cent from 26 per cent.

9. A kilogram of loose red onions (class 2) in Tesco bought online costs £0.95. A kilogram of onions in a market in Mumbai can cost between Rs 60-80 and on occasion more. See Times of India article of 22 December 2010. No onion distribution through ration shops (http://articles.timesofindia.indiatimes. com/2010-12-22/mumbai/28255848_1_onion-prices-onion-crop-onion-stock).

10. European Commission, Trade Sustainability Impact Assessment for the FTA between the EU and the Republic of India, May 2009.

11. Razeen Sally, *Indian Trade Policy after the Crisis*, p. 2, ECIPE Occasional Paper, No. 4/2011.

12. Ibid., p. 9.

13. Sunil Khilnani, Rajiv Kumar, Pratap Bhanu Mehta, Lt. Gen. (Retd.), Prakash Menon, Nandan Nilekani, Srinath Raghavan, Shyam Saran, Siddharth Varadarajan, *Nonalignment 2.0: A Foreign and Strategic Policy for India in the Twenty-First Century*, Centre for Policy Research.

14. 1994 Cooperation Agreement between the European Community and the Republic of India on partnership and development (http://www.europarl. europa.eu/meetdocs/2004_2009/documents/fd/dsaa11102004_002/ dsaa11102004_002en.pdf).

15. *India's Strategic Partners: A Comparative Assessment*, Foundation for National Security Research, November 2011.

16. Karine Lisbonne-de Vergeron, Konrad Adenauer Stiftung and the Global Policy Institute, *Chinese and Indian Views of Europe since the Crisis*: New perspectives from the emerging Asian giants, 2011.

Contributors

SHRABANI BASU is an author and journalist. After graduating in history from St Stephen's College, Delhi, she completed her Masters from Delhi University. In 1983 she joined the *Times of India* working in their offices in Bombay and Delhi. Since 1988 she has been the London correspondent of the Calcutta-based ABP group of newspapers, writing for their publications: *Ananda Bazar Patrika, Sunday, Desh* and *The Telegraph.* She is the author of *Victoria & Abdul, The True Story of the Queen's Closest Confidante* (2010), *Spy Princess, The Life of Noor Inayat Khan* (2006) and *Curry, The Story of the Nation's Favourite Dish* (1999/2003). In 2010 she set up the Noor Inayat Khan Memorial Trust and led a high-profile campaign calling for a personal memorial for WWII heroine Noor Inayat Khan. Her effort was praised in both Houses of Parliament, and in November 2012, the bust of Noor Inayat Khan was unveiled in Gordon Square in London by HRH The Princess Royal. Shrabani is passionate about unravelling stories from the shared histories of India and Britain and preserving these for the next generation.

MIKE KING was born in England and educated at Durham School. In 1968, he joined the City of London Police and left Britain for Canada in 1975. After serving in the Toronto Police and the Canada Border Services Agency, he entered the private sector and spent 25 years working as an investigator on abduction, fraud, international fugitive and asset recovery cases around the world. He has been the subject of a number of newspaper articles and has two books about his work. He has been interviewed on television and has featured in several crime documentaries. He returned to live in England in 2006 and since then has spent much time researching his family's Indian history with a view to writing a book about their lives and times in the days of the Raj.

PHILLIP KNIGHTLEY AM, was a special correspondent for *The Sunday Times* for twenty years (1965-85) and one of the leaders of its *Insight* investigative team. He was named Journalist of the Year (1980 and 1988) in the British Press Awards, one of only two journalists to have won it twice. He is the author of ten non-fiction books including *The First Casualty* (on war and propaganda) which has been published in eight languages. He has lectured on journalism, law, war and espionage at the City University London, Manchester University, the University of Dusseldorf, Penn State, UCLA, Stanford, the Inner Temple, the International Committee of the Red Cross, and at the RMA Sandhurst. He was on the management committee of The Society of Authors, London, for six years. He is the European representative of the International Consortium of Investigative Journalists, Washington. He was awarded the Order of Australia in 2005 for services to journalism and as an author. He has an Honorary Doctorate of Arts from Sydney University and the City University, London. He is currently Visiting Professor of Journalism at Lincoln University, England. He was born in Australia but has worked most of his life in Britain. He divides his time between Britain, Spain, Australia and India.

INDRAJIT HAZRA is a novelist and journalist. His novels *The Burnt Forehead of Max Saul* (2000), *The Garden of Earthly Delights* (2003) and *The Bioscope Man* (2008) have been described by critics as 'stamped by trenchant black humour' and '[original prose with] mad images hyperlinked to other mad images', one reviewer stating that 'few (Bengali) writers writing in English are able to capture that sense of decay and temper it with that quintessential Bengali humour the way Hazra can'. He is a columnist for various publications, including *The Hindustan Times* where he writes 'Red Herring' every Sunday. He lives in New Delhi. English is his second language that he finds it easiest language to write in. He blogs on and off on http://captain-bloodmoney.blogspot.in/

TOM BIRD is the Executive Producer at Shakespeare's Globe. In 2012 he directed the Globe to Globe Festival, which is nominated for a What's On Stage Award for Theatre Event of the Year. In researching the festival he travelled the world from Armenia to Zanzibar in search of new productions of Shakespeare's work.

SANJOY K. ROY is the Managing Director of Teamwork Films and Teamwork Productions which he established in 1989. It is a highly versatile production house with wide ranging interests in the performing and visual arts, social sector and films and television with offices in Cairo, Chicago, Hong Kong, Johannesburg, London, New Delhi, Singapore, Seattle, Tel Aviv and Vancouver. Teamwork designs and produces 19 annual Arts Festivals across 21 cities in 11 countries. He is currently the festival director for Shared History Festival in Johannesburg and Durban, Eye on India – Chicago and Seattle, Celebrating India – Jerusalem and Tel Aviv and is the producer of the Jaipur Literature Festival, META – The Mahindra Excellence in Theatre Awards, Kala Utsavam – Singapore, Kahani Festival, India and The Ishara International Puppet Festival. He has received the National Award for Excellence and Best Director, for the film *Shahjahanabad, The Twilight Years,* the Herald Angel Award and the Spirit of the Fringe Award at the Edinburgh Festival. He is a founder trustee of Salaam Baalak Trust working to provide support services for street and working children in the inner city of Delhi and the Ishara Puppet Theatre Trust. He is advisor for the arts for numerous governmental organizations across the world.

NASREEN MUNNI KABIR is a renowned documentary filmmaker and author of twelve books on Hindi films. Her television programmes, made for Channel 4 TV, UK, include the series *Movie Mahal, In Search of Guru Dutt, Follow that Star – A Profile of Amitabh Bachchan, Lata in her Own Voice,* and *The Inner and Outer World of Shah Rukh Khan.* She had also directed a profile on Bismillah Khan and the making of *Bombay Dreams,* the musical produced by Andrew Lloyd Webber for BBC Television, UK. She authored *A Sideways Glance at Hindi Cinema* (December 2012) to mark 100 years of Indian cinema. Her publications included four dialogue books featuring the dialogue of classics like *Mughal e Azam, Awaara, Mother India* and *Pyaasa.* Her biographical works include *Guru Dutt, A Life in Cinema, Lata Mangeshkar in her own words, A.R. Rahman, The Spirit of Music* and *In the Company of a Poet, Gulzar in Conversation with Nasreen Munni Kabir.* Nasreen won the first Women of Achievement Award in Arts & Culture in 1999 for her promotion of Indian cinema in the UK, and became a governor on the board of the British Film Institute in 2000, serving a six-year term. She continues to curate Channel 4's annual 20-part Indian cinema season.

PRADEEP KAR is the founder, chairman and managing director of Microland, India's leading provider of outsourced IT infrastructure management services. He has been selected by the World Economic Forum as a 'Global Leader for Tomorrow'. A serial entrepreneur, he founded and sold four technology companies notable amongst them was Indya.com, Planetasia. com, India's first Internet Professional Services Company, Media2India and Net Brahma Technologies. He sits on the board of UBM plc, a global live media and B2B communications, marketing service and data provider, on the Advisory Board of Leaders' Quest, an international social enterprise based in London and on the South Asia Board of Trinity College, Dublin. Pradeep is the immediate Past President of The IndUS Entrepreneurs (TiE), Bangalore Chapter and is the Founding Member of the Bangalore Chapter of the Young Presidents Organization. He has been recognized with numerous accolades; notable among these is the Indian Express 'India Young Business Achiever Award'. He has been featured in 'Newsweek International' as 'Stars of Asia' and in 'Business India' as 'Stars of India'.

SITA BRAHMACHARI was born in Derby in 1966. She has a BA in English Literature and an MA in Arts Education. Sita's artistic and academic work has explored cultural diversity and representation within the Arts. Her writing, research work, community theatre, education projects and plays have been commissioned by among others: The Royal Shakespeare Company, The Royal Court Theatre, The Arts Council, London International Festival of Theatre and Tamasha Theatre Company for which she is currently under commission co-creating *Arrival* a theatre-circus production (based on Shaun Tan's graphic novel) with Kristine Landon-Smith. Sita's first Novel *Artichoke Hearts (Macmillan Children's Books)* won the Waterstone's Children's Book Award 2011, and was nominated for The Carnegie Medal and her second novel *Jasmine Skies* was published in March 2012 and has been shortlisted for the Centurion Award and Long Listed for the Carnegie Medal. Her third novel *Kite Spirit* was published in May 2013.

K. VIJAY RAGHAVAN is a developmental biologist whose research interests are in understanding the mechanisms underlying the formation of nerve circuits and the development of animal behaviour. He studied chemical engineering at the Indian Institute of Technology, Kanpur, holds a Ph.D. in molecular biology from the Tata Institute of Fundamental Research (TIFR), Mumbai and was a Research Fellow and then a Senior Research Fellow at the California Institute of Technology, Pasadena. He is currently Distinguished Professor and Director of the National Centre of Biological Sciences-TIFR, Bangalore. Vijay Raghavan also heads the new Institute for Stem Cell Research and Regenerative Biology (*inStem*) in Bangalore. VijayRaghavan is a Fellow of the Indian National Science Academy, The Indian Academy of Sciences and is a J.C. Bose Fellow of the Department of Science and Technology. He is also a fellow of the Academy of Sciences of the Developing World, TWAS and a Foreign Associate of the European Molecular Biology Organization. In 2012 VijayRaghavan was elected a Fellow of the Royal Society.

PROF. NIRMALYA KUMAR was headhunted by the Tata Group and joined them as Head of Strategy from 1 August 2013. He is Professor of Marketing and Director of Aditya Birla India Centre at London Business School. He has previously taught at Harvard Business School, IMD (Switzerland) and Northwestern University (Kellogg School of Management). As an author, Nirmalya has written six books: *Marketing as Strategy* (2004), *Private Label Strategy* (2007), *Value Merchants* (2007), *India's Global Powerhouses* (2009), *India Inside* (2012), and *Brand_Breakout* (2013). He is included in the lists of 50 top business school professors (Poets & Quants), 50 management gurus (Thinkers50), and top 10 Global Indian Thought Leaders (*Economic Times*). In his personal life, Nirmalya is a passionate supporter of the arts. Previously, a patron of the British Museum, he currently serves on the South Asian Acquisition Committee of Tate Modern. In recognition of his patronage and promotion of South Asian Art, SOAS (the School of Oriental and African Studies of University of London) awarded him an Honorary Fellowship in 2012.

PROF. JACK E. SPENCE, OBE, teaches in the Department of War Studies, King's College London. He was educated at Pretoria Boys' High School, South Africa; the University of Witwatersrand (BA 1952); LSE (BSc Econ) 1957. He has lectured at a variety of universities in Britain, South Africa and the United States and was Professor of Politics and Pro-Vice Chancellor at the University of Leicester (1973-1991). He was employed as Director of Studies at the Royal Institute of International Affairs (1991–1997). He has been teaching in the Department of War Studies since 1997 and has specialised in a Post-Graduate course on Diplomacy. He was awarded an OBE in 2003. Professor Spence is a past President of the African Studies Association UK and past Chairman of the British International Studies Association. He is a past editor of International Affairs, the Review of International Studies and the Journal of Southern African Studies. He has published six books on Southern African issues.

MIHIR S. SHARMA was born in Delhi, and educated in Mumbai, Calcutta, Delhi and Boston. He has also lived and worked in Jamshedpur and New York. He intended to be an academic economist, but found he didn't have the patience. So he now works as a writer, policy analyst and journalist. He is currently editor of the opinion pages of *Business Standard*, India's most respected financial daily. He lives in Delhi, in an overpriced rented house, and tells anyone who asks that he'd rather be in Calcutta.

KAPIL KOMIREDDI, a journalist, has written from South Asia, Eastern Europe and the Middle East. His work has appeared, among other publications, in Forbes, Foreign Policy, the Times of India, the New York Times, Ha'aretz, the New Statesman, the Los Angeles Times, the Boston Globe, the Chicago Tribune, the National, the Guardian, and Tablet.

WILLIAM CRAWLEY graduated from Trinity College Cambridge in 1964 and taught history and political science for two years at St Stephens College, Delhi, before taking his doctorate in Modern Indian History from St Antony's College Oxford. He joined the BBC in 1970 and spent twenty years working as a journalist, editor and manager. As head of the BBC Eastern Service from 1986 to 1994, he had responsibility for 10 Asian language services, broadcasting to Iran, South Asia and Burma. Since leaving the BBC, he has written and published articles in academic journals on the media in South Asia and other topics. He was Secretary of the Charles Wallace Pakistan, Bangladesh, and Burma Trusts from 2002-2007. He is on the Editorial Board of *'Asian Affairs'*, the journal of the Royal Society for Asian Affairs.

DAVID PAGE graduated in history from Merton College Oxford in 1966 and spent a year teaching at Edwardes College, Peshawar, in North West Pakistan, where his life-long interest in South Asia began. He later returned to university to write a thesis on pre-Partition politics, which was published as *'Prelude to Partition'* by the Oxford University Press. He joined the BBC World Service in 1972, and worked for more than twenty years in the BBC Eastern Service, where he and William Crawley were colleagues. Since leaving the BBC, David Page has worked as a consultant and researcher on communication issues in South Asia. In 2012, he co-authored (with Shirazuddin Siddiqi) a BBC Media Action publication on *The Media of Afghanistan: the challenges of transition*. He is the Chair of Trustees of Afghanaid, a British charity which works with rural communities in Northern Afghanistan.

JO JOHNSON was elected as the Member of Parliament for Orpington in May 2010. He currently serves as Head of Policy Unit at No 10. He is the Co-Chairman of the Indo-UK All Party Parliamentary Group and Deputy-Chairman of the Conservative Foreign and Commonwealth Council. Between 1997 and his election to Parliament, Jo worked at *The Financial Times* in various roles, including as Associate Editor and Editor of *Lex* (2008-2010), the newspaper's agenda-setting daily business and financial column, as South Asia Bureau Chief (2005-2008) and as Paris Correspondent (2001-2005). He remains a Contributing Editor of *The Financial Times*. His main thematic interests relate to international trade and investment, globalisation and corporate governance. He recently co-edited *Reconnecting Britain and India: Ideas for an Enhanced Partnership* (Academic Foundation 2011), with Dr Rajiv Kumar, Secretary General of FICCI. He is a member of the advisory board of Dishaa, an initiative launched by Prime Minister David Cameron to expand, enrich and energise UK-India relations.

Subject Index

Note: Locators with '*f*' denote figures; 'n' denotes notes.